At the core of bouldering sports

PORTLAND BOULDERING

Volume 2

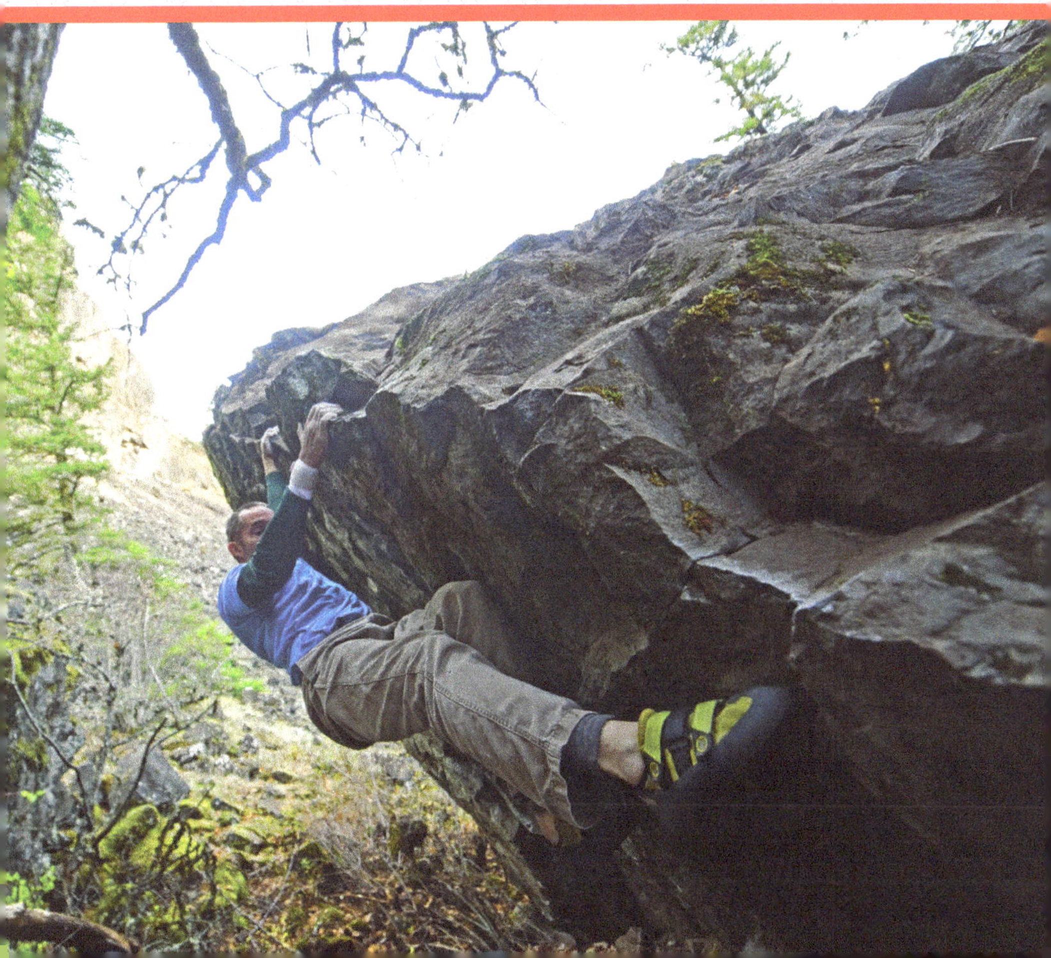

Portland Bouldering™
Copyright © 2024 East Wind Design

All rights reserved. No part of this publication may be reproduced, stored in or introduced into a retrieval system, or transmitted in any form, or by any means (electronic, mechanical, photocopying, recording, etc). Requests for permission must be made in writing to the publisher.

Book Design: East Wind Design
Technical Maps and Illustrations: East Wind Design

Cover Photograph: Sam bouldering on the *Hunchback Boulder*
Frontispiece images: *Rowena* (#1), *Rock Creek* (#2), *LLB* (#3), *High Rocks* (#4)

ISBN-13: 978-0-9997233-8-8
Library of Congress Control Number: 2024917719
Portland Bouldering (PB3 v3.0), **Volume 2**
Printed in the USA

PORTLAND BOULDERING

Table of Contents

Disclaimer vii
Preface viii
Acknowledgments ix

Bouldering Intro 1

Mt Hood Bouldering Areas (southern) 7
Timberline Boulders 7
- Stormin' Norman String 9
- Zippora Group 17
- Magic Mile String 20

Sandy River Boulders 23
East Mosquito Bluff 25
Mud Ridge Boulders 26
White River Boulders 26
Bennett Boulders 29
Hunchback Boulders 32
Boulder Mtn Boulders 35
- Bluebox Group 40
- Lost City 43
- The Rim 57
- Woodlands 64
- Roadside Cluster 65
- Woodlands zone 68
- Top Meadow 81
- Top Meadow - South 85

Mt Hood Bouldering Areas (northern) 89
Cooper Spur Boulders 89
Tamanawas Boulders 102
Lolo Boulders 104
Eliot Boulders 109
West Fork Boulders 115
Pinn Boulders 121
Dee Flat Boulders 123
Lost Lake Boulders 125
- Upper Talus Group 128
- Middle Talus Group 157
- North Talus Group 181

Select Additional Bouldering Sites 199
Sasquatch Hideaway 199
Rowena Boulders 203

Disclaimer

Rock climbing and bouldering contains certain inherent risks that may be dangerous to your health. The sole purpose of this book is to inform rock climbers of the many unique crag climbing opportunities available in and around our corner of Northwest Oregon. Before attempting any bouldering described in these pages you should first be proficient in the use of modern rock climbing and bouldering equipment.

This guidebook is not a substitute for personal insight, time-learned skills, or lessons taught by climbing instructors. There are no warranties, neither express nor implied, that this book contains accurate or reliable information. As the user of this or any guidebook, you assume full responsibility for your own safety. Because the sport is constantly evolving, the author cannot guarantee the accuracy of any of the information in this book, including the V-grades, location of routes, route names, route descriptions, or approach trails. No one can offer you any assurance against natural hazards such as lightning or other weather phenomena, loose or poor quality rock, or the risk of equipment failure. Consider with suspicion all fixed protection (such as bolts). Weathering, metal quality, and impact stress loading are some of the variants that can cause fixed gear to fail.

Only you can know the scope and the upper limit of your rock climbing abilities. Assess your prospective climb shrewdly, and make prudent decisions based on your strengths and weaknesses. If you have any doubt concerning your ability to safely ascend a climbing route today, then stop and consider a climb that is less difficult or dangerous.

This is not a how-to guide but rather a where-to book. This book explains where to rock climb, but you must honestly determine whether you have mastered the most important aspects of the sport before embarking on any rock climbing adventure.

Consult other climbers about the adventure or rock climb you are planning to embark upon. A skilled climber who knows the crag can give quality advice and insight as to proper gear placement as well as impart ideas about climbing technique and balance that will surely be beneficial to you.

Wisely seek assistance and attain good instruction from others such as a diligent climbing instructor who will teach you how to become a safe, intuitive climber.

Exercise good judgment as to where the climbing route ascends the cliff face, and learn to quickly perceive subtle variants you will likely encounter in route difficulty. Know your own strengths and weaknesses; develop a competent understanding of your route-finding abilities and safety skills, for these and the right equipment are your best protection against the hazards of climbing. Confidence and ability gained through many hours of physical and mental preparation are perhaps the most valuable skills you and your climbing partner will need when managing the degree of risk you both are willing to accept.

Preface

This edition of *Portland Bouldering* is the creative expression of several individuals who have brought considerable momentum to the sport of rock climbing and bouldering in this portion of the state. From a core group of persons came forth the primary portions of this little book, which began in younger years when various persons opted to collect their climbing and bouldering activity in a relative format from which to glean a concise storyline to build this book upon. Bringing their ideas and recommendations forward into this project gives it an essential value unmatched locally.

During your quest to tap into outdoor recreational sports, remember that our rock climbing and bouldering actions today impact and influence the future decisions of property owners and land managers alike. We are responsible for keeping ours a friendly, self-managed sport and for acting in full cooperation with land managers so that we will continue to be welcomed for generations to come.

By developing a perceptive, respectful awareness of the environment around us, from the peregrine falcon to *Sedum integrifolium*, we ultimately discover that we are entrusted with the keys to provide a legacy for tomorrow. Hopefully you will find the information bound within these pages both rewarding and fulfilling.

Acknowledgments

The culmination of beta in this book exists primarily because of the shared knowledge and assistance of many friends and individuals. Thank you all for sharing your expertise about the exhilarating edge of this sport.

This guidebook is the end formulation of insight from all those boulderers who relish this sport and choose to maintain valued historical notes on the sport. Numerous tidbits of data exist in various small articles, but a major portion of the information is through close contact with friends and acquintances who have collected a rather impressive amount of bouldering information and data, each focused toward their relative prospective view of the sport.

Over many years various individuals provided expandable authoritative information, or climbing energy, or valued insight about various bouldering sites, persons not specifically referenced here, but who have collectively added to the wealth of knowledge of local bouldering in this region. Photo credits go to several individuals: Mr Abbott, Mr Fields, Mr Jones, etc.

Some of this regions most emphatic players in the game of bouldering are as follows:

From approximately 1990-2000: Mr Bernert, Mr Lyon, Mr Rall, Mr Pajunas, Mr Ryan, Mr Nakahira, Mr Schultz, Mr Chase, Mr Coleman, Mr Scales, Mr Abbott, Mr Alfers, Mr Hill, Mr Kester, etc. From about 2001-2019 onward: Mr Abbott, Mr Sowerby, Mr Polizzano, Mr Slayton, Mr Porter, Mr Davis, Mr Williams, Mr Vitt, Mr Crowder, Mr Cova, Mr Krossen, Mr Svenden, Mr Klesick, Mr Cousins, Mr Fields, Michael Brady, Paul Bishop, etc. The "etc" includes a vast number of additional individuals who did brief select new problems here and there.

A number of individuals were highly instrumental in sharing various crucial aspects of knowledge, ideas and energy that have helped to strengthen the quality and vibrant nature of this book. Those individuals are a virtual walking encyclopedia of superb detailed knowledge on multiple tangents of the sport in this region. Their wealth of local bouldering history, in-depth bouldering beta, extensive photography collection, as well as an express determination to continously explore unknown places to find the next hotspot crag or boulder site were instrumental in this project. Considerable portions of this book are reflective of that energetic personality and invaluable expertise. That information knowledge base yielded data that could be compiled accurately into a quality product that would satisfy the interest of all climbers in this region.

Altogether these people bring a life-time of broad-ranging highly valued climbing skills, indepth local climbing politics knowledge, and a profound interest in the various facets of rock climbing adventures in all its wild flavors. Within the various degrees of climbing, from rock climbing, bouldering to mountain climbing, their shared optimism to explore new crags and find new boulder sites is a unique creative energy that keeps this sport moving forward by promoting an increased wealth of publically accessible rock climbing areas, each person tackling unique ways to continually expand the sport in this region.

World of Bouldering

BOULDERING INTRO

Bouldering Opportunities
Volume 2

This second volume of Portland Bouldering guidebook focuses on the expansive world of bouldering around Mt Hood (at select sites near U.S. Hwy 26 and U.S. Hwy 35), bringing to light an indepth analysis of numerous higher elevation bouldering sites that provide energetic outward bound local boulderers with quality seasonal opportunities.

These chapters take you on a deep analytic tour through each of the key bouldering sites, providing you with a plethora of good reasons to be part of this growing Northwest Oregon bouldering sport. The bouldering information in this volume will hopefully encourage you to step out into the extensive backcountry around Mt Hood to explore and climb at some of the unique and significant bouldering sites here in northwestern Oregon.

CLIMATE

Western Oregon valleys and the snow laden High Cascade Range predominate in douglas fir, spruce and hemlock forests that are often wrapped in misty overcast or drizzly days. The Oregon climate west of the Cascade Range is predominantly wet six months of the year. Pacific marine air weather systems bring an abundance of rainfall that saturates the region, especially from late-October through May. Between the rainy weather patterns when sunshine prevails (May through October) outdoor bouldering recreation ensues in earnest. During this portion of the year mild marine air often mixes with inland Great Basin hot weather to bring a climber-friendly

cycle that keeps the region quite comfortable.

During the summer months temperatures average in the seventies to mid-eighties (Fahrenheit) with occasional short peaks of blazing hot sunny days reaching the nineties in July and August (infrequently peaking near 100°F+).

On stifling hot days in July and August, but don't hide because your favorite bouldering site is a boilerplate. Instead go to high altitude stellar bouldering sites that offer ideal 'heat-escape' locales far better than the low elevation bouldering sites (such as Larch Mtn Boulders, Silver Star Mtn on Ed's Trail, Three Corner Rock Boulders, Timberline Boulders, Cooper Spur Boulders, Bulo Point, Lost Lake Boulders, or Rock Creek Boulders). Some folks are determined to crank only V-hard, so full sunshine bouldering may be too limiting on the hottest summer days, but for those who relish VB-V3 there is an unlimited plethora of stuff at all the higher altitude sites, with minimal to zero moss, and a general lack of mosquitoes (at breezy sites).

By late October, the Pacific marine air storm tracks become more active, usually bringing a consistent series of rain showers. The typical winter storm systems generate frequent cold, rainy days with average temperatures in the 35–50°F range. Average annual precipitation in the Willamette Valley near Portland is about 40 inches.

Nearby, in Central Oregon, the world class destination haven of Smith Rock and its surrounding environ offer a infinite variety of virtual year-round climbing and bouldering on welded tuff (at Smith), and an unlimited supply of lowly rimrock basalt formations scattered liberally across the arrid region in a mixed forest of pine and juniper.

In summation: If it is not raining and it's warm – go bouldering; if it's raining go to the eastside of the Cascade Mtn Range to various bouldering sites.

BASIC GEOLOGY

It's a quirk, at least in the eye of a boulderer, that the greatest percentage of large stone clusters found in this region (of high quality and quantity) are composed of andesitic-basaltic rock characteristics. From a geological perspective, this is readily apparent, simply because most of the Pacific Rim volcanoes (from Japan, to the Alaskan archipelago, and from western Canada / western U.S., to the Andes mountain range of South America) actively expelled (in recent history and to this date) voluminous quantities of igneous lava, some of it being old lava flows with andesitic characteristics. Andesite rock, in essence, is water, gas content, bits of sediment, and a healthy dose of silica

Matt at *Lost Lake Boulders*

TA at *Dee Boulders*

sprinkled in, all previously subducted by an oceanic plate, conveyor belt fashion down beneath the continental plate. These two plates rub and drag sediment material downward, in a process which heats and melts the rock, pooling into massive molten structures that, being lighter than the surrounding older congealed rock structure, rises slowly to the surface venting explosively as volcanic mountain peaks.

The results of this conjunctive igneous mix produce lighter colored silica-rich lava rock types (breccias, tuffs, andesites, dacites, and rhyolites) of volcanoclastics found along the entire Pacific Rim volcanic string. After long periods of erosional and chemical weathering processes, the resultant forested landscape revealed exposed clusters of large andesitic boulders (or short vertical escarpments), in surprisingly extensive quantities throughout the northern Oregon Cascade Mountain range.

Andesite is compositionally a mineral-rich plagioclause matrix, yielding a natural slightly gritty friction-friendly surface of superb quality, including occasional gaseous vesicle pockets, and parallel joint plains that create edges or ribbing for fingertips and foot holds. Many andesite, rhyolite, and dacite boulders originally congealed as larger bulky structures or bluffs, but were tumbled and survived the initial roll remaining relatively intact in variable sizes 7'-25' diameter (occasionally larger). Variables within the compositional matrix of andesite can be extensive and radical, even if just a short distance lay between two sites (i.e. Alpenglow and Super Hero). One site may yield minute bits of pyroxene, feldspar, amphibole, biotite or some quartz, while another site will have ⅔" sized crystalline interstices in the plagioclase matrix.

BOULDERING NOTES

This micro-regions elusive bouldering sites are broadly distributed, but tend to be densely packed with an average of 20-90 boulder problems per site. The scattered boulder sites (or crags) are usually tree-shrouded, seldom of mega size (like the ultra long TLC crag, or the 1,000+ problem LLB site). Most are just small hidden quaint little pocket gems (by Oregonian standards). These bouldering sites offer tantalizing exploratory options for those dedicated resident hunters of the sport, not the fickle rush-job type that wastes the forest to snag a few lines, but for those lifers who know their own backcountry forest like a skilled mushroom hunter who knows the best spot to search for chanterelle mushrooms.

Sandbag ratings are hopefully at a minimum herein, but you may still encounter some old-school V-grades that will throw you off, yet through diligent site research our team has

TA at Cooper Spur Boulders

made lengthy efforts to either know or send many of the boulder problems in this book. In general the ratings aim for consistency on a per zone/area basis only.

Bouldering and rock climbing is an inherently dangerous activity and you could potentially get injured or die from either sport activity. Do not use this book as an instructional manual. Get proper training through a guide service, or an educational class with a local outdoor organization, or with knowledgable friends. Learn the game gradually tutorially with associates who know how to keep you safe and alive and happy so you can go out bouldering again tomorrow.

Textual and visual errors may exist in this book. You assume responsibility for your own safety, not the book author, nor publisher.

If you have historical beta or development information that is missing from this book, and are inclined to share, or provide feedback, contact us via email with your info. We always aim to improve the accuracy of future book editions.

BOULDERING GRADE SCALE

Boulder problems use the well-known Verm or V-rating system. This effective grade comparison scale is designed to articulate a relational comparison involving short bursts of energy typical of concise boulder moves. Though it should relate to actual exact lead rock climbing grades it does not quite parallel, due in part to broad variables encountered in protection based roped climbing. Beta in this book is described as if you are standing in front of the most prominent aspect of a particular boulder, and described from left to right, unless otherwise noted (such as if it's a boulder with problems 360° around).

Beta Nuances (Sit Start, Grades, etc)

In this bouldering book the V-scale grading units have meaning (sometimes subtle). VB means anything 5.9 and below. If it's shown as V2 (V4) the left rating is 'standing start' and the parenthesis is a 'sit start' rating. A single grade, like V2ss, is used if sit start is the common way its done, thus 'ss' is Sit Start. If no parenthesis grade follows the first grade then the listed grade is generally assumed to be sent as a standing start (typical for tall boulders).

Broadly listed ratings (such as V5-7 or V6-V9) are merely an approximation, but its probably within that range. And that

type of graded problem may (or may not) be done. If done, it's usually narrowed to one single V-grade (but not always) or at the most two (V4/5) side by side grades.

A question mark '?' after the grade indicates an unknown rating (or possibly not yet seen an ascent). If the grade has a plus '+' symbol it's an open-ended grade assumed to be a minimum of that grade (or stouter); its a mere generic estimate not intended to indicate its final real difficulty. Any V-number may, theoretically, be off a bit. Lastly, some V-numerics on the topo are mere generic approximations, not implicatory of finality. What is not science is science fiction.

Bouldering is all about the moves (not the length), involving short bursts of energy, whether it's either V-crux power, or V-classic movement. That's the essense of the game.

INFO SYMBOLS

A selection of boulder problem descriptions may have additional icons representative of other potential challenges found at that particular boulder or problem. The ⚠ symbol indicates our cutting edge of real high-ball problems at 17' (5-meters) and above. Tall problems below that range may still be spicy, but are not indicated in this guide. A jagged edge ⌒ symbol indicates a rocky or hard to protect landing (where extra crashpads and spotters are wise protocol).

USING THIS BOOK

1. **Green** problems range: VB-V2
2. **Blue** problems range: V3-V6
3. **Orange** problems range: V7-V10
4. **Red** problems range: V11-V17

This book uses a four-star system to indicate problem quality:
No stars. The problem exists.
★ The problem is minor, but interesting.
★★ The problem is average quality, but worth doing.
★★★ An excellent problem, and it's well worth doing.
★★★★ A stellar problem (if you climb at the grade, then definitely do it).

Grade Comparison Chart

V Rating	YDS scale
VB	5.9 and under
V0	5.10a/b
V1	5.10c/d
V2	5.11a/b
V3	5.11c/d
V4	5.12-
V5	5.12b/c
V6	5.12+
V7	5.13-
V8	5.13b/c
V9	5.13+
V10	5.14a
V11	5.14b
V12	5.14c
V13	5.14d
V14	5.15a
V15	5.15b
V16	5.15c
V17	5.15d

TA at *Badger Boulders*

6 INTRODUCTION

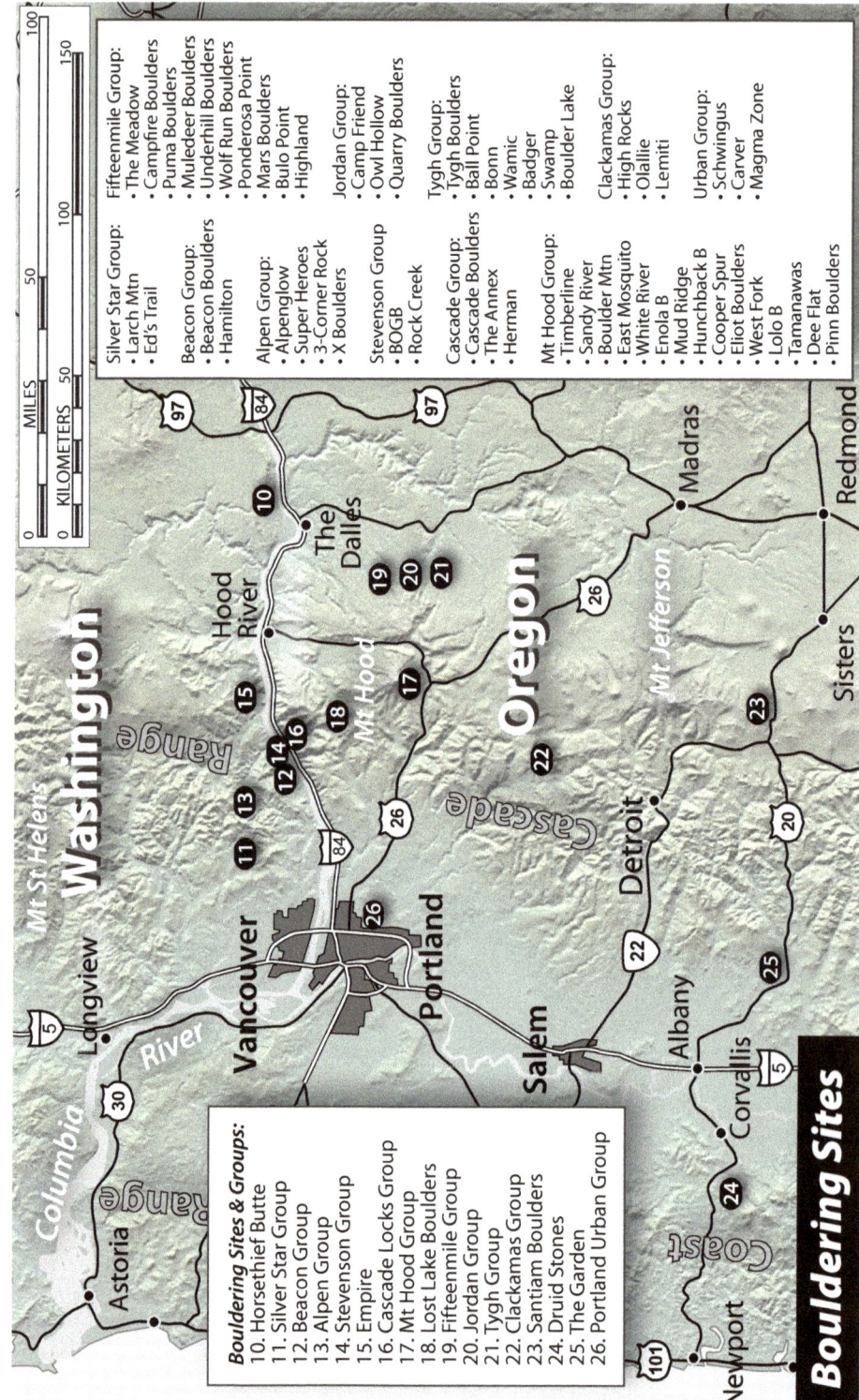

Silver Star Group:
- Larch Mtn
- Ed's Trail

Beacon Group:
- Beacon Boulders
- Hamilton

Alpen Group:
- Alpenglow
- Super Heroes
- 3-Corner Rock
- X Boulders

Stevenson Group
- BOGB
- Rock Creek

Cascade Group:
- Cascade Boulders
- The Annex
- Herman

Mt Hood Group:
- Timberline
- Sandy River
- Boulder Mtn
- East Mosquito
- White River
- Enola B
- Mud Ridge
- Hunchback B
- Cooper Spur
- Eliot Boulders
- West Fork
- Lolo B
- Tamanawas
- Dee Flat
- Pinn Boulders

Fifteenmile Group:
- The Meadow
- Campfire Boulders
- Puma Boulders
- Muledeer Boulders
- Underhill Boulders
- Wolf Run Boulders
- Ponderosa Point
- Mars Boulders
- Bulo Point
- Highland

Jordan Group:
- Camp Friend
- Owl Hollow
- Quarry Boulders

Tygh Group:
- Tygh Boulders
- Ball Point
- Bonn
- Wamic
- Badger
- Swamp
- Boulder Lake

Clackamas Group:
- High Rocks
- Olallie
- Lemiti

Urban Group:
- Schwingus
- Carver
- Magma Zone

Bouldering Sites & Groups:
10. Horsethief Butte
11. Silver Star Group
12. Beacon Group
13. Alpen Group
14. Stevenson Group
15. Empire
16. Cascade Locks Group
17. Mt Hood Group
18. Lost Lake Boulders
19. Fifteenmile Group
20. Jordan Group
21. Tygh Group
22. Clackamas Group
23. Santiam Boulders
24. Druid Stones
25. The Garden
26. Portland Urban Group

Bouldering Sites

Mt Hood Bouldering Areas (southern)

This section details bouldering sites on the southern slopes and valleys of Mt Hood, sites that are generally found along the US Highway 26 corridor (and up to White River on Hwy 35).

TIMBERLINE BOULDERS

Timberline Boulders offer a extensive quality string of high-altitude dacite and andesite boulders scattered widely across the south-facing alpine slope on Mt Hood. The greatest concentration of boulders is found between the 6000' to 7100' elevation, in a rough square mile northwest from Timberline Lodge and west of the Magic Mile Chairlift. Several other prominent stones exist east, and north, of Silcox Hut. The boulders range from little spit balls to large behemoths up to 24' tall, with the greatest concentration of lines ranging from VB-V4 (and a tiny score up to V6). The seasonal weather elements have fiercely and abrasively scoured the rock surface, thus keeping virtually all the boulders spotless of moss. Some of the larger stones remain above the snow pack year-round, and tend to have some black colored lichen growing on top portion of the block. The vivid high-altitude scenery of jet blue skies and strata-cumulus clouds combined with twisted clusters of mountain hemlock and alpine whitebark pine create a visually appealing, photographic destination.

History: The site has seen brief exploration by a few Lodge employees who scrambled on a few stones. Spread over a dozen years Mr O combined many day hikes with visits to all of the boulders, tapping various lines a little bit at a time. By about 2011 he had literally sent about 90% of all known problems at this site. Additional stout sends were established by Mr A in about 2011.

Season

The optimal season to access this area is from late June through late October. The sunshine and steady breezes tend to dry out the boulders very quickly, so even on an overcast day you may find bouldering feasible. Bring adequate clothing if the weather is cold. A light crashpad, or even a small satellite crashpad may be suitable if you plan to walk to the further destinations, because it is over one mile distance to reach the furthest boulders. Many boulder problems are tall, so expect committing lines with careful assessment. A typical daily tour usually yields 20-30 lines before the sharp weather-resistant phenocryst crystals gradually peal your finger pads raw. Several likely bouldering choices to aim for are Stormin' Normin, Blacktop, Zelda, or Zig boulders.

Directions

From Portland drive east on US Hwy 26 to Government Camp, then drive up Timberline Road to the parking lot at Timberline Lodge. The area is virtually treeless above the lodge, so getting visual bearings on certain large stones is relatively easy. Most of the time you will be in a big triangular zone above Pacific Crest Trail (PCT), west of the Magic Mile Chairlift (unless you went to Silcox), and east of Little Zigzag Canyon (unless you went all the way to Zippora). There is one north-south trail just west of the Stormin' Normin Chairlift that a lot of day hiker's use, and this can be a valuable access tool, if need.

To start, walk north from the lodge, initially on a generic trail till you locate the junction of the Magic Mile Chairlift dirt maintenance road and the PCT Skyline trail. Once you are here... there are several logical tour direction choices.

1.) Hike up the Magic Mile Chairlift (MMC) dirt access road a short distance to Zephyr Boulder, and onward up the road to Zeppelin and Zola Boulders, all generally near various chairlift

8 MT HOOD ZONE (SOUTH)

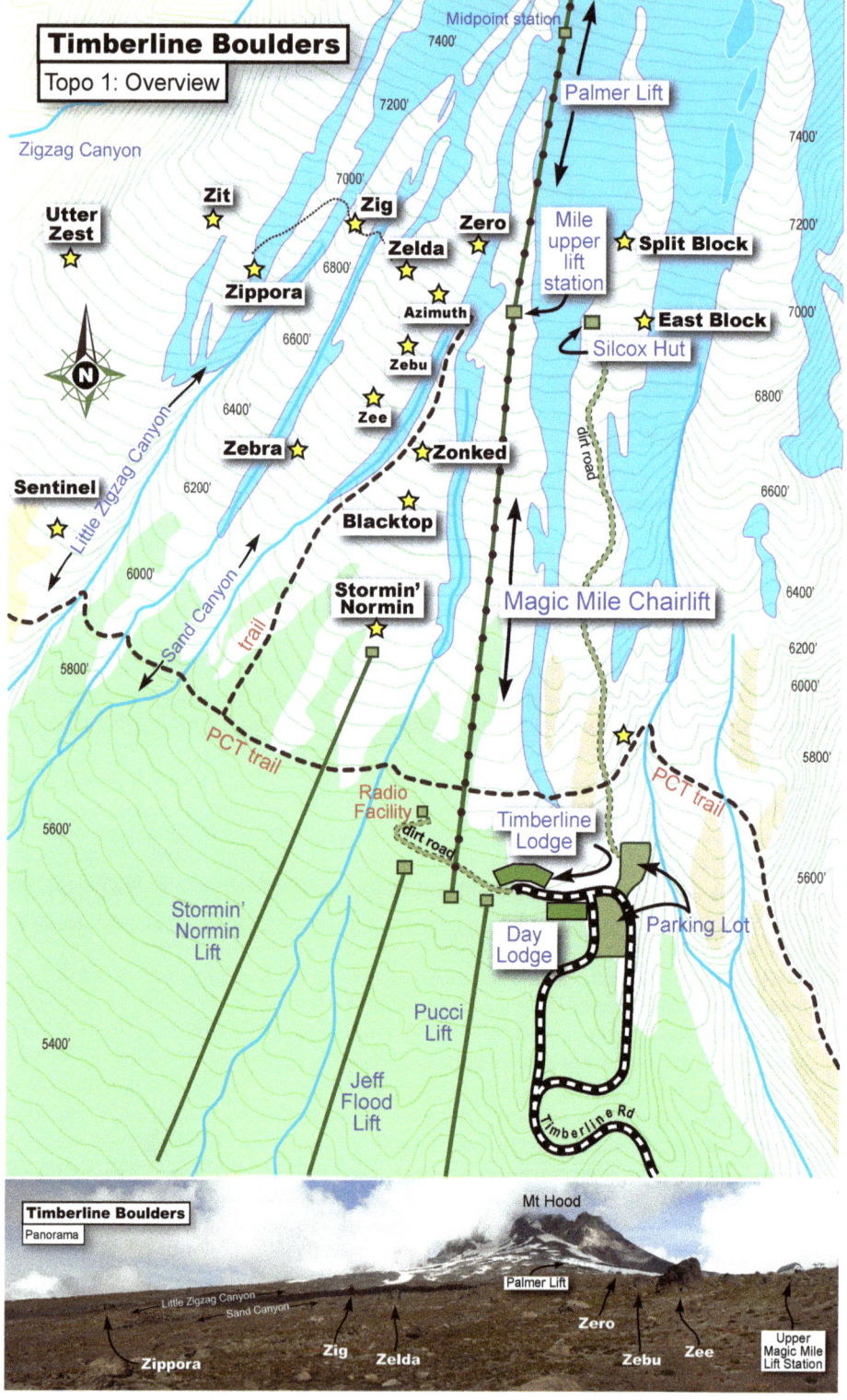

Timberline Boulders — Topo 1: Overview

Timberline Boulders Panorama

pole sets.

2.) Take PCT Skyline trail west a short distance, then follow this uphill to the upper lift station of Stormin' Normin Chairlift (SNC). A few yards above this upper lift station is the the Stormin' Normin Boulder, an obvious introductory stone, followed by Blacktop further uphill, then Black Gold, Zonked, etc. From Blacktop Boulder aim uphill (passing Black Gold, and Zonked) northwest to Zelda. From Zelda aim northwest across Sand Canyon to Zig Boulder, then across Little Zigzag Canyon and downhill 400' to a side branch where the low sitting Zippora Boulders. These two canyons are steep sloped when crossing them at a lower elevation, but still feasible if you want to do it.

Several 'way-out-there' options exist beyond Zippora Boulders, which are Zit Boulder, Utter Zest Boulder, and the south most oddity Sentinel Boulder, if you are so inclined. Most other stones in that region are low angle or too short. You can descend from Sentinel downhill several hundred feet to the PCT (Skyline) trail and hike back to the east directly to Timberline Lodge.

STORMIN' NORMAN STRING

Stormin' Normin Boulder

Stormin' Normin is the lowest of the string of boulders at this section. Start here first, and then hike uphill to the next boulder in the string. There are several good problems on this short stone, which are considered to be the entrance exam for TLB. This string starts immediately above the upper chairlift station called Stormin' Normin. You can reach here by walking on the dirt road from Timberline Lodge west and slightly uphill to this site.

V1 First Run
Waltz up the minor groove on left.

V1 (V2ss) Stormin' Normin
Start on the jugs below the arête, and power up the hung prow to the top nose. Exit variants exist.

V2 Infinite Light
Low start same as Stormin' Normin, then climb up exiting via the right seam onto the slab to the right.

V4ss Thundercloud
On the eastside, slither onto the smooth slab rightward.

Razor Stone

A minor 10' tall stone about 80' directly west of the Stormin' Normin' Chairlift upper station in a main snow channel. The surficial texture has sharp as blades crystals that make sending anything on this unit a delicate matter. About six lines (L to R): **VB** face, **VB** crack, **V0** face, **V0** prow, **VB** corner crack, **V0**, **V0**. Nothing special here.

Lightning Bolt Boulder

A minor slump located a few yards north of the

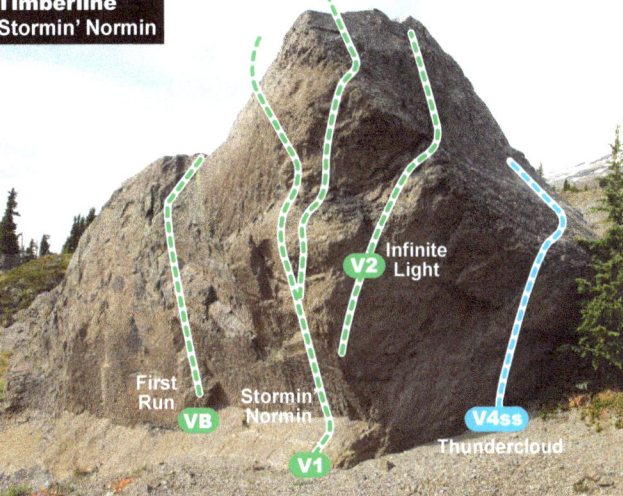

Timberline Stormin' Normin

10 MT HOOD ZONE (SOUTH)

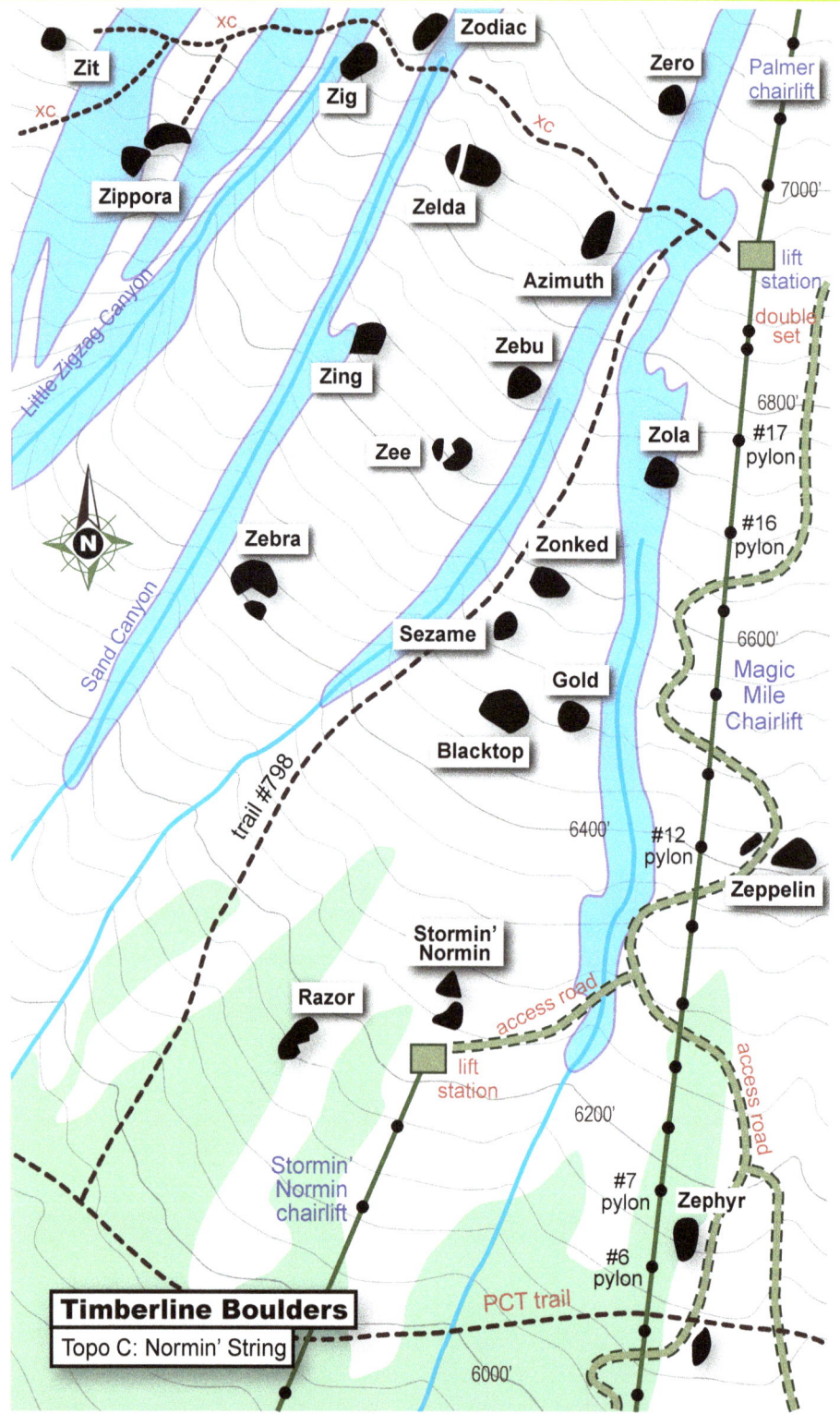

Timberline Boulders
Topo C: Normin' String

Timberline Boulders ✦ PB 11

On Stormin' Normin' boulder

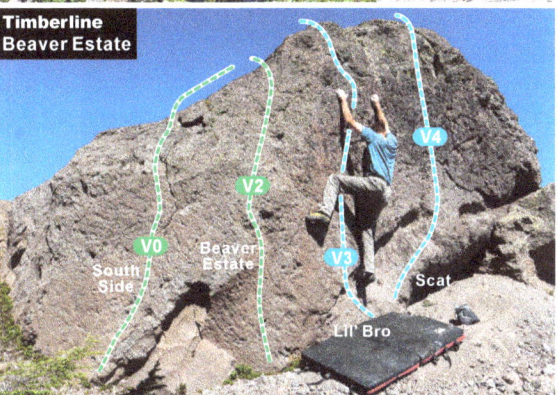

main Stormin' Normin boulder.

V4ss Lightning Bolt ❏
V2ss Stuck Like Glue ❏
VBss Free Ride ❏

Beaver Estate Boulder

A short distance below Blacktop Boulder is a large SE facing vertical stone (10' tall by 20' long) with a big rodent nest at the base.

V0 South Side ❏
V3 Beaver Estate ❏
V2 Lil' Bro ❏
V4 Scat ❏

Blacktop Boulder

Blacktop Behemoth is a classic 16' tall stone (part of the Stormin' Normin string of boulders). It's a good place to view the other boulders from the top of this monster so as to coordinate your direction of travel.

V0 Sunrise ❏
Facing west-*ish*. Power up the initial steep face on slopers and up black lichen holds to the top.

V0 Sunset ❏
The 2" wide curved rail. Start up the low angle slab on the left side of the monolith. Dance up

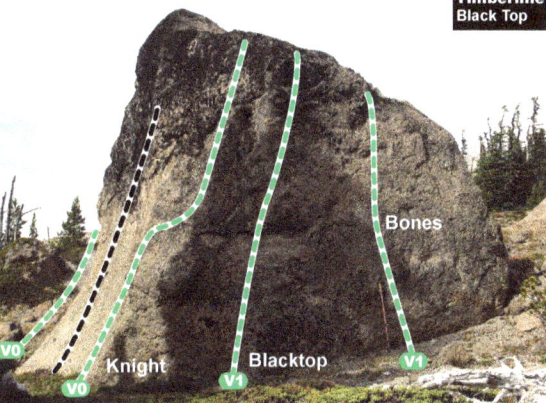

the obvious curving rail and exit up left onto the black lichen slopers near the top.

V_ Black Lichen ❏
Tall slab loaded with black lichen.

V0 Knight ❏
A fun line, start on the low angle slab. Aim up right onto the top of a tiny rock knob, then di-

12 MT HOOD ZONE (SOUTH)

rectly up to the top on good holds.

V1 Blacktop
The classic line with tech moves that keep you on edge to the top.

V1 Bones
A minor balance on the right most flat section of face.

Black Gold Boulder

This one sits about 40' to the east of Blacktop. There are 2-3 minor VB's other than the 3 following power lines listed below.

V2ss Vermiculite
Sit start on the east most side

V6 Black Gold
Crux necessitates palming onto smooth sloped slab on south side of block.

V1 Spring Flower
Ascend a seam on the SW side of the block

Sezame Street Boulder

A minor block in between Blacktop and Zonked, with eight slab VB's (most are stubby 'sit starts').

Zonked Boulder

Zonked Boulder is about 300' uphill from Blacktop and is identified by the graffiti. Though about 13' high, route scrounging is limited. Beta L to R.

V3ss Zoned Out
Thin seam on left side at hung prow.

VB Blackhole of Anti-Knowledge
The obvious crack.

V0 Agent of Influence
A slightly hung break in the rock.

VB Zonked
Minor stubby prow near graffiti.

One Stripe Zebra

One Stripe Zebra is a quality 14' tall splitter finger crack on a southeast facing vertical face and goes at **V1** with sharp jams, a hollow block at the top, and tricky mantle. Limited opps.

Zee Boulder

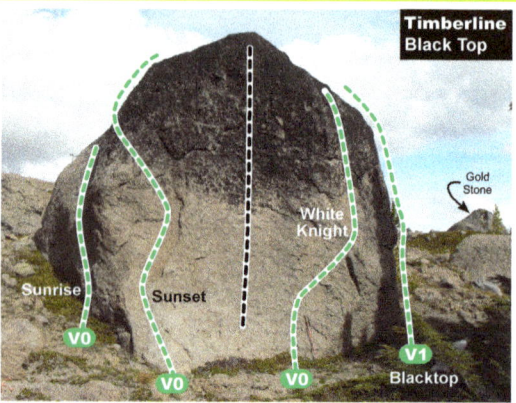
Timberline Black Top

Timberline Gold Stone

Timberline One Stripe Zebra

A broken small block with a nook tucked under the west side of the larger stone.

V4ss Zen Master
Sit start; power out a thin finger locks crack (well overhung); punch past the lip and cruise up right on better edges to the top.

Zelda Boulder ⚠

Big Zelda is a classic 24' tall broken-in-half

Timberline Boulders ✦ PB 13

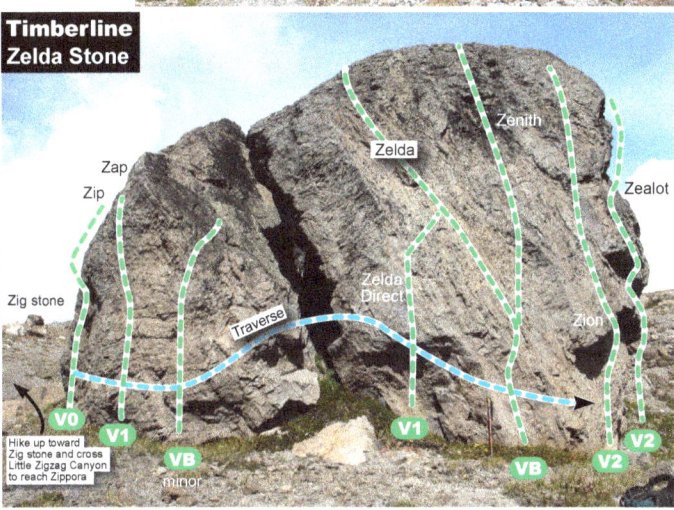

double chunk mega block. The south face is a tall aspect with cool lines, and the east face notably overhangs. The west block is a bit crumbly in places:

West Block

V3 Zurich ❏
Small Roof on west side

V0 Zip ❏
Nice basic crack or face. Several variants all about the same.

V1 Zap ❏
Full south face using right hand on the arête prow and fluted holds.

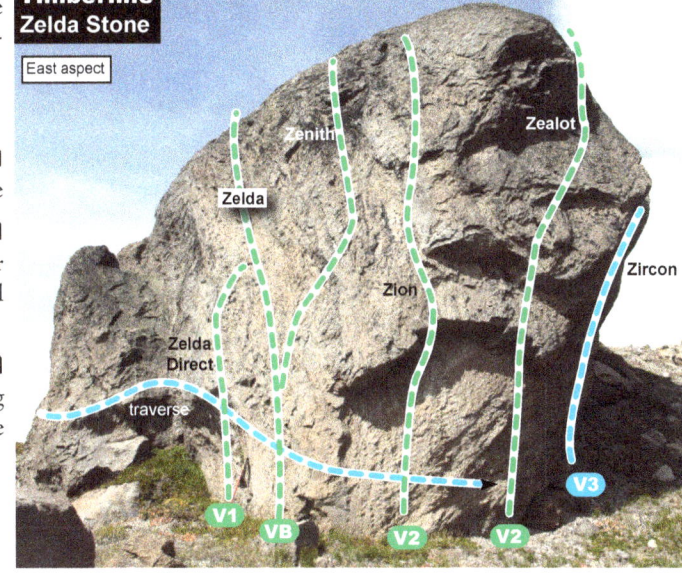

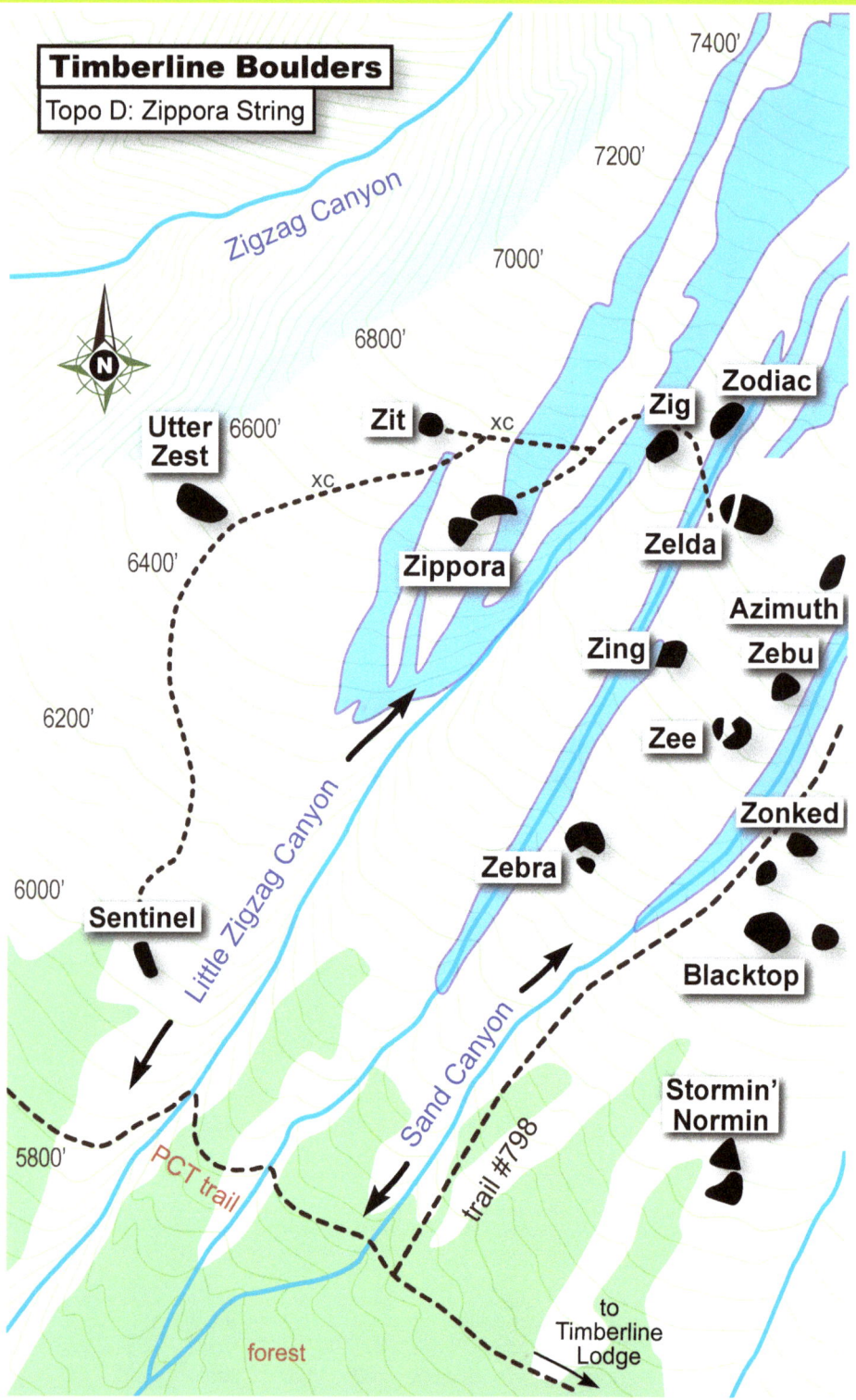

Main Block

VB Zelda
The classic line. Dance up the initial moves to a tiny stance, then move up leftward following the slight groove. Starts powerful, stays steep, and has a rounded top out.

V1 Zelda Direct
A minor direct using semi-hollow holds.

VB Zenith
Another classic line. Start same as Zelda but move up right to next groove then up to top.

V2 Zion
Start at a minor roof and triangle pocket above lip, then use side-pulls and aim left till you can join Zenith

V2 Zealot
Starts same as Zion but over all four obvious small lips directly to the top.

V2+ Zircon
Variant start up past the initial two small lips, merges with left line.

V3 Zither
Ascends a steep overhung (hollow rock) crack to sloped face.

V3 Zelda Traverse
Is harder if including the east face.

Zodiac Boulder

This stone sits just uphill from Zelda on the west edge of a lesser arm of Sand Canyon, immediately above the east-west hiker's path. The beta, beginning with the north-most line. The stone is a bit flakey.

V3 Zodiac
A quality smooth andesite sequence on low overhung side-pulls, launch for the top jug, and mantle crux.

V3 Celestial Dreams
Start on the VB, traverse left to join the V3 line, then mantle up.

VB (west groove), **VB** (the SW nose), **VB** (the east groove).

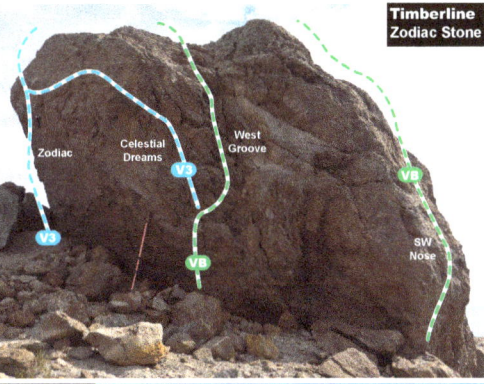

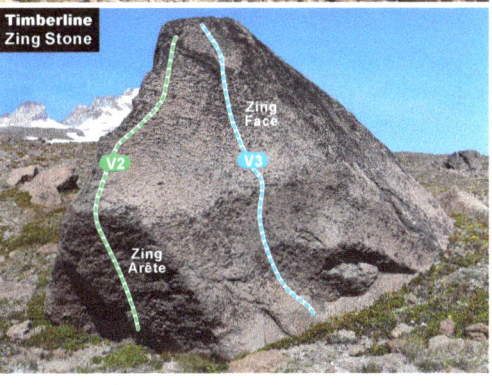

Zing Boulder

An 11' tall loner stone located about 250' downhill from Zelda stone. A quality stone with a rounded rib that starts as a rounded overhang.

V2 Zing Arête
Standing start, high wide foot edges over a bulge to get established on the arête.

V3 Zing Face
A very smooth almost featureless slope on the

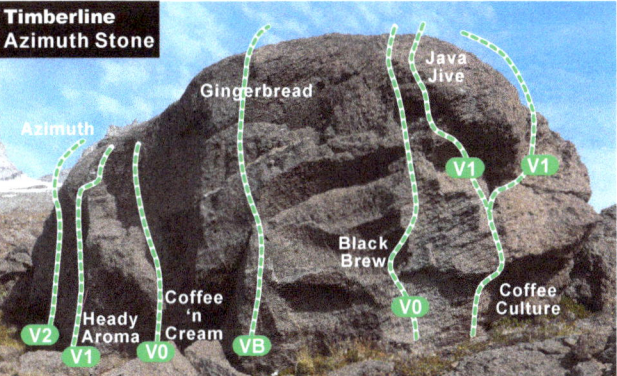

16 MT HOOD ZONE (SOUTH)

right side.

Azimuth Boulder

Azimuth Stone is a flat laying (9' tall by 20' long by 15' wide) stone difficult to distinguish from a distance, composed of grainy dacite rock. All routes overhang as starting move, except the VB. Located west of the ski boundary signs, west of the initial snow ravine. Located 200' west of chairlift, and 100' below the rough horizontal hiker's path that runs west from the chairlift building. Beta is from the north aspect counterclockwise (most are on west side). All routes opening move bulge except the VB.

V2 Azimuth
Sends up the rounded bulge

V1 Heady Aroma
Up overhung center into low angle scoop.

V0 Coffee n' Cream
Minor stuff.

VB Gingerbread Eggnog Machiato
Incuts and steps on west side.

V0 Black Brew
A good line that starts low on left on overhang, run jugs to top.

V1 Java Jive
Start low on overhang, and move up left.

V1 Coffee Culture
Start low on overhang, and move up right.
And a traverse (**V4**) starting at the VB.

Zig Boulder

Zig Boulder is overhung on the west and east sides. This is reached by continuing west on the faint path (which extends west from the Mile Lift Station) just uphill from Zelda. Zig Boulder is perched on the east edge of Little Zigzag Canyon.

Timberline Zig Stone

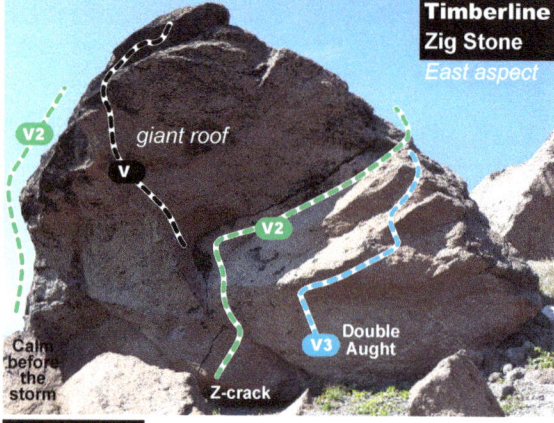

Timberline Zig Stone — East aspect

Timberline Zig Stone — West aspect

VB Zig Arête
Fun basic run on the SW nose.

Timberline Boulders ✦ PB

V2 Zillion
An elusive delicate balancy face that starts with a high right step (south aspect).

V3 Calm before the Storm
Two high steps, then onto a long smooth lichen covered slab (south aspect).

V4 (?) High Roof
The big overhung roof on the east side.

V2ss Z-Crack
Obvious eastside low starter going into a crack (sit start).

V3ss Double Aught
Eastside low lip move (sit start).

V4ss Zoroaster
Thin crimps angling up left (briefly) on west side in a minor overhung nook.

V2 (V3ss) Pacific Pearl
Cool line on west side in overhung nook on round nose. Start on tiny crimps, dyno to jug, then mantle up.

ZIPPORA GROUP

Zippora Boulder ⚠

The Zippora cluster has several superb bouldering problems. The stone offers powerful, quality, hi-ball problems on steep, overhanging rock. Get there by hiking west from Upper Zig Boulder across the Zigzag Canyon, then descend about 200' downhill to the site.

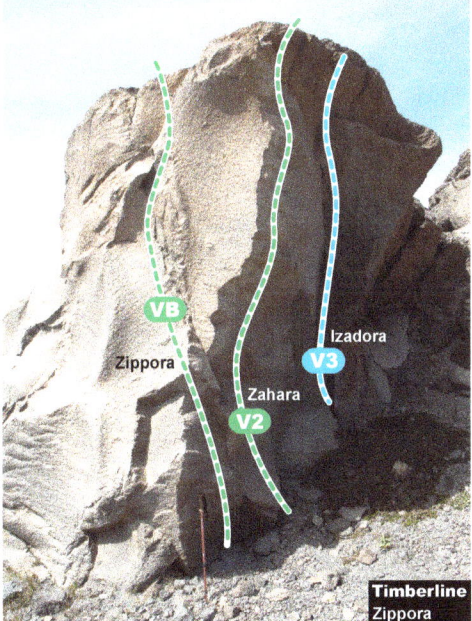

18 MT HOOD ZONE (SOUTH)

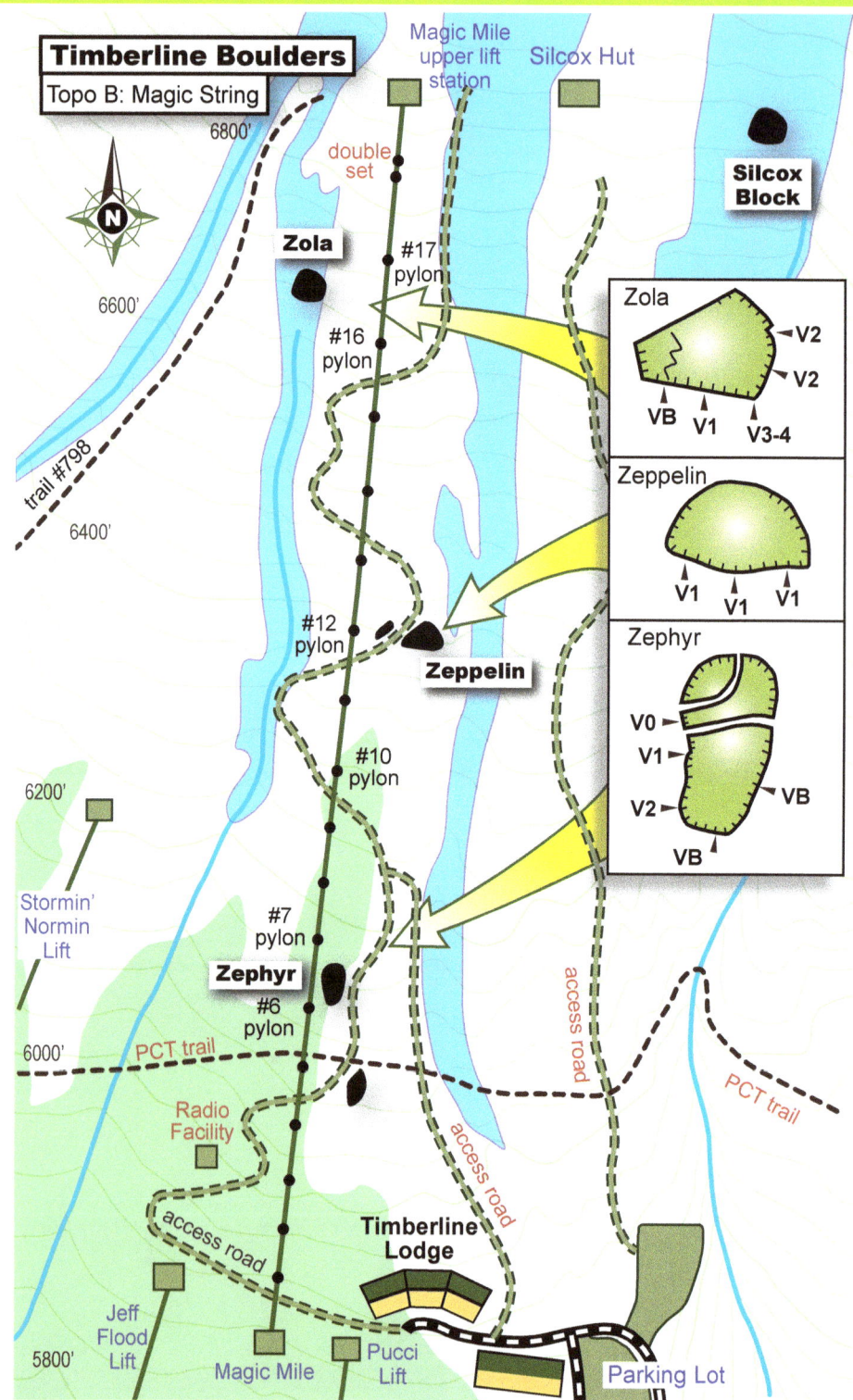

Timberline Boulders ✦ PB 19

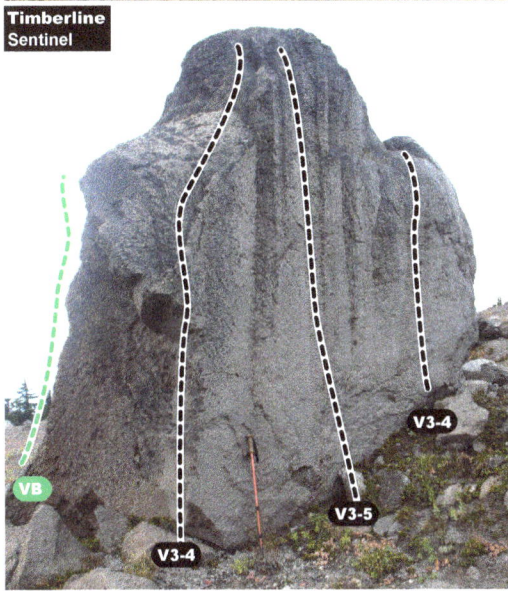

The lower boulder offers smooth crisp features with a super overhung east side. The upper boulder is rough textured with a steep southeast aspect.

VB Zippora ☐
A quality fun face. At the arête base move up left onto face using small edges.

V2 Zahara ☐
Superb arête with slightly hung power crimps.

V4 Izadora ☐
A cool upside down crimps power line.

V0 Nth Degree ☐
A great awakening. Start under overhang on crack underclings, move up right into hung scoop, then up left to better crack holds.

V2 Weapons Grade Stupidity ☐
A steep series of crimps on tallest section.

VB Secular Myopia ☐
Minor problem with a hollow block to start, mostly large holds.

Zit Boulder

Zit Boulder is visible further west as you cross the Little Zigzag canyon near Zig boulder. It is like a little round bump out west-ish and appears to be big, but in reality is just a short 8' tall rock with a flat smooth south side.

V0ss One Zit ☐
Starting with right hand on incut in center face, and go up left.

V1ss Two Zits ☐
Start with left hand on center face incut, right hand in a triangle incut pocket, go up right.

Utter Zest Boulder

Can be reached by hiking way out west from Zippora. It's situated on the rounded ridge crest overlooking Big Zigzag Canyon. The long traverse line is about 60' long.

V3 Utter Zest ☐
A traverse cruise combining considerable sustained effort. Start the traverse high on the

far east side by using the top slopers to palm down going left, descending down past a crux (onto the south side), then go left along the low hand rail (4' off the ground & minor hollowness) around to the west side, then up to a stance, then finish up brief vertical moves with incut jugs on the far upper left west side, ending on the top of the boulder.

Sentinel Boulder

Sentinel Boulder is a unique oddity about 300' above the PCT Skyline trail and immediately west of the Little Zigzag Canyon. It stands tall, providing a northeast face that is flat and smooth.

VB _____ ☐
V_ _____ ☐
V_ _____ ☐
V_ _____ ☐

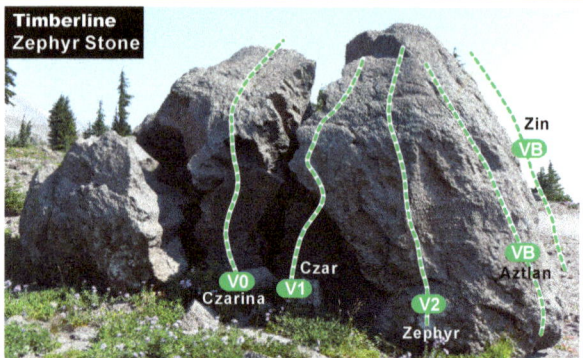

Timberline Zephyr Stone

Zero Boulder

Zero Boulder is a highly visible round boulder on a prominent knoll 2 pylons up and northwest of the upper Magic Mile chairlift station about 200'. It is immediately west of a deep snow filled ravine used by skiers. The out of bounds ski signs run downhill along that same knoll.

VB Afterglow ☐
Can jog up left onto the rib to top out.

V3 Zero ☐
Power up the center of the east face on nothing and finish on nothing slopers.

V0 Roman Nose ☐
On prow, several tight moves to a series of slopers to finish.

VB Jug Haul ☐
A west side, slightly hung series of jugs.

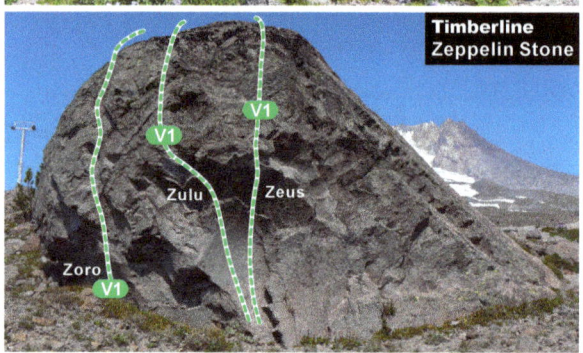

Timberline Zeppelin Stone

MAGIC MILE STRING

The following boulders are located by walking north of Timberline Lodge up a trail to the PCT trail, then continue walking up the dirt maintenance road.

Zephyr Boulder

Located 80' downhill from pole set #7. Excellent rock, 11' tall, broken in three pieces, and is a good introductory block for the area. About 200' above the PCT trail, located between pole

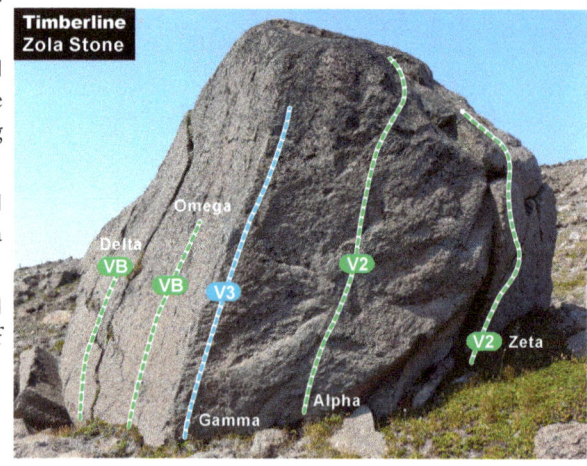

Timberline Zola Stone

set #6 and #7 on the Mile Chairlift.

V0ss Czarina ☐
Sit start and use both edges of this narrow center block.

V1ss Czar ☐
Start under the minor angled lip and pop up right, then use the left arête to top up. Good line.

V2 Zephyr ☐
Techy, balancy on a slight overhang, then up to a rounded easier top out. High quality.

VB Aztlan ☐
Fun slabby face, a basic introductory standing start problem.

VB Zin ☐
Standing start with pinches and small edges.

Zeppelin Boulder

Continue walking up the access road (from Zephyr) to a set of two boulders next to the road, and about 200' east of pole set #12. The east block is the largest (about 11' tall) and rounded for its upper portion. Composed of andesite with prominent cut surfaces and edges.

V1 Zorro ☐
Start low, and pop for the horn jug, then upward as it rounds out.

V1 Zulu ☐
Start low in the overhung scoop on south face, and work up left on positive edges. Cool line.

V1 Zeus ☐
Start low in the same overhung scoop, but go directly up to the top. Cool line.

Zola Boulder

Continue to walk up the access road and aim for a prominent block 200' west and halfway between pole set #16 and pole set #17. The rock has a prominent crack on its south face slab. Height is 11'

tall, with a 75° south face slab.

VB Delta ☐
The basic obviously easy jam crack.

VB Omega ☐
Cool delicate face problem on the south slab. Start on arête, move up left to face.

V3 Gamma ☐
Climb the arête using very thin tech edges and tiny features.

V2 Alpha ☐
Standing start using good side pulls. Power up and over the minor bulge. Cool line.

V2 Zeta ☐
Sit start and pop for jug and a jug (detached but solid block). Cool line.

Zebu Boulder

A boulder about 11' tall on east side with three minor problems. Located directly west of Zola.

VB Zebu ☐
Jugs on rounded SE nose.

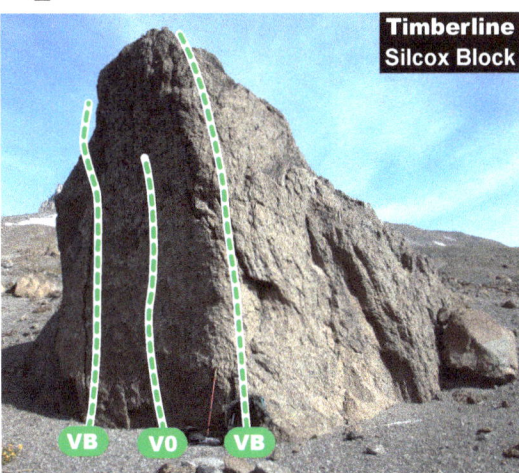

22 MT HOOD ZONE (SOUTH)

V0 Coffee n' Cream
On scoop on center east face.

VB (on jugs on uphill line).

Black Pearl Boulder

If you like to hike, continue up along the west side of the Palmer Chairlift to the 3rd pole set down from the Palmer Mid-point lift house, and 300' west of the lift. An overhung 40' long west facing boulder with a flat lip running the entire length of the west aspect, low at both ends, and 11' tall at center. Difficult to see due to its flat top. All lines are full mantle exits.

V_ (?) ___
A vertical tips seam on the upper left section of overhung west face.

V1 Black Pearl
This is the center flake rail. Start low on obvious center flake, run rail up left, mantle out.

VB Hubris Greed & Ignorance
The basic fat jug run on right.

THE TRAVERSE:

V3 Pearl Hunter
Do the entire 40' long lip traverse from right to left.

The following boulders are located east of the top lift station of the Magic Mile chairlift in the vicinity of the Silcox Hut.

Silcox Boulder ⚠

Silcox Boulder is located about 300' east of the Silcox Hut at the same elevation. Highly visible from all angles and located near a major snow ravine.

VB The Nose
The basic rounded nose with plenty of holds.

V0 Lichen
A steep lichen covered face just left of the nose.

V0 Detached Flake
Yup a detached flake.

Split Block Boulder

Split Block Boulder is to the north of Silcox Hut (about 300' uphill) at the level of the Palmer Chairlift at the 3rd pylon. A low **Split Traverse (V2)** exists on the W-S-E side. The rock is split in half east-to-west (encompasses 30' diameter).

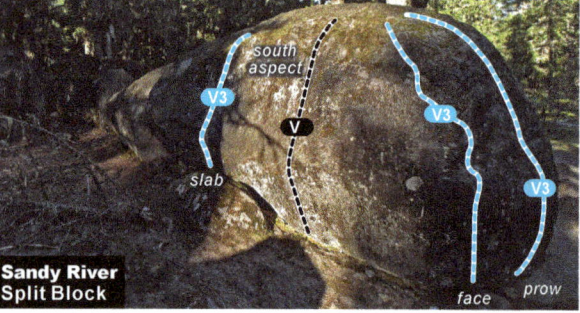

SANDY RIVER BOULDERS

Along the ever popular Ramona Falls trail are several boulders near the hiker's trail. These are erratic stones swept into their present location by floods long ago. Most stones are slick-as-snot basaltic rock (micro-crystalline plagioclase in deep black-gray matrix), well smoothed from tumbling and weathering, scattered in three clusters on flat sandy terrain about ½ mile apart. The stones have good flat landings (single crashpad viable site), some mossy aspects, though very limited total problems (less than 25). Other stones alongside the river tend to get shifted by the river flow.

Directions
Drive east from Sandy, Oregon on U.S. Hwy 26 to Zigzag, then drive north on NF18, turning

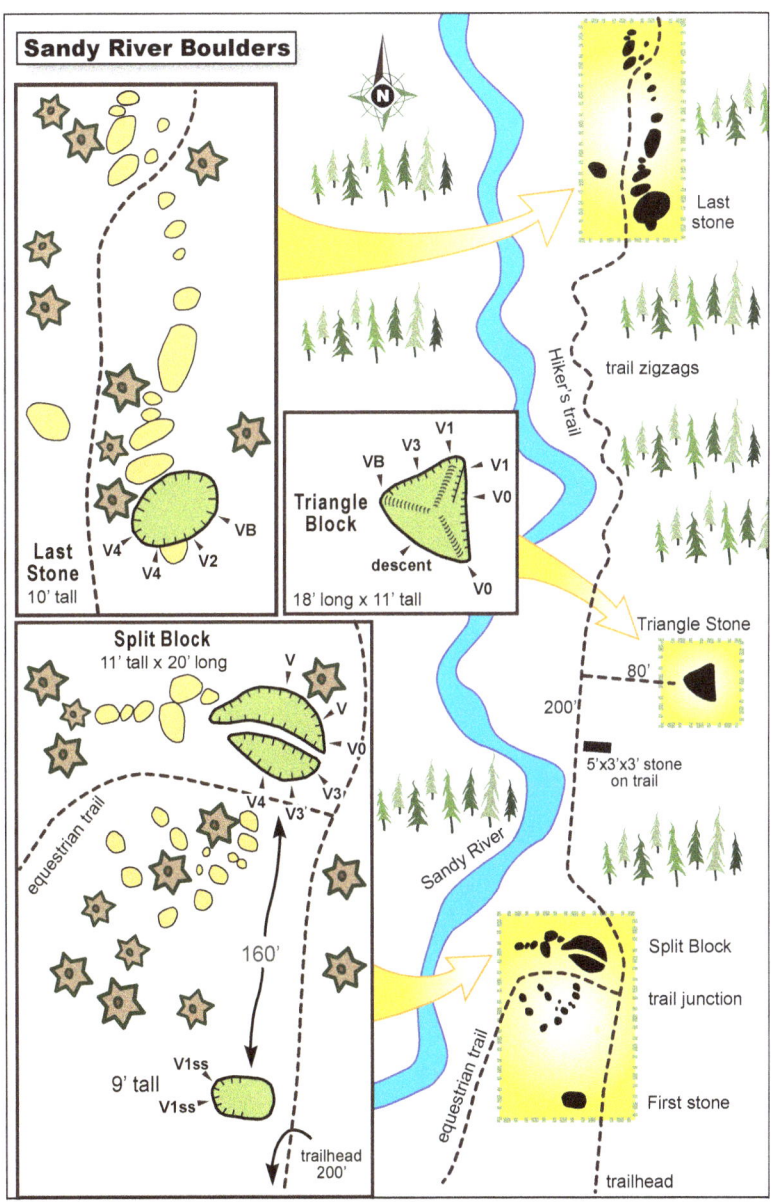

right on NF1825 and drive to the Sandy River trailhead #797. See diagram for more info

Split Boulder

The obvious large set of split stones.

V3/V4 _____ ❑
Short face on leftmost part of smaller stone.

V_ _____ ❑
Shorty immediately right of previous problem.

V3 _____ ❑
Round face (just left of next problem).

V3 _____ ❑
Round nose just left of OW (on smaller stone).

VB _____ ❑
Off-width between both stones.

V0 _____ ❑
Quality rib with pocket (on big stone).

Triangle Boulder

V0 _____ *(minor south rib)* ❑

V2ss _____ *(east face)* ❑

V0 _____ *(east ramp)* ❑

V1 _____ ❑
Rib left of tree

V1 _____ ❑
Rib right of tree

V2ss ___ *(north side)* ❑

VB *(low angle rib)* ❑

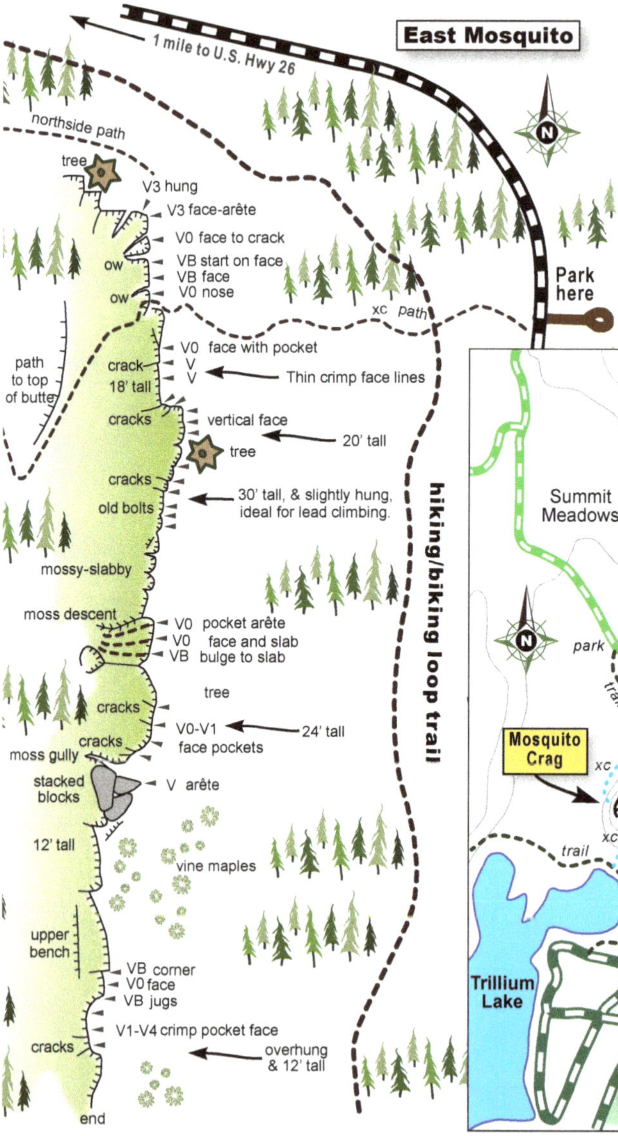
East Mosquito
1 mile to U.S. Hwy 26
northside path
tree
V3 hung
V3 face-arête
V0 face to crack
VB start on face
VB face
V0 nose
ow
ow
xc path
Park here
V0 face with pocket
V
V
Thin crimp face lines
path to top of butte
crack
18' tall
cracks
vertical face
tree
20' tall
cracks
30' tall, & slightly hung, ideal for lead climbing.
old bolts
hiking/biking loop trail
mossy-slabby
moss descent
V0 pocket arête
V0 face and slab
VB bulge to slab
tree
cracks
V0-V1 face pockets
24' tall
cracks
moss gully
stacked blocks
V arête
12' tall
vine maples
upper bench
VB corner
V0 face
VB jugs
V1-V4 crimp pocket face
cracks
overhung & 12' tall
end

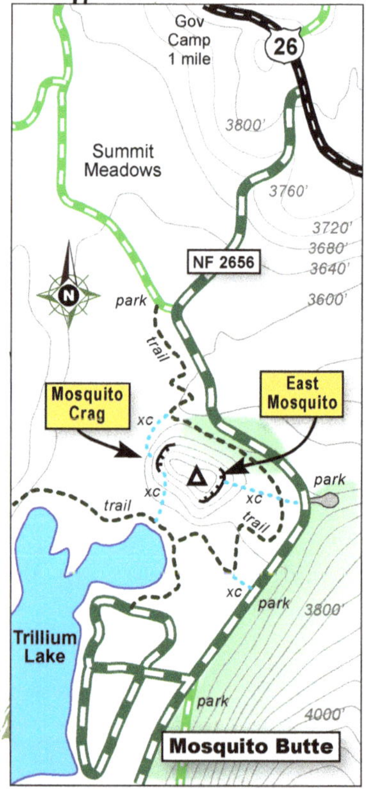
Gov Camp 1 mile
26
3800'
Summit Meadows
3760'
3720'
3680'
3640'
NF 2656
3600'
park
trail
Mosquito Crag
East Mosquito
xc
xc
park
trail
xc
trail
xc
park
3800'
Trillium Lake
park
4000'
Mosquito Butte

EAST MOSQUITO BLUFF

Trillium Lake is a popular scenic camping and hiking area, but it's also known for a quality secluded rock climbing bluff on the west end of Mosquito Butte. On the east end of the same butte (3,800' elevation) you'll find a short bluff conducive for bouldering. There are about a dozen existing problems (VB-V3 to date), but future room for about 15+ problems (though some of the taller stuff is rope terrain). The rock is a grainy textured, well-weathered, vertical basalt outcrop, ranging in height from 12' to 30' tall. Some minor moss or lichen growth (particularly near the cracks). Tucked in a forest shaded setting the 200' long bluff sees minimal use. Seasonal access from mid-May through October, and it's a 1-2 crashpad minimum recommended site.

History: the site was tapped initially by well-known local Govie hardman [JT] who also utilized a nearby rock climbing bluff. The northernmost lines are tapped. Most of the V-ratings south of Antfarm are merely raw estimates.

Directions

Drive Trillium Lake road NF 2656 for ¾ mile south from U.S. Hwy 26. Park at the east end of the butte, and walk cross-country westward a few hundred feet to the butte (you will cross a hike/bike trail that circles the butte). Beta is north to south (beta R to L).

North End

- **V3** Right side of overhung prow. ☐
- **V3** Face & arête; left side of prow. ☐
- **V0** Face to big edges; crack at top. ☐
- **VB** Face merging with slot. ☐
- **VB** The short gully. ☐
- **VB** The short nose. ☐

The cross-country path cuts up several steep steps here onto the knoll.

- **V0 Ant Farm** ☐
Start on giant pocket, reach to lip face edges, finish to top.
- **V2 (?) _____** 👑 ☐
Thin face and crack.
- **V4 (?) _____** ☐
Tall slightly hung flat crimpy face.

Southward is a very tall section that may yield about 10 lead climbs (some old bolts exist). Then a brief gap to the next cluster.

Tall Slab

Tall 16' slab with a bulge along the base.

- **V0 Pocket Pretense** ☐
Tackles the vertical rounded nose prow with big pockets.

- **VB Riplets** ☐
Tackles the bulge then a thin slab.
- **VB Double Deception** ☐
Get over initial bulge; cruise up slab.

Large tree

South of the tree is a 24' tall section that may yield 3-4 lead climbs. Just beyond it is a tall stacked blocks section.

South End Nook

The Nook (12' tall problems).

- **VB** _____ moss corner. ☐
- **V0** _____ thin face. ☐
- **VB** _____ jugs on face. ☐
- **V_ (?)** pocket crimps on overhung face. ☐
- **V_ (?)** pocket face. ☐
- **V_ (?)** the crack. ☐

MT HOOD ZONE (SOUTH)

MUD RIDGE BOULDERS

Nothing to write home about, but if you're utterly desperate - it exists. About 20 possible lines on weathered textured black basaltic rock (some with lichen/moss) with a light surface textural grain for friction, all perched on a minor wooded knoll at the 3,800' elevation. A few of the problems are easy, some are not. Minimally explored to date (by Mr O).

Directions
Drive the Trillium Lake road NF 2656, then drive south 1 mile on Mud Creek Road (prior to reaching the quarry) and park when you see a minor rock slope on the east side of road. Walk uphill angling rightward, off-trail scrambling up a steep slope from road to the knoll, then proceed south 200' to the south end cluster. See diagram for some of the beta (some grades are estimates).

WHITE RIVER BOULDERS

An idyllic scenic setting in an open pine tree lightly forested sandy flat area (where winter x-country skiers frequently tour) you will find two boulders that may interest a beginner boulderer. A scenic hike along the river on a closed gravel road, then up a brief slope to the pine tree flats. The first stone is the largest and offers a 360° circuit. The stone surface is well textured with crimps, holds, and smears. The north and northeast side is surprisingly overhung at the base (on the lower 2'-3' of the stone). Some routes offer sit start feasibility.

Where is the second smaller stone? Walk further north up the trail till you reach the power line, then walk west 100' to the second minor 8' tall moss-free andesite stone with rounded crimps, a short stout rail run, and several basic lines. Seasonal access is June to early November.

Directions
Drive U.S. Hwy 26 east past Government Camp, then on Hwy 35 to the White River parking lot on the north side of the road. Walk north on a gated dirt road. Hiking distance is about ¾ mile from parking lot.

Big Beluga
Beta begins on the westside at the basic descent (and goes counter-clockwise [L to R] around it).

VB Git Down
An easy basic line on the west side (closest to the north overhang).

VB Get Down
The standard descent on the west side (at a slight groove).

V0 Face
Tall face on the west side.

V1 Round Face
Thin holds on a rounded bulge.

V2 Minor Hung Nose
Crouch low, and climb the outside of a slightly hung nose.

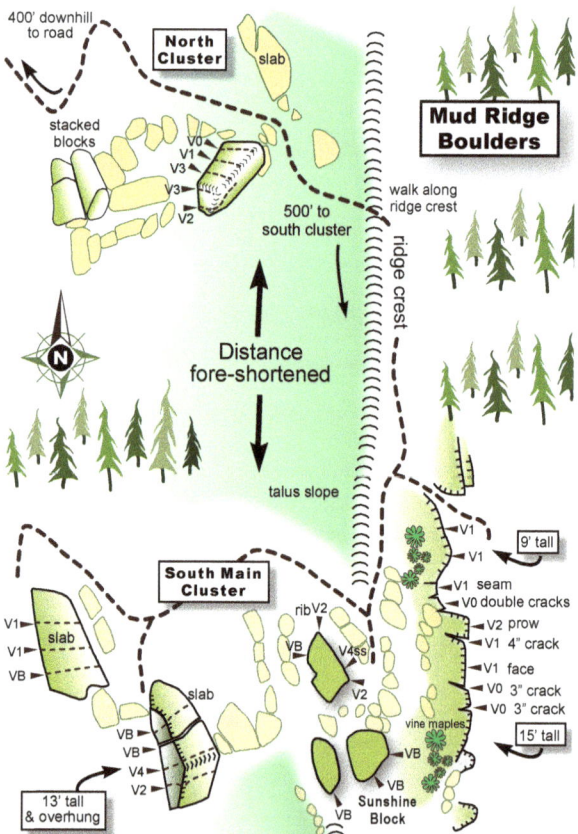

White River Boulders   PB   27

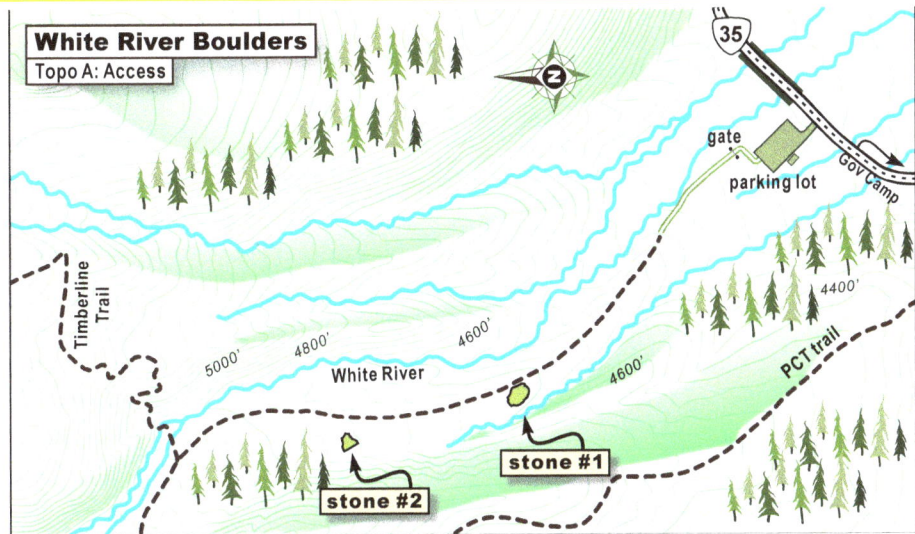

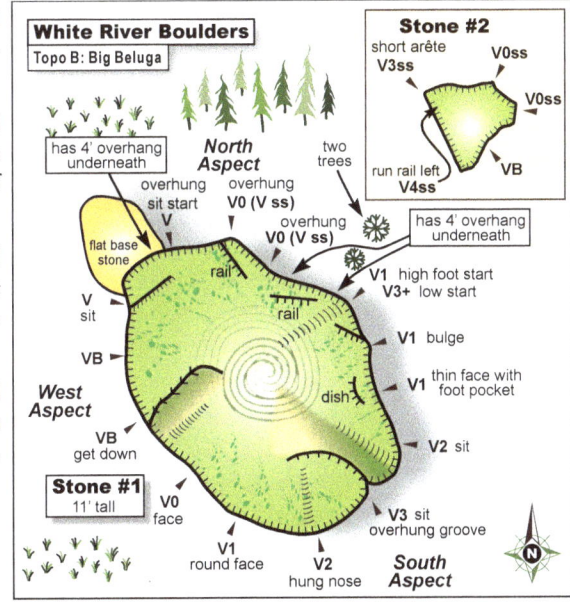

V3ss In to a groove
Sit start, and climb the small overhung nook up in to a groove.

V2ss Thin Face
Sit start, and use small crimps on a rounded face (the outer right part of the previous line).

V1 High Foot Knob
Thin face with a single high foot pocket on the east side, and goes up over a slight bulge at the top.

V1 High Foot Smear
Starts with a low round bulge with a series a face holds on the east side.

The next series of lines are where the notable overhang becomes more undercut with each subsequent problem.

V1 (V3ss ?) Left of Tree
Just left of a thin tree. High foot start on a slight bulge on the east side. Sit start underneath the notable overhang bumps grade.

V0 (V_ss ?) High Rail
Just right of a small tree. Standing is from the obvious high rail. Sit start would be stout.

V0 (V_ss ?) Low Rail
Squatting start is from obvious low rail hold. The sit start is via crawling underneath the large overhang and starting on tiny crimps and bumping up to the better holds.

V_ss Super Hung
The deepest part of the overhang starting full under as a sit start. Power out and over the outer lip onto the top.

V_ss Super Hung
The rightmost end of the deep overhang (on the west side of a flat base stone). Power the overhang on thin crimps, over the round top lip.

Powerline Boulder

Just a minor 8' tall stone. Nothing special and

28 MT HOOD ZONE (SOUTH)

nothing to write home about.

VBss Basic ☐
The basic descent (on south side).

V0ss Tainted ☐
Minor short move on the east nose.

V0ss Jillion Flies ☐
Smears just right of east nose (on north side).

V3ss Reflections ☐
Sit start side pull on an arête, then mantle.

V4ss Infinite Regress ☐
Start low on right, run rail to the left, merge into the arête, then top out.

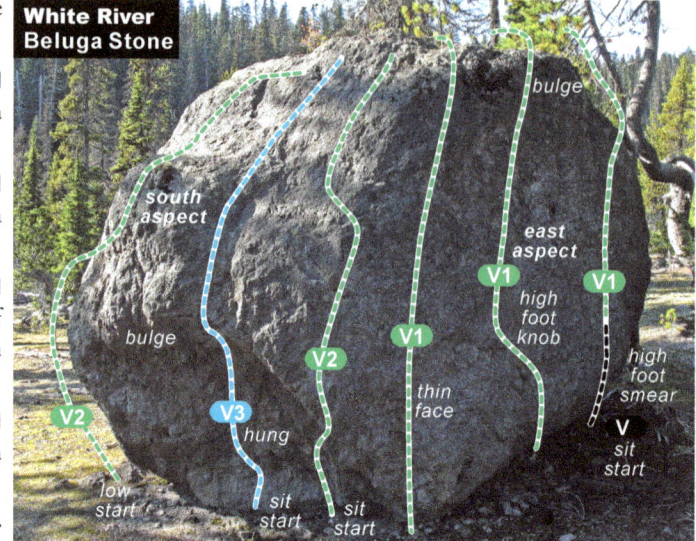

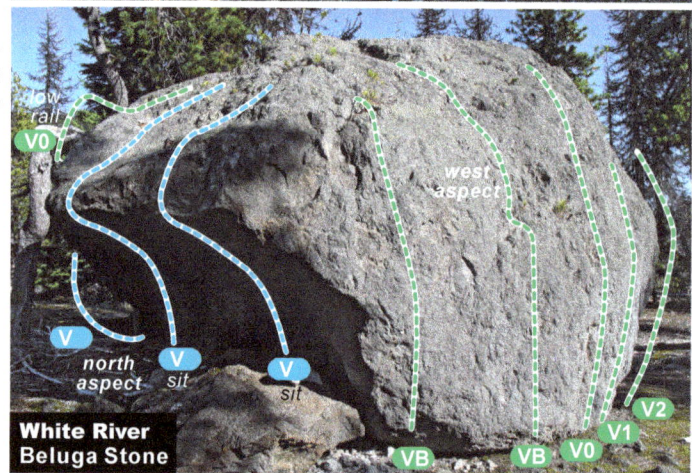

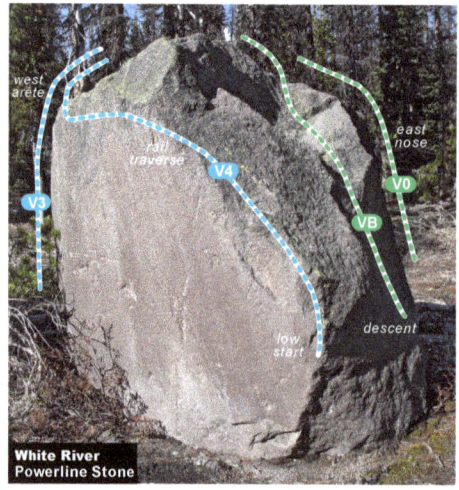

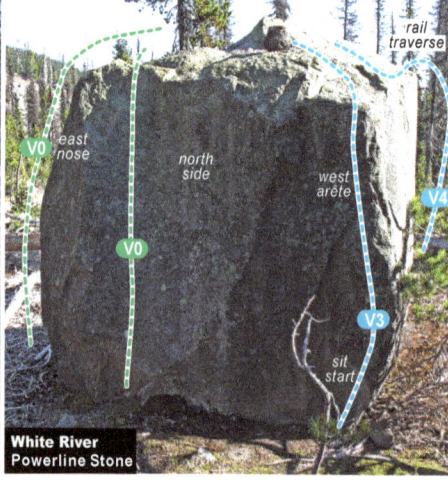

BENNETT BOULDERS

A quality, compact andesitic bouldering area hidden in the back country of the Mt Hood National Forest. At the ideal altitude where moss or lichen are minimized, this tiny site provides an enjoyable days workout for any dedicated boulderer. Were it located anywhere else (on a paved road) it would surely be a mega hit for locals.

At the core spot, the tallest stone is about 13' tall, while the girth on a few are roughly 20' diameter. Mostly moss free andesite rock with a lightly aged surface factor, yielding great friction on small sandpaper surface textured granules. Site has several classic lines, and about 40 problems total. Only 1-2 crashpads are needed.

The site is well tapped and most grades are VB to V7. Being located at the 5,400' elevation it's snow covered during winter months. General access is viable from July to October.

Other nearby boulder options: a few boulders are scattered above the road (just below a small cliff). A small orange tinted vertical flat face exists at the *Terrible Traverse* (*see map*) can provide some VB-V0 brief entertainment.

Now the stickler...getting there. The gravel road is not maintained, thus its a AWD or 4WD only road (high clearance) and a slow careful drive on a road that has some narrow sections (at *Terrible Traverse*). The road at the site is planned for closure sometime in about the year 2023-2025. Alternative? Yes....and more enjoyable. Rack up your mountain bike on the top of your vehicle and you are ready to go. The road is fairly level (with minor inclines).

Directions

Drive US Hwy 26 east of Gov Camp, then east on Highway 35 to Bennett Pass. Exit here, and turn into a large paved parking area with a rest room. Drive south on Bennett Pass road, which is a good gravel road for 1.7 miles to a junction. Park here (especially if its a low city car). The 'S' curves section is just ahead. Get on your bike, latch your crashpad on your back (and water), and south you go. At .7 miles you reach *Terrible Traverse* at a notch. (several VB-V0 on west side). At 2.25 miles you reach the 'T' junction of Bennett Pass and Bonney Meadows road. Continue south briefly on Bonney road (the talus slope becomes obvious immediately on your left (east). Stash your bike, and descend a 100' down slope to the main cluster (at the south end of the talus slope).

Mileage: 1.7 miles good gravel, 2.4 miles poor non-maintained road; total is 4.1 miles to reach the bouldering site.

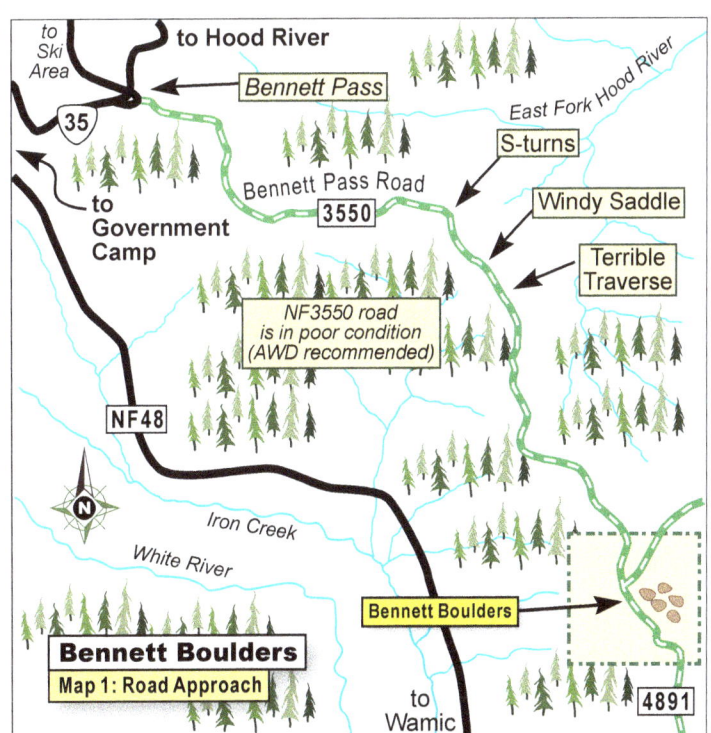

Bennett Boulders
Map 1: Road Approach

MT HOOD ZONE (SOUTH)

Bennett Boulder

It's the real reason you came here. Tall, hi-ball, and all quality lines from VB to V-hard. Beta is described L to R.

V1 _____
Left part of this large flat east face. Go up onto a left rib.

V6 _____
Center left face (starts almost same as previous but stays on flat face.

V7 _____
Thin seam on the center of the tall east face.

V9 (?) _____
Dimples to a sloped small rail on a tall flat face. Project?

V2 Bennett Classic _____
This is the double-sloped rail on the flat tall east face. This is the reason to visit this cool place.

V0 _____
This is a basic arête (rightmost line).

Fin Boulder

A cool tall triangle shaped boulder with several easier lines.

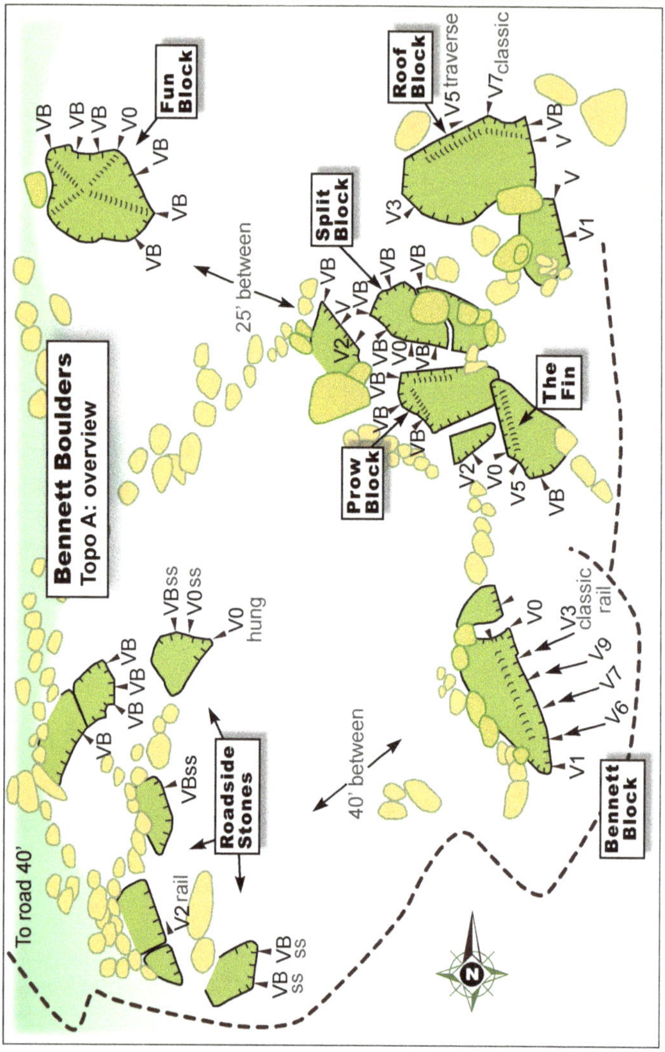

Bennett Boulders — Roof stone

VB _____ *(the slab)*

V5ss _____

Classic route. Sit start, and power a slight hung section onto a tall clean smooth face with small crimps.

V0 _____

The leftmost part of the tall face.

Roof Boulder

A cool boulder. Several classic lines, all sit start, on an overhung crimp routes on its north aspect. Beta is described R to L (starting on the north aspect):

V4ss _____

On the west side of this same large stone in a low hung spot.

V7ss Mega Morph

Several eliminate options, some with good holds, some tiny holds on this north-facing overhung cool cave-ish nook. Eliminates vary the grade.

V5ss Traverse

Traverse the same overhung cave-ish nook from L to R at mid-height using incuts below the lip.

Split Boulder

Offers several simple one move shorty's.

VB/V0 Prow Stone

Prow Boulder

Fun basic momentary things all **VB**.

VB Prow Stone

Fun Boulder

Virtually all **VB** and nice for a warmup.

VB/V0 Fun Stone

Roadside Stones

A group of five small boulders, some quite low, and all range from VB to V2, some as sit start.

VB/V2 Roadside

Bennett Boulders — The Bennett Stone

Bennett Boulders — Fin stone

Bennett Boulders — Roadside bluff

HUNCHBACK BOULDERS

The Hunchback Boulders are nestled quietly in a tantalizing tall Douglas fir forest which invites boulderer's to experience a little andesite bouldering near the elusive mega wall known as the Hunckback Wall. A gentle forest breeze generally keeps the place at a comfortable temperature even on hot summer days. This is a place where the sounds of nature predominate.

The problems range from VB to V8 (to date), are generally limited in totality mainly because there are only three boulders. The largest is of behemoth size (30' x 18') with a serious overhang on two aspects. The ultra cool main mega-stone has about 15 lines (one aspect is a superb 30' long traverse with a 45° undercut). Both nearby smaller stones have been tapped as well. Just 1-2 crash-pads recommended, no ticks, no poison oak, cell reception (yes), low altitude (2600'), season from May-Oct, and sometimes accessible even into the winter months (if its dry).

The site has a convenient proximity to Portland (1-hour drive) with paved road access to the parking spot. A 25-minute steep uphill grunt on a narrow path gets you to the boulders, though due to the stout uphill grunt hike from the road it may keep some individuals at bay.

History: First tap by Mr O (2016); the punchy V's were tapped by Abbott/Anglin team.

Directions:
Drive east on U.S. Hwy 26 from Sandy, Oregon till you reach Welches. Turn south at the Subway store onto Salmon River Road (NF2618). Continue about 9/10 mile south passing a guardrail on the right, a small rotten roadside bluff on the left, and a deeply cut ravine also on the left. Park immediately on the west side of the road at a minor pullout. Step into the dry ravine for a few yards, then angle up right onto the south slope into a grove of cedar trees. A faint path begins there and zigzags gently uphill, and gradually steepens for the remainder of the uphill hike.

Hunchback Boulder ⚠

Starting on the south aspect. Beta from L to R (lower to upper):

1. VB Imperialism ☐
The basic get-down method on the slab.

2. VB Liquid Desire ☐
Easy face / slab variation.

3. VB Royalty ☐
Crimps on the low angle slab.

4. V2 (V_ss) Exploited Class ☐
Lip mantle onto slab.

5. V2 (V_ss) Ruling Class ☐
Hole mantle onto slab.

6. V_ss [?] _____ ☐
A sit start project.

7. V3 (V_ss) Lemming Lore ☐
Hung crimp pull.

8. V4 (V_ss) The Abyss ☐
Overhung prow onto steep slab.

9. VB Noob ☐
Fat dirty slot (uppermost problem).

10. V7 Circuit Traverse ☐
The long cool uphill stellar traverse (the lower ½ is done).

The following are on the overhung west aspect (beta is right to left):

1. V3 Of Noble Birth ☐
Jug start. The rightmost line.

2. V5ss ONB Extension ☐
The sit start extension of the above.

3. V5 Bell Ringer ☐
Do just the high start.

4. V6 Bell Ringer ☐
The standing start.

5. V7ss Bell Ringer ☐
The full low traverse going right, then up to top.

6. V7ss Acceptable Losses ☐
Dyno straight up to high hold; continue to top.

7. V7-9 [?] _____ ☐
Project.

8. V5 Quasi Moto ☐
High jug start, up and out right.

9. V__ _____ ☐
Project.

Hunchback Boulders ✦ PB 33

10. V__ _____
Project.

11. V8 Full Moto
Thin moves right to jug, then up right and out.

12. V__ _____
Project.

13. V0ss Megalonia
Leftmost line. Layback and mantle over the lip.

Quasimodo Boulder

A few yards SW of the big boulder. To date (beta L to R):

VB Basic
Short flat face on left.

VB Basic
Outer easy steps.

V_ (?) _____
Overhung power crimps.

V5 (V_ss) Ex Libris
Rightmost overhung power line.

Esmeralda Boulder

Located about 100' north of the Hunchback stone along the trail. Problems done to date (beta is right to left):

V2 Zeno's
Short rounded face / rib.

V2 Esmeralda
Short verrtical seam up onto slab.

V7+ _____
Center face starting on crimps, but as it rounds onto a slab the holds virtually vanish.

V5/6 Antiquo
The leftmost rounded face on thin crimps.

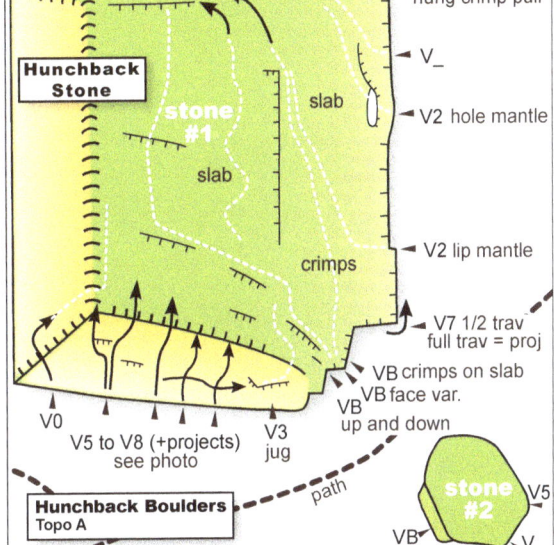

Hunchback Boulders
Topo A

The HUNCHBACK STONE
- south aspect -

MT HOOD ZONE (SOUTH)

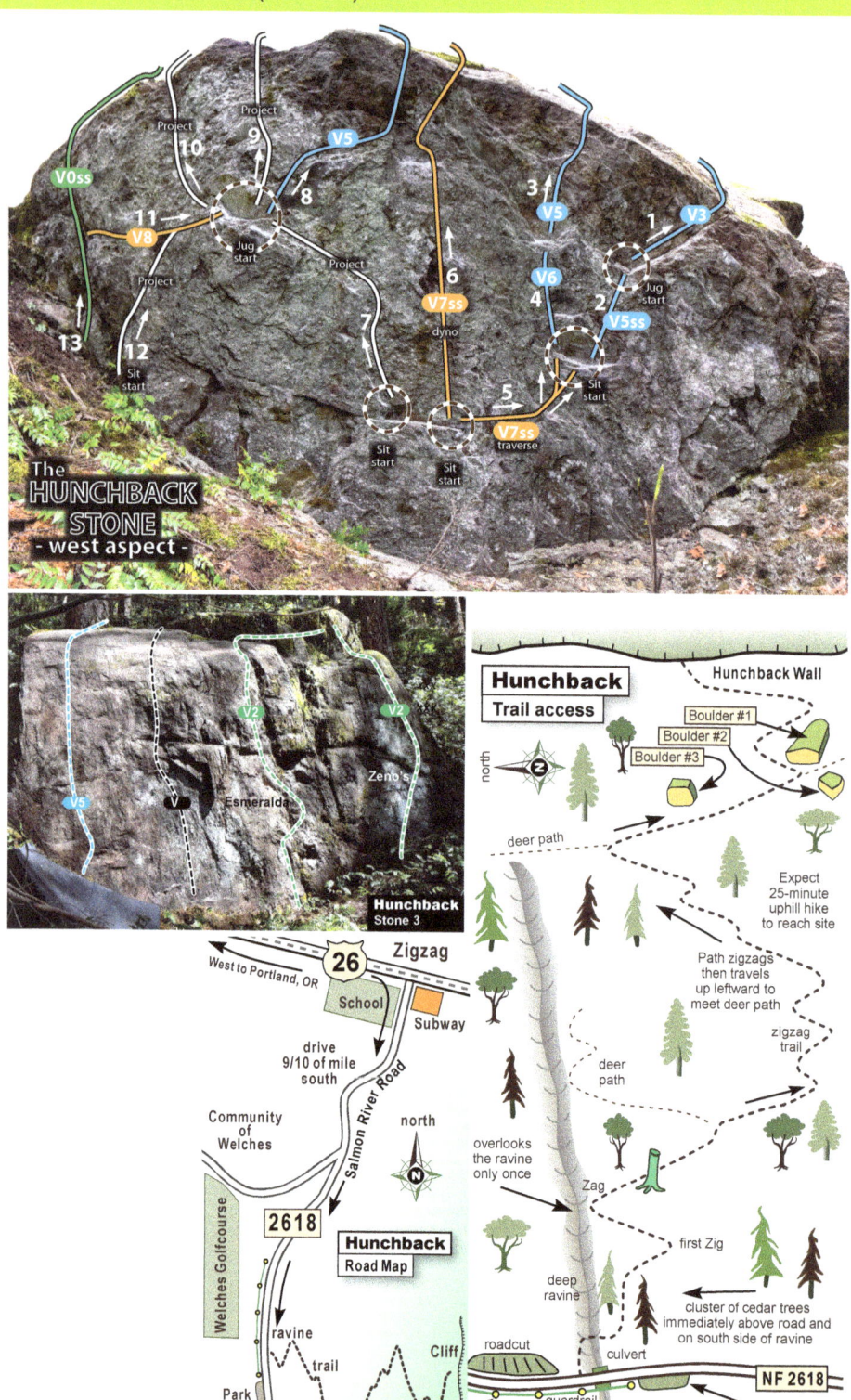

BOULDER MTN BOULDERS

Quality andesite bouldering in a scenic High Cascade Mtns forested setting just off the road at Bluebox Pass on US Highway 26. The name 'Boulder Mtn' is a bit of a misnomer; the site has far more trees and it's the trees that keep you from seeing the next stone cluster (though topo maps do help). This site is a unique aesthetic destination worth visiting by any veteran of the game.

Boulder Mtn has three primary boulder talus fields, while the remainder of the stones lay scattered in random clusters in open forested terrain. Some boulders tend to be fairly isolated from the next batch, making the search a bit more adventurous than what the average person might willingly endure. So initially focus where the established problems are best in the primary boulder zones (like the stellar Lost City). The entire Boulder Mtn Boulders zone will eventually yield 300+ boulder problems after it's more thoroughly tapped. Due to sporadic route sending anticipate moss or lichen growth on certain problems for a while.

By far the best quality string of boulders is the extensive Lost City with its panoramic views of Mt Hood. This spot offers a fine quality set of stone beasts ranging in height from 8'-12' tall in an idyllic open forest sunny setting wrapped along the edge of a large talus field. This extensive cluster has minimal tumbling, thus most of the crimps and features are still well formed.

The eastern Bluebox Talus Cluster offers some very well-rounded stones on a southeasterly facing slope surrounded by an open forest. Some stones are so well tumbled to be almost bowling ball round scattered along the lower perimeter of the talus field zone in a string of stones which range from 8'-12' tall. The rock offers numerous gaseous air pockets, dishes, and scoops. The Bluebox Cluster (VB-V6+) may eventually yield a limited 25+ problems.

Seasonal access to this entire bouldering haven is viable from late-May through October (longer if it's snow free [4,100' elev]).

General History

The quality Lost City zone and numerous other isolated quaility stones in the area were discovered and tapped into by Mr Holzman (nice find dude!), Mr Cousins, Mr Krossen (and numerous others) starting in about 2011. The Bluebox Group was first explored and various V's were tagged by Mr O in about 2011. This entire site is now seeing considerable expansion by multiple local teams. The overall expansion of the remaining assortment of problems at the site will involve an array of dedicated locals scattered over several more years.

Directions

Drive U.S. Hwy 26 to Government Camp, then seven more miles south to Bluebox Pass (Frog Lake). Turn west onto NF 2660, then immediately northwest onto a rough gravel logging road. Drive for ¼ mile to the switchback, and park at a wide pullout at the edge of an open forested area. Walk horizontally west (best to have GPS or map) for 200' to the boulder field. Future road access is not assured, but if it gets a closure berm, the walk is short.

To reach the popular Northwest String drive up the same gravel road, but continue past the first switchback uphill till it levels off and it curls westerly to a 'Y' intersection. Go right, and drive for another ¼ mile till you encounter a roadside cluster with sweeping views to the northwest of Mt Hood. The Southwest String is reached by continuing to drive south on this old road for another ¼ mile, then hiking briefly uphill eastward.

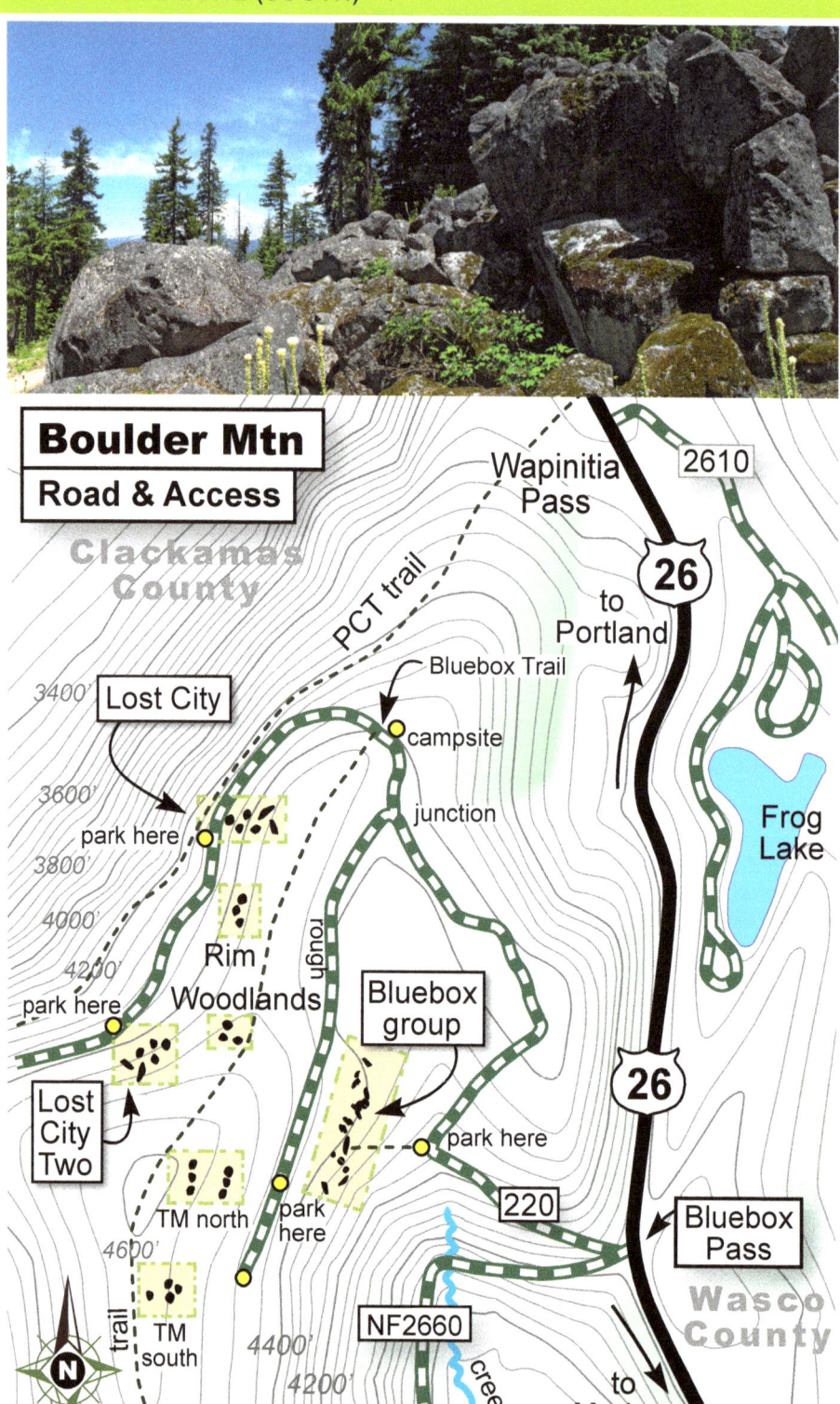

Boulder Mtn Boulders ✦ PB 37

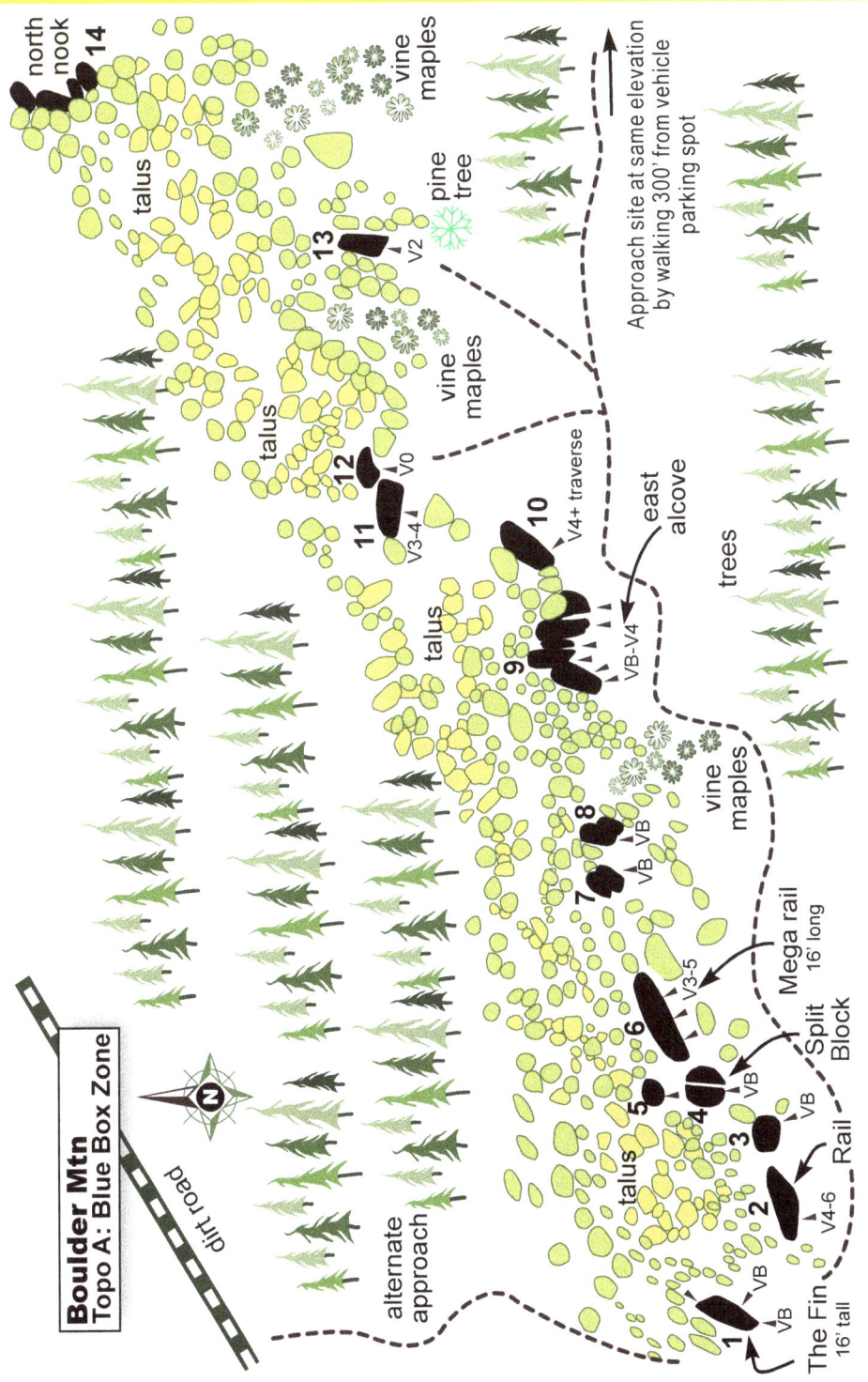

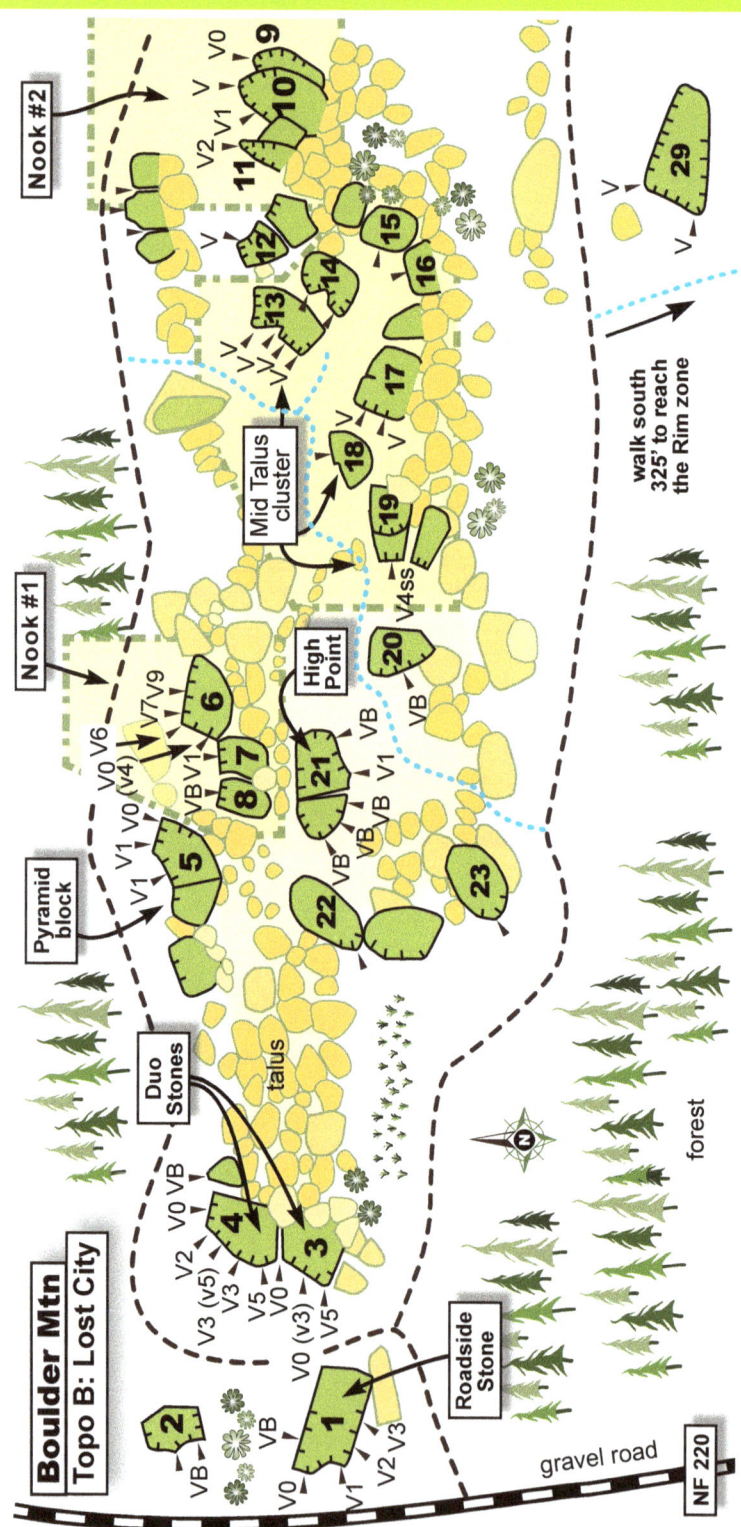

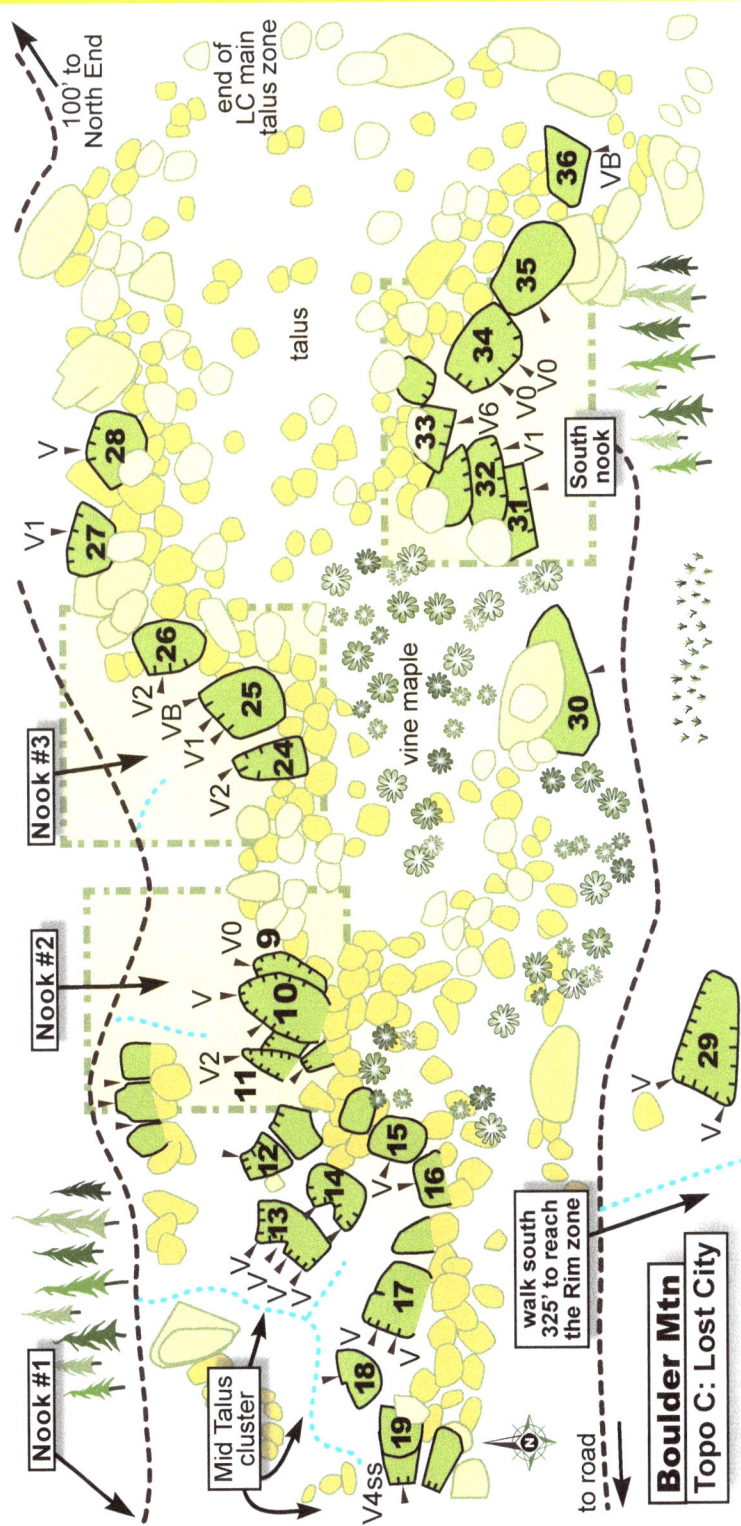

40 MT HOOD ZONE (SOUTH) ✦

BLUEBOX GROUP

(Topo A)

This minor cluster of boulders can be accessed from gravel roads on either the east or west side (see map). Broad talus field of stones, a few low grade problems, and some stones with well-rounded features. This cluster is facing southeast and most of the large boulders are situated along its lower flank. GPS UTM 10T 601400 5007225.

Midnight Fin (#1)

The giant 15' tall fin loaded with pockets and some moss, at far west end of talus field.

VB Midnight Ride ☐
Tackles the east side starting low on arête fin.

VB _____ ☐
On the east side face.

VB _____ ☐
Located at the north end..

Stone 2

V4-5 (?) _____ ☐
To the east of Midnight Fin is a rounded rail stone traverse.

Stone 3

VB Basic ☐
The nose of another round block nearby.

Stone 4

VB Pocket Pretense ☐
Climb the Split Block using mega pockets on left block.

Double Stack (5)

VB Contrivance ☐
It's a vertical double-stacker block, one on top

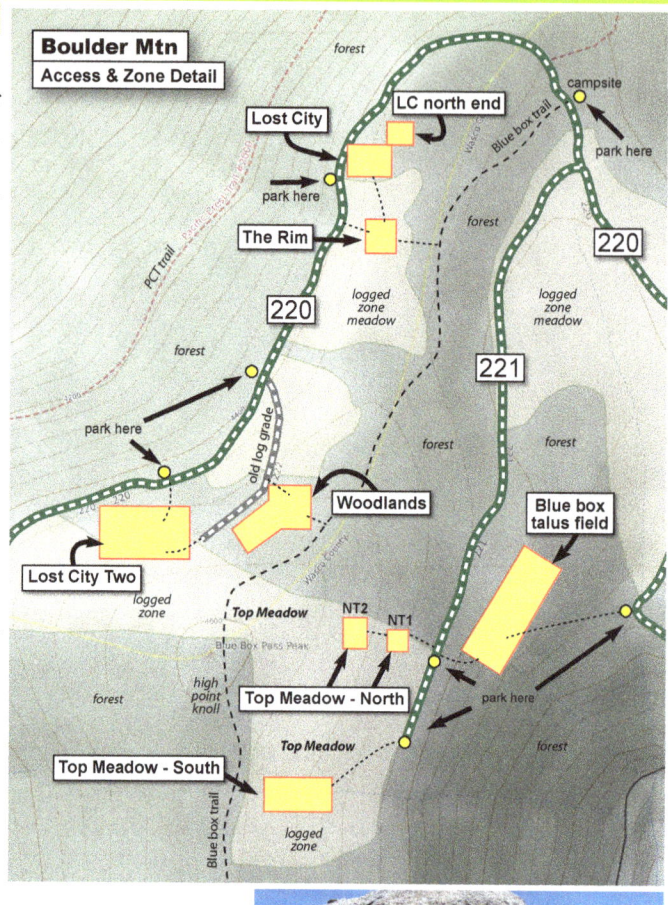

Boulder Mtn Boulders ✦ PB 41

of the other with nice holds.

Stone 6

Offers about 3 problems, sit start going over a bulge, ranging from V3-V6-ish, and a traverse option. Rumored to be done.

V_ (?) _____ ☐
V_ (?) _____ ☐
V_ (?) _____ ☐

Stone 7 & 8

VB Basic ☐
A brief combo of blocks that make a slab n' crack run.

East Alcove (9)

A cluster of blocks jammed together offering short sit start vertical or overhung lines.

V4 (?) _____ ☐
Short prow.

V5 (?) _____ ☐
Short face.

V2 (?) _____ ☐
Short corner.

V7 (?) _____ ☐
A hung arête.

V3 (?) _____ ☐
Hung prow-corner-slot combo.

V3 (?) _____ ☐
A short prow.

VB _____ ☐
A blunt arête.

Stone 10

V4 (?) _____ ☐
Traverse rounded low traverse.

Stone #1

V3/4ss _____ ☐
Go up a hung short flat face to a round top.

Stone 12

V0 _____ ☐
Short vertical nose next door to the right.

Vine Maple Stone (13)

A single 2' wide prow about 11' tall.

The classic zone at the Woodlands

The core zone at Boulder Mtn - Lost City

V2ss Treason
Quality run, face crimps, lip, small backside sloper pocket, hi-step, done.

North Nook (14)

Minor alcove with a brief pack of future potential problems.

LOST CITY

Certainly the best zone for your first visit. Convenient parking spot, and zero approach time to get to the first few stones. The talus slope trends uphill away from the road northward for several hundred feet. Access the problems by walking on either side of the talus field. GPS UTM 10T 601140 5008050.

Topo B & C

The Lost City section begins at the roadside stones, then describes stones along the north side of the LC talus field (including in the middle part of the talus), then describes the remaining few stones scattered along the south perimeter of the LC talus field. The LC section is numbered from 1-to-39.

Roadside Stones

Stone 1

Some fun roadside stuff. Beta is listed right to left.

V3 Dynomite
Begin low and power pockets and face holds up right onto slab.

V2 Roadside
Pockets going up onto an angled slab.

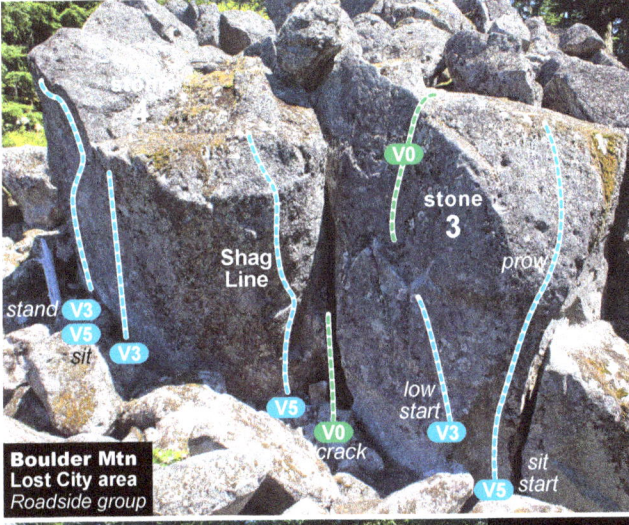

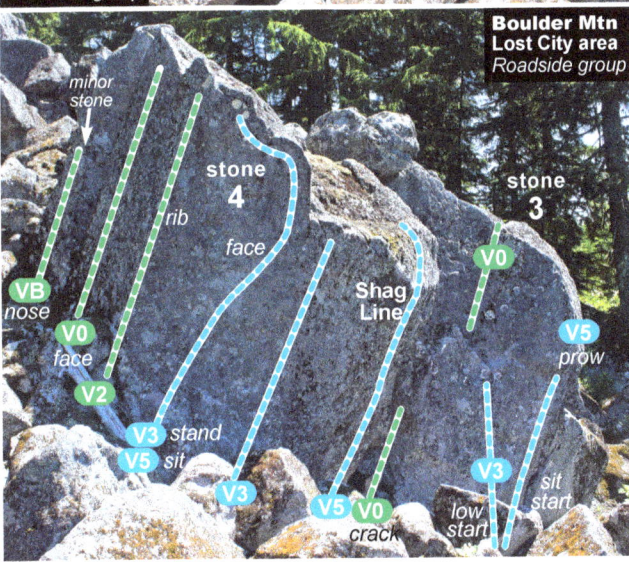

MT HOOD ZONE (SOUTH)

V1
Go up face onto a slabby groove.

V0
Go up onto an outer round prow (leftmost problem).

Stone 2

VB
Just a minor short pocket problem.

Duo Stones

Stone 3

A set of dual large stones (#3 and #4) with a treasure trove of stellar problems (all part of the Roadside Group). Beta is detailed right to left.

V5ss Austin Powers
Cool and powerful prow done as a sit start.

V0 (V3) Warmup
Standing begins on the obvious mid-height jug; sitting start is down closer to the prow (on the right).

V0ss
Climb the fat crack that separates stone #3 and stone #4.

Stone 4

V5ss Shag Line
The round prow immediately left of the crack.

V3
A brief face move to a high lip jug.

V3 (V5) Spank
Face crimps to same high lip jug, then up left along the lip. Sitting start is V5.

V2
Climb a slight outer rib (with left hand on it).

V0
A short face (with your right hand near the the slight rib).

VB Other Stone
A minor short outer nose on a minor block next door to the duo stones.

Pyramid Stone (5)
Tall with cool quality easy lines. Beta is left to right.

V0ss _____
Left hand on left arete, then up high turn around onto the easier foot holds on high left side.

V1ss _____
Sit start at low crack and power up the face directly by staying on this outer hung aspect all the way (using the left arete near the top).

V1ss _____
Begin low and climb past the horizontal cracks up the slightly hung face.

MAIN ATTRACTION - NOOK ONE

Stones 6, 7 & 8
One of the finest core classic zones to explore on your first visit here at Lost City. Beta is described left to right.

V_ _____
Something project on the left (maybe).

V9 Kerosene Hat
A direct on the overhung face going straight up.

V7 Bugatti
Begin on the low rail, bump right to arête, and climb the pocketed arête.

V6 Five-star Arête
One of the great classic lines. Climb just the pocketed arête directly up.

V0 (V4) Frosted Flake
Climb the flake near a corner crack (sit start is V4 using face only).

Stone 7

V1 Lichen It
Climb the easy flat face using both outer edges for holds. Rules alter grade slightly (V0/V1).

Stone 8

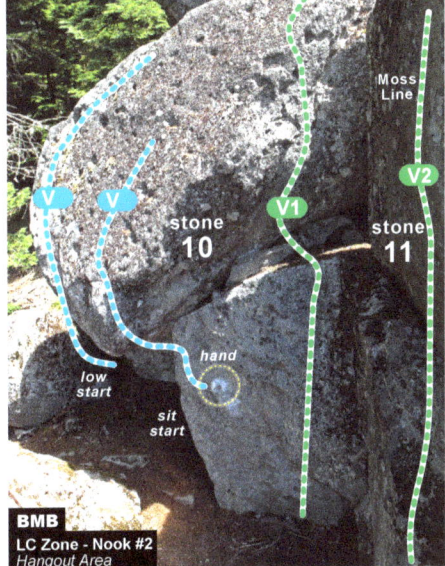

VB _____
Fun easy problem on a tall face to prow.

HANGOUT AREA - NOOK TWO

STONES 9, 10, & 11
Some powerful problems on well overhung stones. Beta is listed left to right.

Stone 9

VB (V0) _____
On the leftmost stone, climb a series of pockets and holds (standing or sitting).

Stone 10

46 MT HOOD ZONE (SOUTH)

V5/V6ss
Sit start low on the right underneath this very overhung boulder, then power along a series of pockets and round hand holds, topping out high onto a pronounced rib and gas pockets at the top. Superb problem.

V1/V2ss
Begin sit start low on the right (right hand as marked on photo), then power up over the overhung next boulder onto the top slab.

V1
Start low (hands on flat ledge), then power onto the upper stone.

Stone 11

V2 Moss Prow
Climb the obvious sharp leaning arete.

MID-TALUS CLUSTER

STONES 12 TO 21 (AKA THE EXTENSION)

This section entails a string of boulders that trend from near Nook Two and goes rightward up onto the center of the main talus field (ending at the High Point boulder).

Stone 12

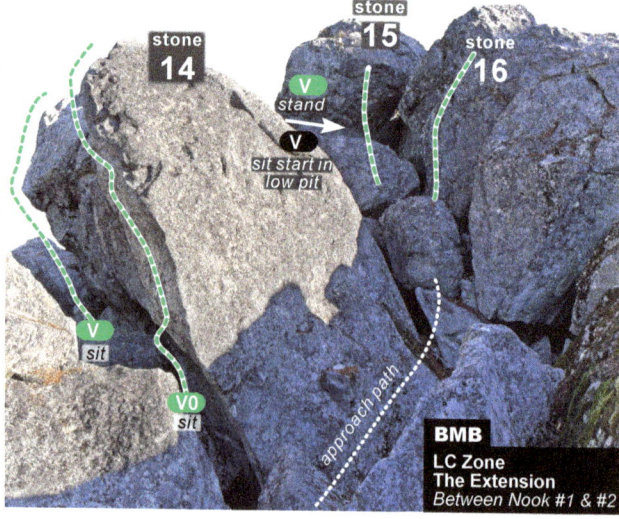

V_ss
Minor sit start potential.

Stone 13 (Cool hung prow)

This stone appears as a big jutting out high prow from below. Cool quality boulder with a string of overhung shorty problems all in a row.

V0/1ss (?) _____ ☐
Stellar overhung pocketed pointed prow.

V0/1ss (?) _____ ☐
Sit start up a short crack.

V0/1ss (?) _____ ☐
Overhung short face.

V0/1 (V2) _____ ☐
Sit start would bump the grade up. The rightmost problem on this stone.

Stone 14

This stone is located directly behind (uphill of) the previous stone.

V_ss _____ ☐
Short crimpy problem (leftmost line).

V0ss _____ ☐
Short left leaning prow (rightmost line).

Stone 15

V1 (?) (V_) _____ ☐
Standing is done on this well hung high perched boulder. But a sit start is possible with more pads.

Stone 16

V_ss _____ ☐

Stone 17

V_ss _____ ☐
Left hand on left prow. Short problem.

V_ss _____ ☐
Right hand on right rail. Short problem.

Stone 18

V_ss _____ ☐
A potential powerful overhung line.

Stone 19

V4ss Nemesis _____ ☐
Sit start low in the hole; crimp up face, then over the top stone.

Stone 21 (High Point)

Fun stone and the highest point on the talus field in this section. Beta is described left to right starting on the south sunny aspect. All are juggy fun runs.

VB _____ ☐
Dance up the large holds (leftmost problem facing west). Stone 21a.

48 MT HOOD ZONE (SOUTH) ✦

VB _____ ☐
Dance up large holds on south side. Stone 21b.

VB _____ ☐
Dance up large holds on south side. Stone 21b.

V1ss _____ ☐
Sit start low at low lip, then use crimps and holds up steep face directly to the summit of this high point stone. Stone 21c.

VB _____ ☐
The rightmost problem.

LC - NOOK THREE
Beta is listed right to left for this section.

Stone 24

V2ss _____ ☐
Brief shorty on a low stone.

Stone 25

V1ss Classy ☐
Sit start and power up the seam, going up right to the top.

V1 _____ ☐
Start at the same seam (as previous line) and power up to the left.

VB _____ ☐
Short prominent prow. Leftmost line.

Stone 26

V2ss Gaplander ☐
Short crimps and pocket face.

Two Random Stones

Stone 27

V1 _____ ☐
Located a few yards north of Nook #3 on a single lone stone.

Stone 28

V_ _____ ☐

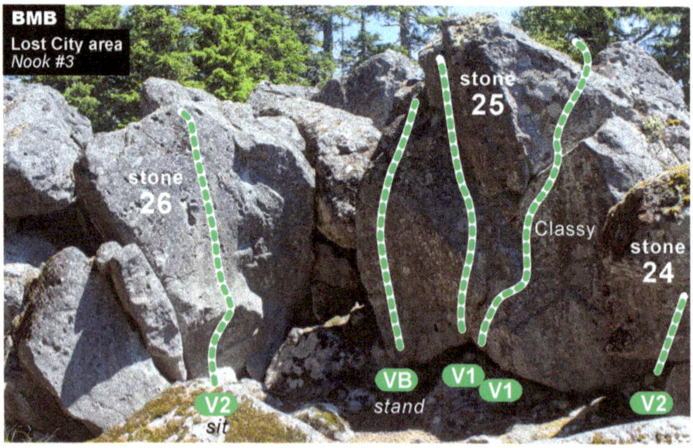

LC - SOUTH SIDE
Stone 29

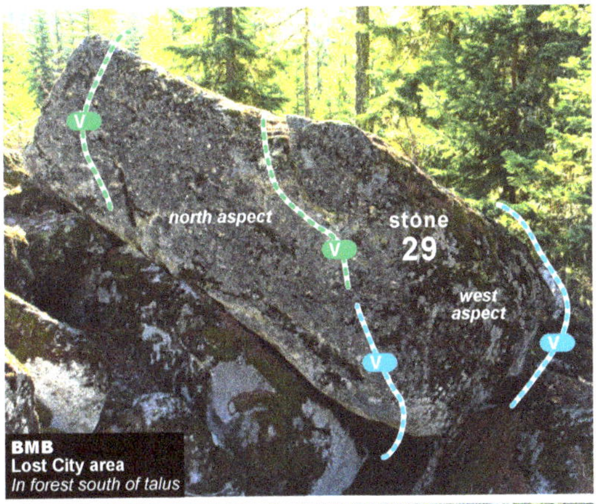

V_ss ☐

A short crimp problem on the north aspect that starts at a rounded bulge overhang as a sit start. This may also be a combo-traverse (?).

V_ss ☐

Sit start problem low on the right rounded point (at the west end of the stone).

V_ss ☐

Leftmost minor shorty.

LC - SOUTH NOOK
Stone 31

V_ss ☐

Short flat face.

Stone 32

V1ss ☐

Sit start; climb a short flat face using crimps and a right hand rail.

Stone 33

V6ss ☐

Sit start; powerful crimps and small scoops on a flat face.

Stone 34

V0ss ☐

This and the next start the same low start. This goes up left.

V0ss ☐

Goes up right from same low start.

Stone 35

V_ ☐

Stone 36

VB Juggy Thing ☐

Minor problem on a lone stone.

50 MT HOOD ZONE (SOUTH)

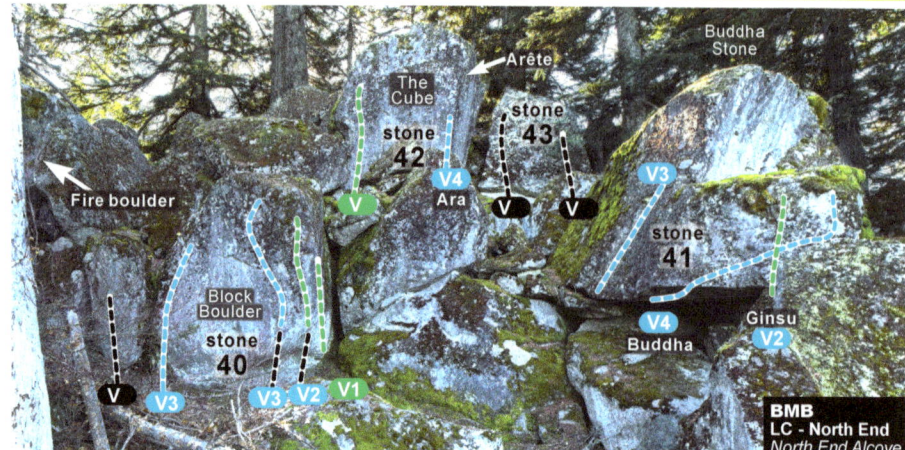

LC - NORTH END

Topo D

North End Group is the utter north end of the Lost City boulder field. To get there (from the parking spot) walk along the north edge of the talus boulder field in the open forest.

GPS UTM 10t 601203 5008100.

The LC North End uses numerical sequence from 40- to-60 for each stone.

North End Alcove

Stone 40 (The Block)

Some tricky stuff on this little unit, and some that'll require a 2-3 pad stack. Beta is described from left to right.

V_ _____ ☐
On the far left; a potential project (on its own well hung jutting out rounded prow).

V2/3 _____ ☐
Climb thin crimps on the left rounded outer edge of the stone.

V3 _____ ☐
Pad stack. Reach a small rail,

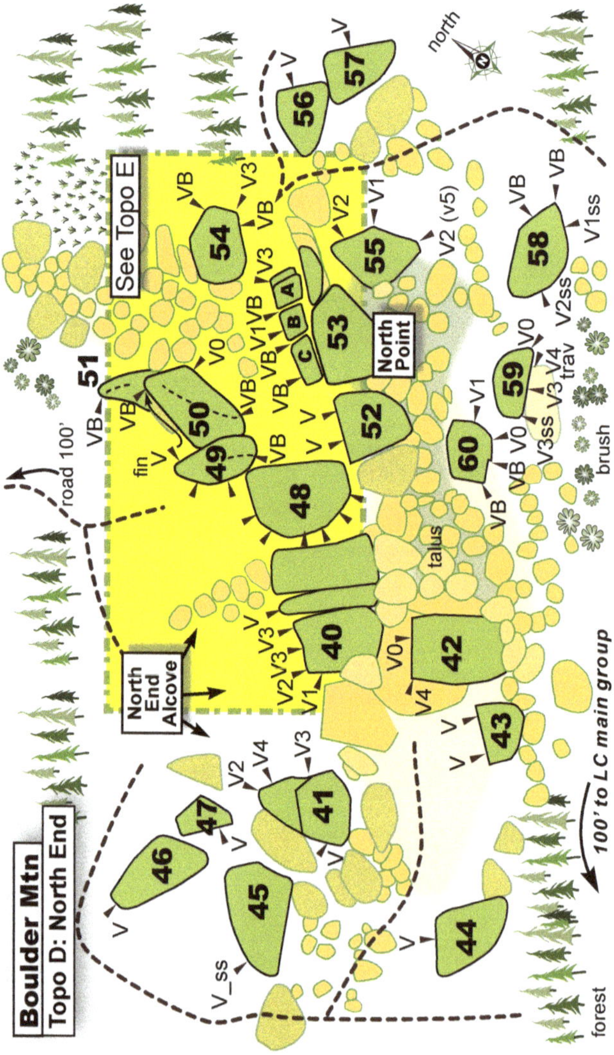

then aim for the pocket up left, then head to the top round lip.

V2 The Arête ☐
Pad stack. The round prow beginning at the midway hold.

V1 Right Face ☐
Something minor on the rightmost aspect tucked in with the offwidth.

Stone 41 (Buddha)

This stone, though parts of it are tall, the front aspect juts straight out as a roof (yielding several short unusual problems). Beta is listed left to right.

V3 Time Capsule ☐
An angled seam on the left aspect, lands quickly onto a flat ledge.

V4 Buddha ☐
Wild roof problem. Begin on its left aspect, and power out a few moves rightward, then at the outermost point go up onto the flat ledge.

V2 Ginsu ☐
Just start at the outermost point and power up onto the ledge.

V4/5ss _____ ☐
Something as a sit start in a hole on the far backside (westside).

Stone 42

THE CUBE

V0/1 _____ ☐
The leftmost problem with only a few moves up the left prow.

V4ss Ara ☐
Tricky setup to start onto the arête, but the final upper holds are better.

V_ _____ ☐
Blank right aspect (maybe).

Stone 43

V_ _____ ☐
Short brief crimp moves.

V_ _____ ☐
Several brief crimp moves.

Stone 44

V_ _____ ☐

Stone 45

V_ss _____ ☐
Something low is done on the west point of this stone.

Stone 46

V_ _____ ☐

Stone 47

V_ss _____ ☐

Stone 48

FIRE BOULDER

A cool tiny stone with a tight squeeze nook on its immediate south aspect. Most lines use repeated holds (i.e. left hand uses right hand of next problem, etc).

V2ss Fire in the Hole ☐
Low on the right in the very depth of the narrow nook. Rightmost problem.

V0ss Burn Baby Burn ☐
Start on the knob and climb up.

52 MT HOOD ZONE (SOUTH)

V0ss Straddle the Saddle
Obviously straddle the stone.

V2 (V4ss) Riptide
Pocket and left hand on crimp, working right, then traversing using top lip till knob then up. The classic line on this stone by either start.

V5ss Aquifer
Crimps up to tiny incut then merge right all way to route #2 knob.

V5ss ____
The leftmost line.

Stone 48b
A minor next door neighbor problem.

V2ss Illusion
On other minor stone behind you to the south.

Stone 49

Fin Boulder
The obvious tall skinny fin with a futuristic line awaiting.

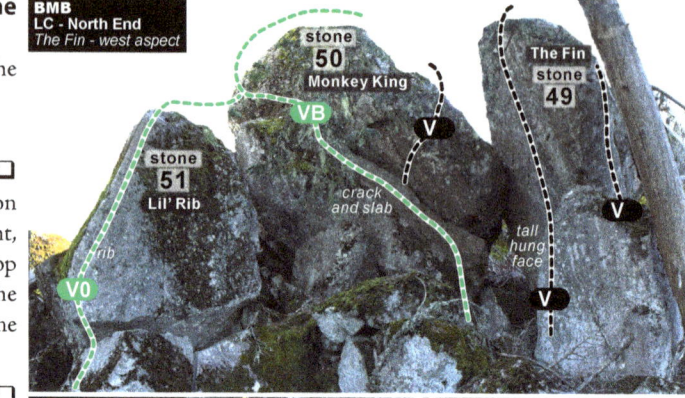

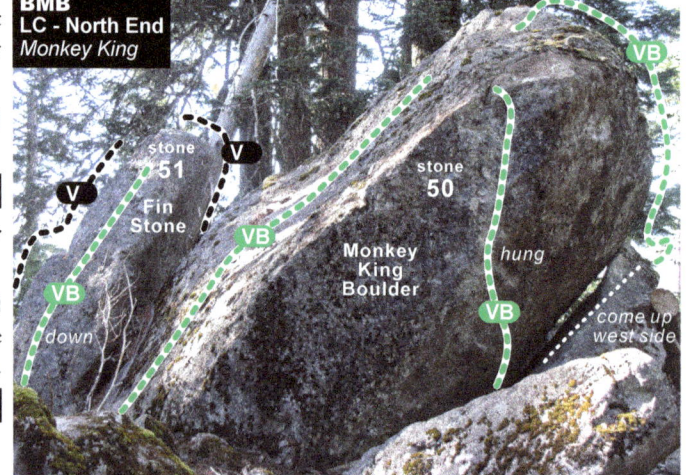

V5-8 The Fin
Potential powerful route on north hung aspect.

VB
On the westside is a one move stepper.

V2ss [?]
On the south side are a few brief moves.

VB
The get down slab.

Stone 50

MONKEY KING BOULDER
A few basic entertaining lines on block just north of The Fin.

VB Slithering Sycophant
Run the horizontal left trending slab crack (on west side) to the outer point then up the final big pockets to the top.

V0ss Monkey King
Short fast east face crimp problem.

Stone 51

V0/1 'Lil Rib
This short 'lil rib prow is on located another minor stone tucked under the immediate northwest side of Stone K.

Stone 52

DIAMOND FACE
Two excellent quality problems on a wide flat diamond-shaped face.

V1/2
The left standing start is just a few moves going straight up.

V3-5 (?)
Powerful crossover move going from right to the left (using the midway pocket), then several more reach moves to catch the final top edges. This is a high quality problem.

Stone 53

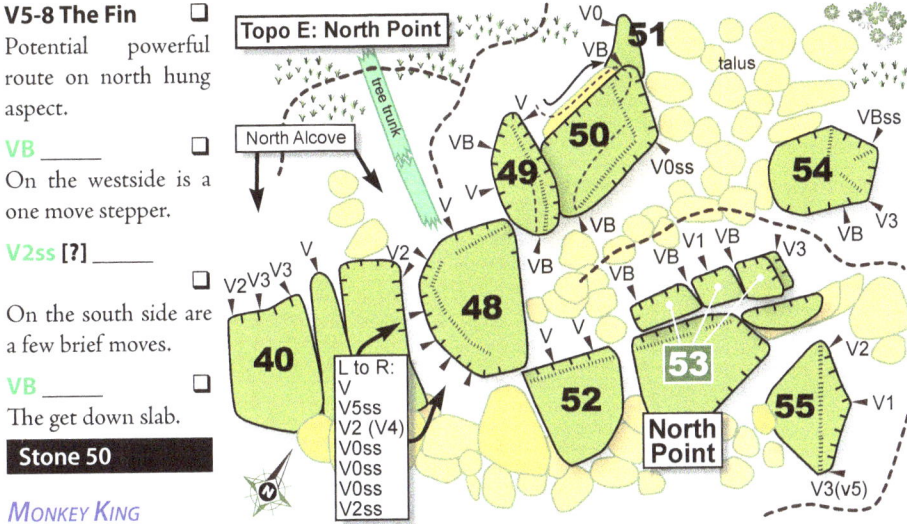

THREE DOMINOES
The obvious flat vertical west facing stones (beta is right to left).

VB Domino
The right outer point (on stone #N3).

VB Domino Right Crack

V1 Lemming Lore
A few short face moves (on stone #N2).

VB Domino Left Crack

V3 Domino Effect
The leftmost outer point (on stone #N1).

Stone 54

VBss Williwaw
Minor short hung bump problem (N aspect).

V3 FlatEarther
Brief power crimp moves on the north point.

VBss Rumor Mill
Minor moves getting onto the east slab.

Stone 55

THE WEDGE
The Wedge stone leans to slightly overhung on its north aspect. The left route is quite popular. Beta is described left to right.

V2 (V5ss) The Wedge
The popular left rib direct; do it standing, or sit start.

54 MT HOOD ZONE (SOUTH)

V1 ___
A single move in the middle of face on north aspect to catch the top lip and mantle.

V2 ___
Start on the right, traverse along lip to the left, merge at middle, mantle.

Stone 56

V_ _____
Project

Stone 57

Project.

V_ _____

Stone 58

BMB
LC - North End
The Wedge

stone 55

ascend left lip

V1

V2 stand start

V2 ascend right lip

The Wedge

stand

V5

sit start

Fun Times

VB _____
Easy jug pockets on the north side.

VB _____
Easy holds on the north point.

V1ss _____
Sit start on a steep slightly hung aspect and power up several small holds.

V2ss _____
Begin sit start under the weather overhang and power up several small pockets.

Stone 59

Excel Stone

A great stone with several quality lines. Located near the north point area. A left leaning compact little pig with a vertical south aspect that holds a fine string of sit starts.

V0ss _____
On far lower right, make a single move, then prance up low angle fat rib.

V0ss _____
Alternate start onto the same rib above.

V3ss _____
Low and up slight hung face on crimps in center of face.

BMB
LC - North End
Excel stone

stone 59

traverse

V0

V3ss   V3ss   V0

hung face

V4ss

V3ss _____
On far left. Crimp up slight hung rounded face.

V4ss Reason To Be _____
Indeed a cool line. Start low on right, run entire slightly hung face up leftward to merge with previous line and top out.

Stone 60

Greek Goddess

Mostly basic fun runs. Beta is left to right.

Boulder Mtn Boulders ✦ PB 55

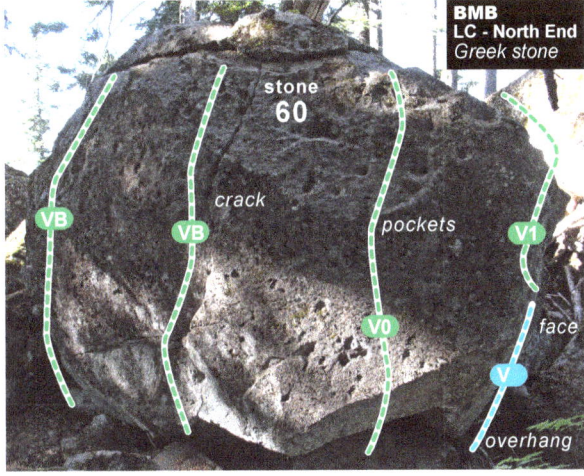

VB ☐
Jugs and pockets on the leftmost line (on the south aspect).

VB ☐
Jugs and pockets at the slight seam/groove/rail.

V0 ☐
Start low, climb pockets and edges, going straight up.

V1 (V_ss) ☐
Standing begins at the obvious large sloped rail, then a crimps or so to catch the top lip, and its over. Sit start is stouter. Located on the north aspect of this stone.

56 MT HOOD ZONE (SOUTH)

THE RIM

A notable compact zone, and certainly a high quality haven worth visiting. If you opt to visit this tiny spot it's actually quite close to the main Lost City zone. Beta is described left to right on each stone (unless otherwise noted). Locale: GPS UTM 10t 601170 5007930

Two options for getting there:

1.) From the parking spot at the LC zone just walk south on the gravel road for 300', then hike uphill 200' in the forest to this compact, quality string of boulders facing west in a old logged zone (partially regrown).

2.) Or approach it by walking along the south edge of the LC talus, then cutting south from LC stone #29 (for 325' south of it to reach "The Rim" zone).

Stone 1

V3/4 [?] _____ ❏
North aspect. Sit start using crimp face holds, while your right hand is near the right prow.

VB _____ ❏
West aspect. Left variant.

VB _____ ❏
West aspect. Middle standard line.

VB _____ ❏
South aspect using the prow with left hand.

Stone 2

V_ss _____ ❏
On north side. Climb short brief moves on a prow.

V_ss _____ ❏
On north side. Climb the other minor outer prow.

V6 Artist Arête ❏
Classic overhung prow. Certainly one of the coolest problems here at the 'Rim zone'. The problem begins on the west aspect as a sit start. Power crimp going up a hung prow (with right hand using the rounded prow).

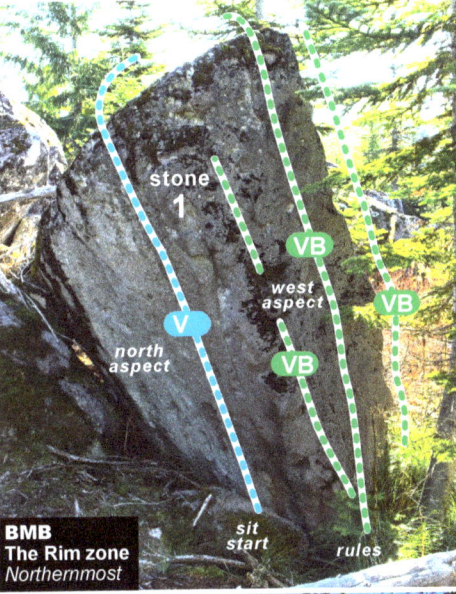

BMB **The Rim zone** *Northernmost*

BMB **The Rim** *Classic Arête Stone 2 & 3*

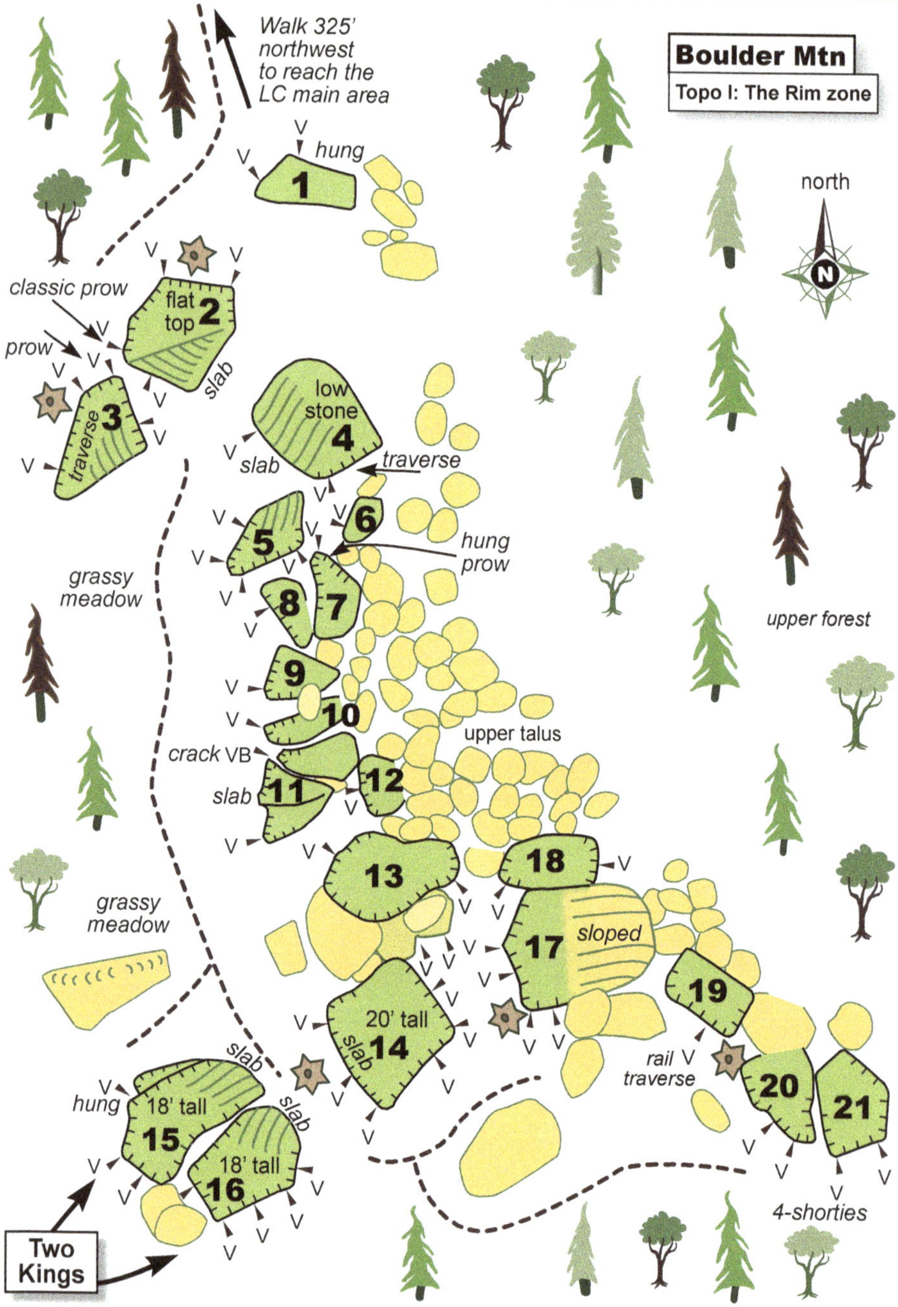

58 MT HOOD ZONE (SOUTH)

Boulder Mtn
Topo I: The Rim zone

Walk 325' northwest to reach the LC main area

hung 1
classic prow
flat top 2
prow
3 traverse
slab
low stone 4
slab — traverse
5 6
hung prow
8 7
grassy meadow
9
10
crack VB
slab 11 12
upper talus
13 18
sloped
17
grassy meadow
20' tall
slab 14
19
rail traverse
hung 18' tall
15
slab
20 21
18' tall
16
Two Kings
4-shorties

upper forest

north

V1 ☐
Brief crimpy face on the south aspect (to the right of the prow).

Stone 3
Beta is described left to right beginning on the east side problem.

V__ ☐
Leftmost problem on the NE aspect of the stone. Start low in a slight trough, and climb crimps up flat face onto slab.

V4 Land Before Time

Quality well-hung nose shaped prow. Sit start low, and power past the hung nose, then up the sharp rib (all on the right side - the west side).

V1 Dishes at Dawn

Traverse left beginning on the south end quite low, and traverse leftward till you reach the hung prow, then go up to the top.

Stone 4

VB Basic

Just a low angle slab nothingness.

V_

A very low sit start lip traverse going from left to right (on the east aspect), but there's some kind of contortion master game to it.

Stone 5

A very low stone - all sit start.

V1/V2

Sit start going left to right along a low lip rail.

V1/V2

Sit start low on the hung south aspect and bump out to merge with the previous lip traverse route near the outermost tip top point.

V1

Ultra shorty on east side.

Stone 6

V_

Very short squiggle problem.

Stone 7

V3/V4 [?]

An impressive high quality overhung prow. Sit start un-

BMB The Rim
Classic Arête area
Stone 2 & 3

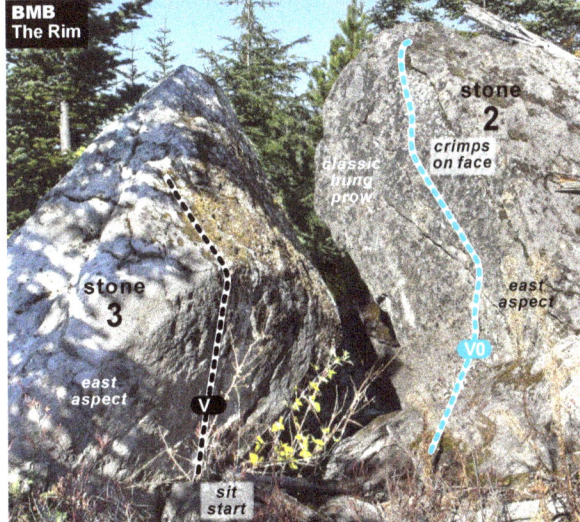

BMB The Rim

BMB The Rim

60 MT HOOD ZONE (SOUTH)

derneath the beast and power hug your way out and up to the top.

Shorty's Stone Gang:

This is a group of 4-5 stones in a row that offer a string of quite short, mostly sit start boulder problems, all quite basic.

Stone 8

V3 ____
The left shorty on the south aspect.

V_ ____
The right shorty on the south aspect.

Stone 9

V0 ____
Shorty at the sharp point (stay on the prow).

V0 ____
Climb the right aspect face of the same prow and the corner.

Stone 10

VB ____
A left leaning rib shorty. Sit start.

Stone 11

VB ____
Minor short jam crack. Sit start.

VB ____
Minor basic nothingness on the slab.

Stone 12

V2 [?] ____
Very low shorty tucked in a slight trough. Crawl under it and use pockets to get out and up.

Stone 13

V_ ____
Problem located on the west aspect.

V_ ____
Located on far back side (the east side) is this unique well overhung short low pig.

Stone 14

This is a tall 20' high boulder with a host of fine fun problems.

Boulder Mtn Boulders ✦ PB 61

South Aspect:

V1/V2 [?] _____ ☐
Tall slab problem (the leftmost problem). This is height dependent, and sticking that first high right hold is not simple.

V0/V1 _____ ☐
Tall slab smears (in the center of tall face).

VB _____ ☐
Tall slab smear problem that merges in with the next at about mid height.

VB _____ ☐
Long angled slab ridge problem with edges and steps, plus over the perched top small stone.

East Aspect:

VB _____ ☐
A tall long slab problem beginning next to a small base stone. This enters a broken set of perched stones up high near top.

V0 _____ ☐
Tall face with power crimps on a steep quality face. This line is surprisingly fun, and the small holds are all user friendly, making the entire line a unique fun run.

V2/V3 (?) _____ ☐
Tall thin power crimps face.

VB _____ ☐
Short crack corner.

VB _____ ☐
Short brief face moves on an outside prow.

Stone 15

Two Huge Pillars

This is the impressive double set giant 20' tall pillars of stone - a unique quality dual behemoth treasure for this particular compact zone.

BMB The Rim — Big Slab - South Side
stone 14 — South Aspect
start is height dependent

BMB The Rim — Big Slab - East Side
Big Slab South Face
stone 14 — East Aspect

The beta is described starting on the west side going left to right (counter-clockwise).

VB/V0 (?) _____ ☐
An easy west side problem starting at a large flat block step.

V_ (V_ss) _____ ☐
Standing is at the outermost part of the overhung cave nook; just go directly up the prow. The sit start begins low inside underneath the

beast and powers out on thin holds to join into the standing start.

V0/V1 ____

Standing start gets a jug rail first hold then power onto it and go up onto the slab toward the top.

VB ____

South aspect has this easy jugs and buckets fun run. By the time you get to the top you feel like you've climbed a mountain.

Stone 16

V2 ____

Tucked in a trough on the south aspect; sit start in the pit and power up the face using crimps on this vertical tall pillar.

EAST ASPECT:

V2 ____

Classic tall pockets and crimps on the east aspect at the slight round prow.

V1 ____

Climb only the flat east face directly up (on all the thin crimps and small edges).

V0 ____

Though it begins on the east face, the right hand grapples the rib and quickly transition onto the steep slab face on the north aspect.

VB ____

The north side low angle slab.

Stone 17

V0/V1 (?) ____

Leftmost sit start problem. Minor problem at the point (on the west aspect).

V1/V2 (?) ____

Immediately right of the previous problem on the same west-facing aspect. Sit start; crimp a few face moves past the bulge onto the slab going to the top.

V_ ____ ☐
Immediately right of the tree. Sit start and power thin crimps directly up the face to the slabby top out.

V_ ____ ☐
Begin as a sit start the same method as the previous problem (under the overhang) and power up going rightward slightly on thin crimpy holds to the top.

Stone 18

THE OTHER EGG

V_ ____ ☐
Located on the west aspect. Sit start and power a series of pockety crimps on a bulge.

V5 ____ ☐
Located on the east aspect of the same stone. A well overhung sit start; power out the pockets and crimps over the round egg.

Stone 19

V_ ____ ☐
A brief rail traverse going from the left to the right. Tucked in behind a cluster of trees.

Stone 20

V_ ____ ☐
A short sit start minor.

V_ ____ ☐
Sit start short minor.

Stone 21 (Last stone)

V_ ____ ☐
Sit start short minor problem.

V_ ____ ☐
Sit start short minor problem.

64 MT HOOD ZONE (SOUTH)

WOODLANDS

The ideal approach to reach the Woodlands cluster is to continue driving south past the main Lost City zone on gravel road NF220 for about ⅓ mile further, then park at a minor wide pullout on the east side of the road. Park here at GPS UTM 10t 600974 5007683.

From this parking spot pullout on road NF220, walk 750' southeast up a gentle incline using an old bulldozer grade.

The first cluster of stones that you'll encounter are the **Roadside Cluster** of boulders tucked in a minor talus field. Just downhill (not visible) are the **Campfire Cluster**, a minor pack with minimal goals. From that same spot along the bulldozer access road, a faint user path cuts around the roadside talus field heading east uphill in the open forest for about 180' to the primary **Woodlands Cluster**, which includes the 'The Twins' (aka Twin Giants) and the grandly large and famous Goliath stone.

From that same parking spot it's possible to walk up the same old bulldozer grade southward for a total of 1500' to reach the upper edge of the LC2 zone (we refer to this southern zone as the '**LC2 - South Talus Group**'.) From this scenic vantage point you can access any of the LC2 South Talus Group of boulders quite easily. Thus, from one single parking spot all of the zones are within easily walkable distance.

The Woodlands and LC2 South Talus zones combined are a vast network of boulders, some in a fairly open forested setting, with the remainder located on an extensive talus field. The forested stones tend to be somewhat masked by all the trees. The GPS coordinates UTM 10t 601019 5007457 is the approximate locale of Goliath Stone and the 'Twin Giants'.

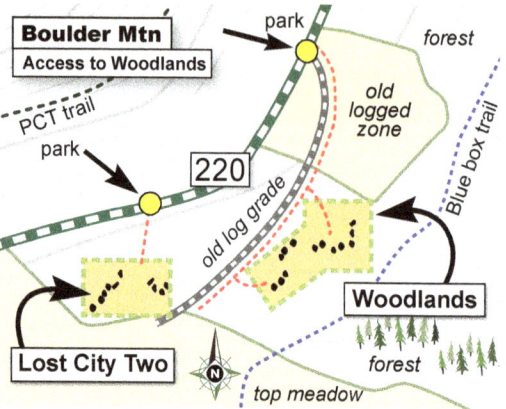

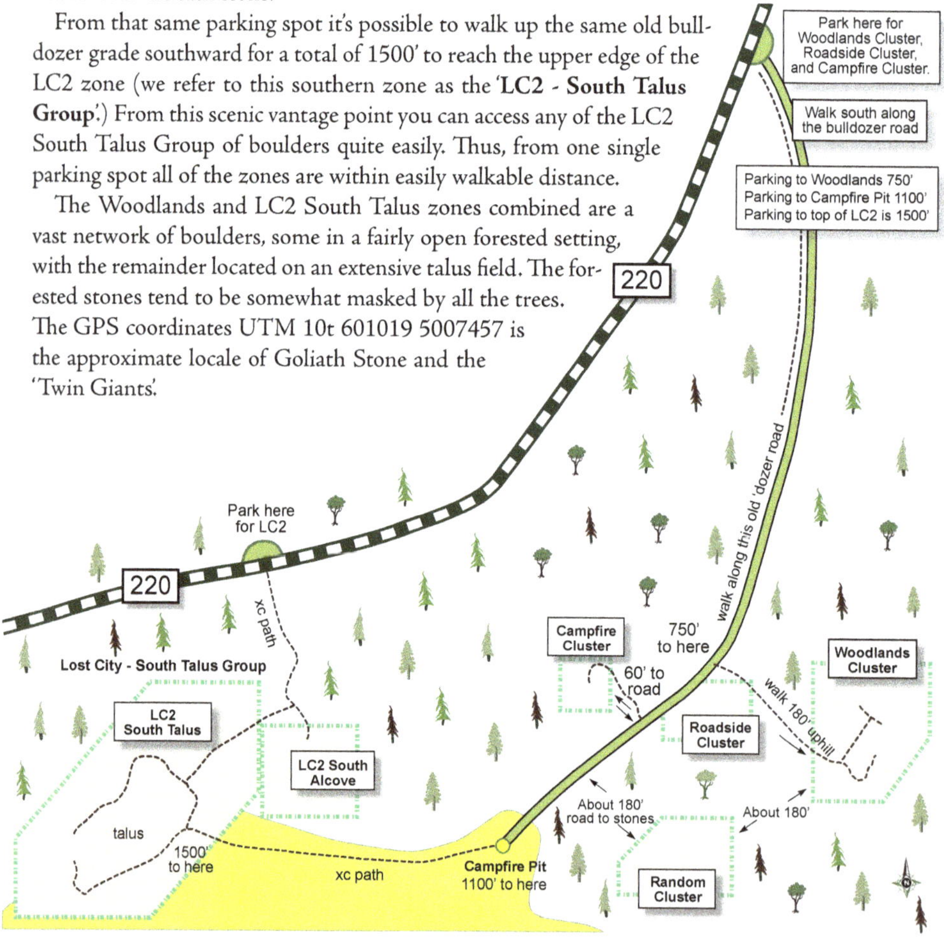

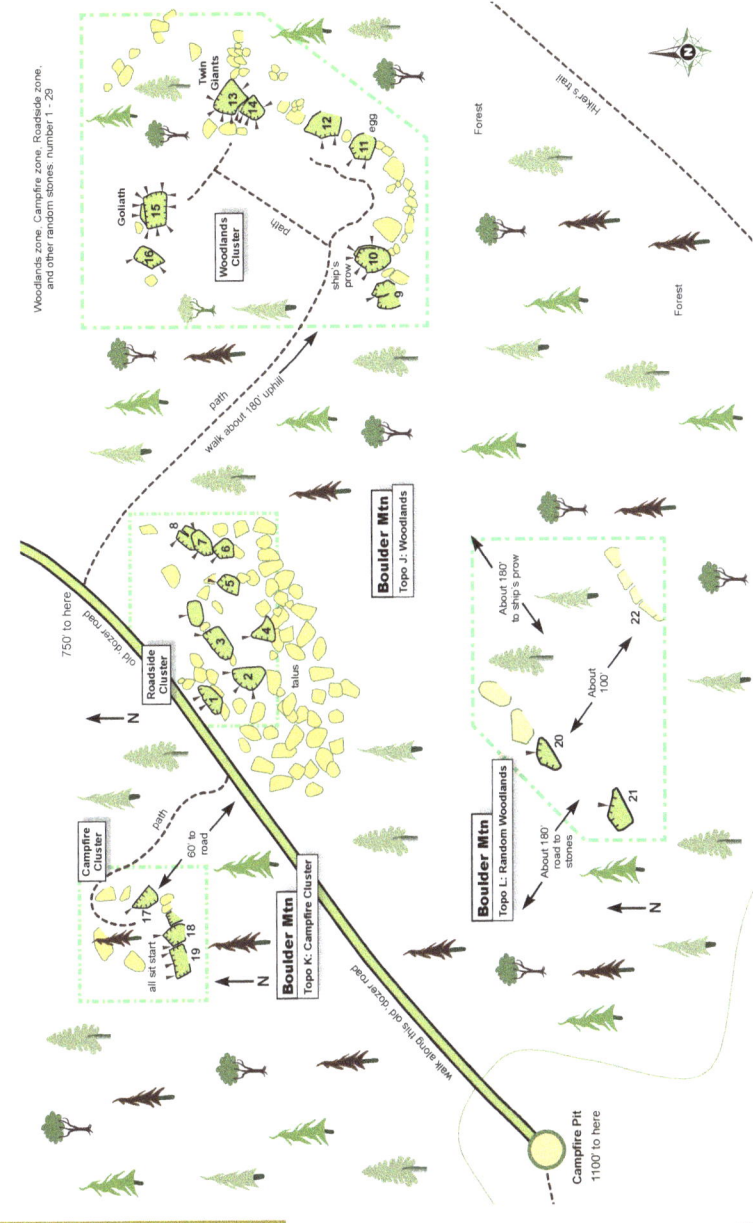

ROADSIDE CLUSTER

This is the first cluster of stones in the midst of a broad uphill talus field that you will arrive at when walking south along the bulldozer access road. Though limited in quantity the brief selection of large boulders can entertain you for an hour or so.

Stone 1

V_ _____ ☐
Minor possible line on a slab.

Stone 2

V_ _____ ☐
Sit start, crimps a few rounded small holds, catch top lip, and move rightward.

V_ _____ ☐
Sit start, crimps and pockets on face.

66   MT HOOD ZONE (SOUTH)

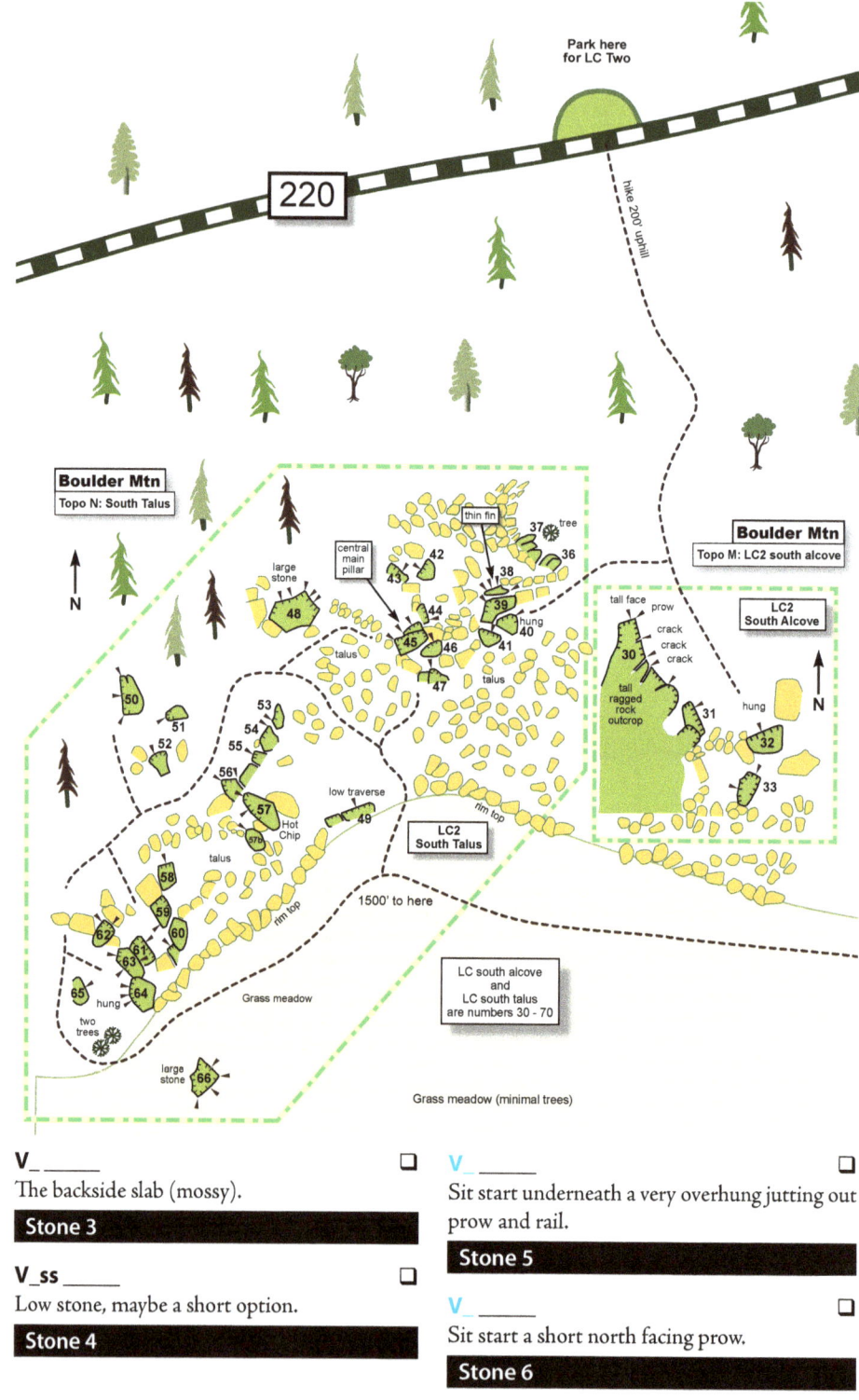

V_ _____
The backside slab (mossy).
Stone 3

V_ss _____
Low stone, maybe a short option.
Stone 4

V_ _____
Sit start underneath a very overhung jutting out prow and rail.
Stone 5

V_ _____
Sit start a short north facing prow.
Stone 6

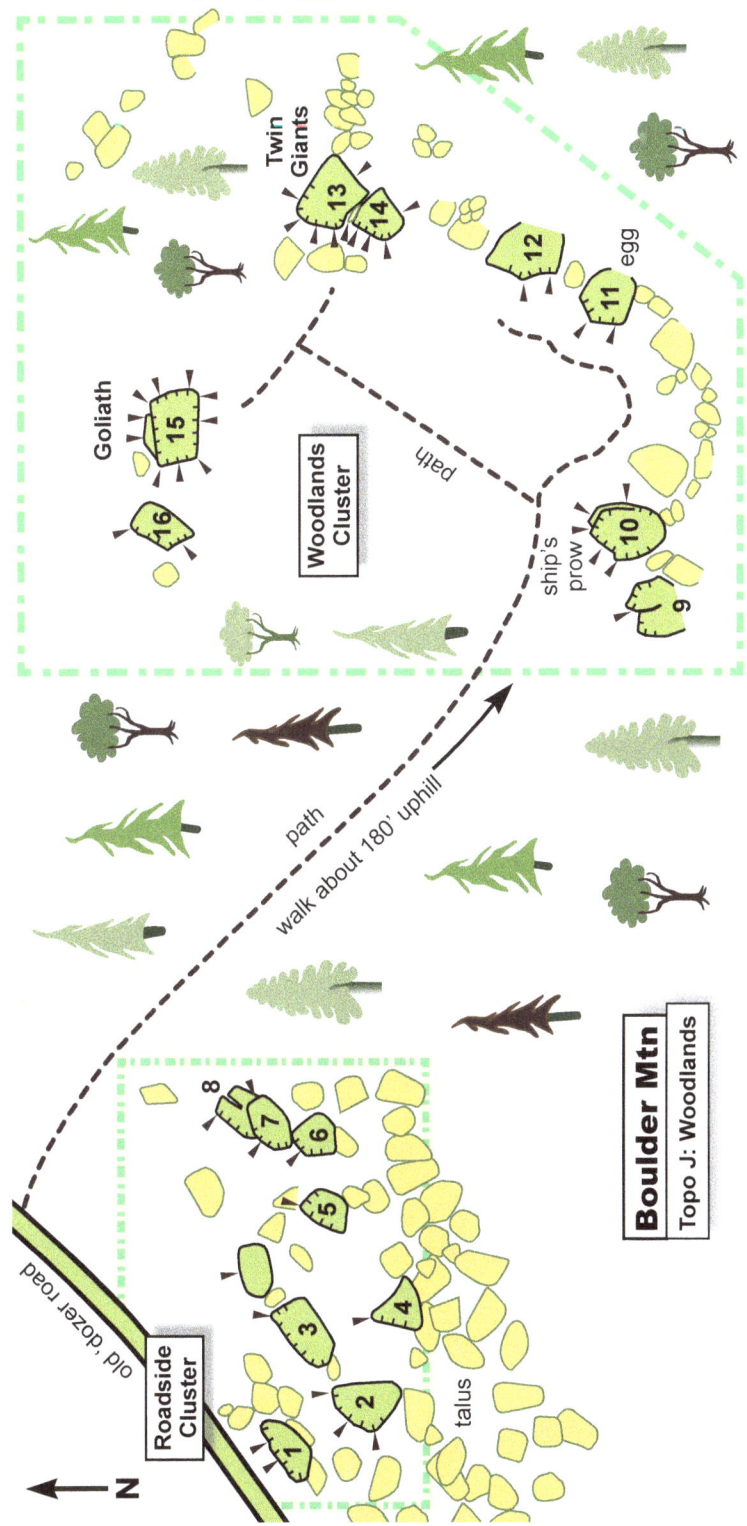

68 MT HOOD ZONE (SOUTH)

V_ _____

V_ _____

Stone 7

V_ _____

Angled block with one rising traverse.

Stone 8

V_ _____

Double block (the upper is Stone #7). Sit start on outer aspect of lower stone, climb with left hand on arête; at top of that block move over onto the higher block and pull over that top lip.

WOODLANDS ZONE

The Woodlands of Boulder Mtn are certainly going to be on your prime destination hit list for exhilerating bouldering opportunities. The problems range from seriously overhung beasts, to a cool string of high-ball lines, all on a plethora of boulders in a uniquely compact zone.

Stone 9

V0/V1 _____

Sit start in a low spot, then jam out the overhung short hand jam crack. Tougher variations exist by starting the same, but going left onto the face.

THE SHIP'S PROW BOULDER

Perhaps the most amazing reason you will want to visit the Woodlands zone. This one stone can certainly entertain any serious boulderer with several virtual classic wild and powerfully bold problems. The beta is described from right to left.

Stone 10 (Ship's Prow)

V3 Hammock Heaven

Sit start, climb short hung face on the far left section of stone.

V6 Camp Chair Catastrophe

Sit start, climb thin pinch holds just left of the ship's prow on a substantial overhang, then either top out straight up.

BMB Woodlands
Roadside cluster

BMB Woodlands
Roadside Cluster

BMB Woodlands
Roadside talus zone

V3 Fire Brigade

Sit start directly beneath the amazing jutting out prow, and all the way climb out the powerful overhung ship's prow, then up over the very tip of it onto flat top of the stone.

Boulder Mtn Boulders ✦ PB 69

BMB Woodlands zone
Ship's Prow

V6 Stone Cold Cookout ❑

Sit start on the right side of the jutting out prow, crimp tiny incut right hand holds, right foot pressing against a pressure point, aim with your left hand high to catch a long reach, then cut loose, then reposition, and muscle over the outer lip onto the flat top of the stone.

Stone 11 (Egg)

V6 Faberge ❑

Sit start, climb out the well-rounded quite small and substantially overhung stone.

V_ _____ ❑

Possible second future line on the left of the same stone.

Stone 12

A minor little stone that is briefly entertaining. Beta is described from left to right:

V0 _____ ❑

Begin on the left as a sit start, but after the initial opening move, wiggle up left onto the slab

BMB Woodlands zone
Stone 9 & 10

BMB Woodlands zone
Ship's prow

and go up the short slab.

V1 _____ ❑

Begin on the left as a sit start, and run the lip up rightward.

70 MT HOOD ZONE (SOUTH)

V1 ☐
Very contrived sit start straight up.

BOULDERS 13 & 14

Twin Giants is an impressive set of huge stones. Most of the tall problems are located on the outer west aspects of both stones. Many lines are done, though a few are still untapped. Beta is described from left to right starting on stone #13, then #14.

Stone 13

V_ ☐
North side slab. The long tall slab, and it's quiet mossy.

V_ ☐
Initial flat face crimps, then rounded angled slab for remainder.

V5 Gin Gin Mule ☐
Sit start, and crimp the thin crack edges, variable holds on face.

V2 Moondance ☐
Climb the tallest central part of the face.

V3/V4 The Prow ☐
Climb the right slightly hung prow (of the left boulder). This is immediately left of the wide chimney.

V1 Chumly Chimney ☐
The obvious chimney on the west aspect.

V2 Intimate Corner ☐
Immediately right of the chimney is this thin face climb.

V4 Primal Scream ☐
The tall vertical center face (on the south boulder).

V2 Insta-classic ☐
Climb the short face (near a stump), then continue up angled terrain to the top.

V_ ☐
Possible line on back side.

V_ ☐
Another possible line on back side.

Stone 15 (Goliath)

Another famous giant stone at the Woodlands well worth visiting. Beta is described clockwise, beginning on the eastside lines.

V_ ☐
This is the NE facing overhung prow. Climb the left aspect of a cool looking overhung prow, then go up a low angle easy slab.

MT HOOD ZONE (SOUTH)

V4 Stereophonic
Sit start, climb over a bulge using the pockets, then run up an easy slab to the top.

V1 Slide
Climb the center tall slab bypassing the overhung part.

VB Descent
The easiest way down off from this big stone.

V_ _____
Located on the south face.

V_ _____
On the south face.

V_ _____
On the outh face.

V1 Stinger
Start at same sharp arête/prow as Singapore Sling, but continue up the prow all the way.

V2 Singapore Sling
Start with right hand on the right sharp prow, make a move up, then traverse hard left along a slight overhung bulge, and merge with Moss Carpet line.

V0 Moss Carpet
The tall west side slab (the long mossy slab). Variants exist.

V_ _____
Brief problem on west aspect just left of Moss Carpet; finish up mossy slab.

V_ _____
Overhung bulge on crimps, then easy slab.

V_ _____
Cool looking overhung prow landing upon an easy mossy slab for remainder of ascent.

Stone 16

V2 Sleet
This is a short low hung stone a few yards south of Goliath stone. The sit start will be harder.

Stone __

Boulder Mtn Boulders ✦ PB 73

V5ss Weaver
Stone __

V7ss Infinite Bliss
An eliminate problem on a single stone.
Stone __

V0/V1 Future Not Choss
A mossy boulder located a short distance uphill east of the Egg Boulder.

CAMPFIRE CLUSTER

Not much to say about this tiny brief cluster. From the bulldozer access road, walk down slope for about 80' to reach this compact cluster. The stones can entertain you for an hour or so. Everything here at this cluster is a sit start boulder problem.

Stone 17
The northernmost hung stone.

V_ ____

Stone 18
The middle stone has a short problem.

V_ ____

Stone 19
Southern flat faced stone.

V_ ____
V_ ____
V_ ____
V_ ____
V_ ____

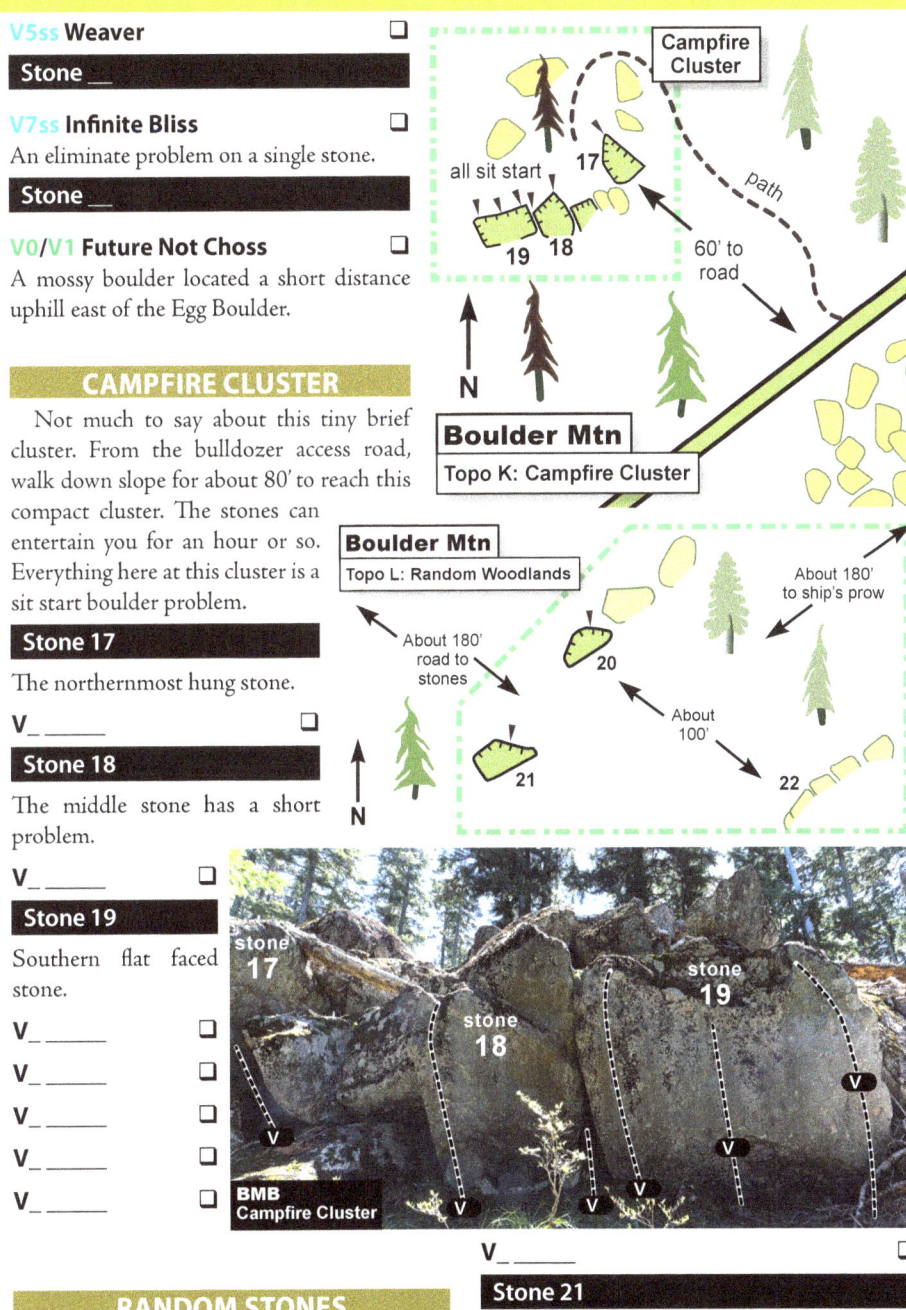

RANDOM STONES

Several minor random stones occur in the open forest (see topo), and any one of those might be of interest briefly for bouldering purposes.

Stone 20
Northernmost stone is a maybe.

V_ ____

Stone 21
Southernmost stone; brief sit start on short flat face.

V_ ____

74 MT HOOD ZONE (SOUTH)

LC2 - SOUTH ALCOVE

This major alcove was tapped by locals due to its fully entertaining value. The entire series of problems - mostly hi-ball lines - are well worth their weight in virtual digital gold.

It's best to access this zone by hiking up from NF220 road for several hundred feet in open forest to reach this super cool alcove.

Stone 30

Technically this zone is a large single massive rock outcrop broken into definitive hunks, all still well attached. The rock formation is about 25' tall and juts up like a prominent yet brief rock rooster's comb. On its north and east aspects are a treasure of lines worth ascending.

V1 ☐
Rightmost outer aspect of the Rooster

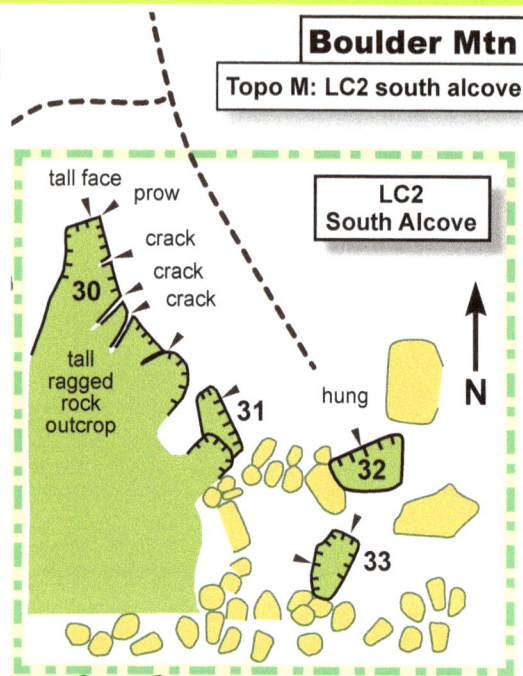

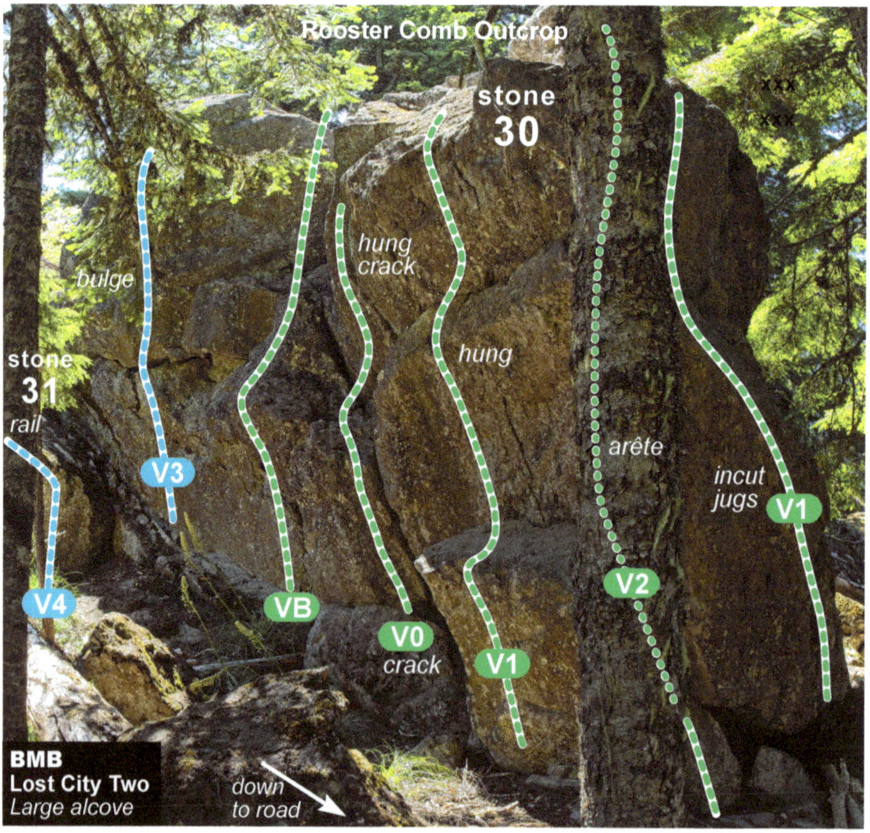

Boulder Mtn Boulders ✦ PB 75

Comb Outcrop. Climb a steep angled ramp up a vertical cliff, surmount the slight hung top part, and waltz along the top crest till you reach easier descent terrain.

V2 ____ ❏
A cool vertical arete with a slight hung lean to it.

V1 ____ ❏
A slightly overhung face. Begin as sit start, power over initial bulge, grab crack, make a few moves up crack till feet are on the stance, then make several overhung face moves over the high top bulge, till you land on the upper easy slab. Traverse along the tip top SE to easier terrain.

V0 ____ ❏
A big wandering crack system (that is slightly overhung) with plenty of holds, jams, and edges.

VB ____ ❏
Starts slightly overhung. Jam the crack a few moves into a wider slot. Ends quickly at a notch.

V3/V4 [?] ____ ❏
Sit start, crimp a series of overhung powerful moves up to a final bulge, that lands onto an angled slab for the final moves at the top.

Stone 31

V4 [?] ____ ❏
Single long stone also attached to the main massif, but slightly independent of it. The problem begins low on the right as a sit start, traverses left, then goes up over a second higher block.

Stone 32

V_ ____ ❏
Odd saucer shaped block perched atop several other large blocks, yielding either a standing start, or a powerful sit start under it.

Stone 33

The tall blocky formation a few yards uphill from the previous stone has several lines on it.

V_ ____ ❏
V_ ____ ❏

BMB
Lost City Two
Large Alcove

LC2 - SOUTH TALUS

aka Lost City Two

Access this by hiking up from NF220 road, or walking the bulldozer access road to the top meadow, then descend down to it. This third major talus field at Boulder Mtn Boulders is the southernmost talus group, and has a fair number of cool problems well worth visiting.

The beta for this extensive boulder talus field is described starting near the LC2 Alcove, then proceeds out onto the talus field to the cool central pillar, then southwestward ending near the Moonwalk boulder., and lastly a minor large random stone located in the meadow above the talus field.

Drive NF220 gravel road south till you see the large LC2 talus field (visible from road on your uphill left side). Park here and walk uphill to the the primary large stones or the tall alcove (on left side of the talus field).

GPS info: UTM 10T 600779 5007433.

Stone 36

V_ _____ ☐

Next to a tall tree.

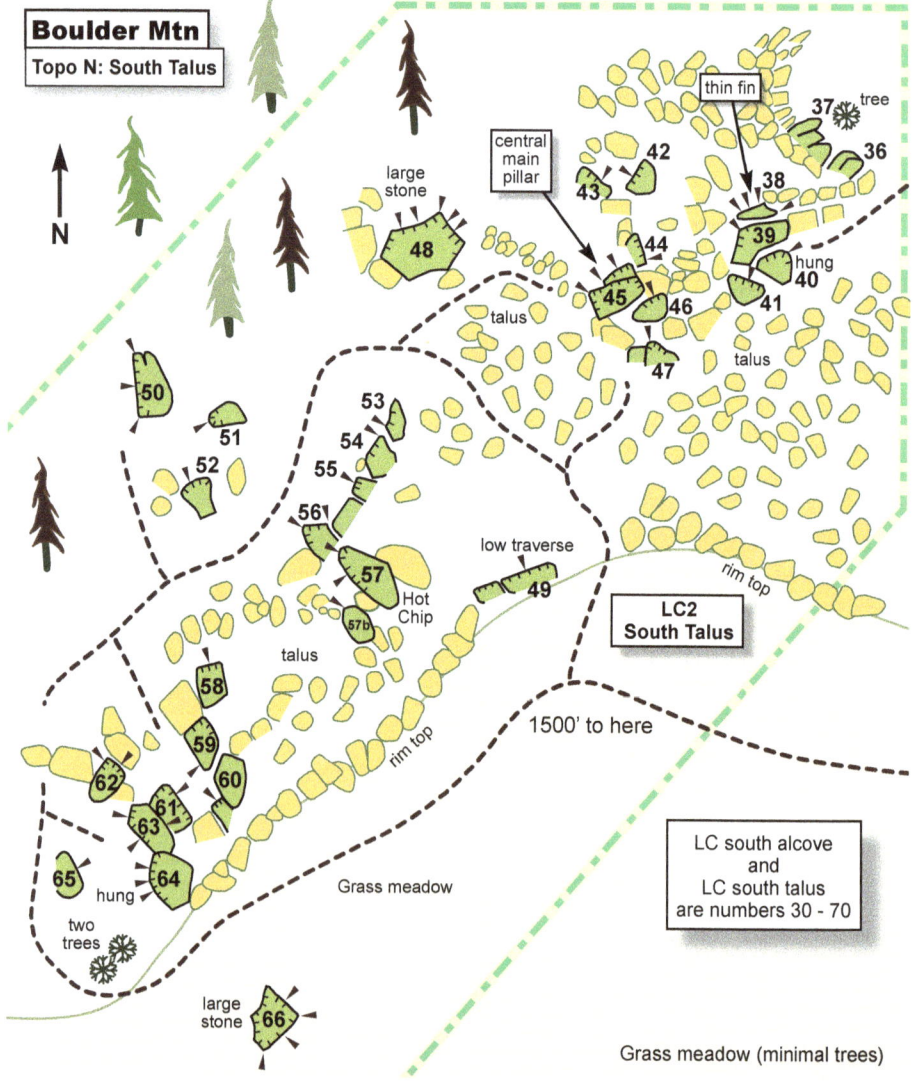

Stone 37

V_ _____ ☐
Near the same tall tree.

Stone 38 (Thin Fin)

Unique wafer thin fin of rock with several cool lines on it.

V_ _____ ☐
The eastmost sharp arete fin.

V_ _____ ☐
North face.

V_ _____ ☐
North face.

V_ _____ ☐
West arete / face.

Stone 39

V_ _____ ☐
A minor prow facing northwest-ish.

Stone 40

V_ _____ ☐
An overhung rounded NE face.

Stone 41

V_ _____ ☐
Short flat face.

Stone 42

V_ _____ ☐
Short flat face.

Stone 43

V_ _____ ☐
Short flat face.

Stone 44

V_ _____ ☐
Short face.

TALL CENTRAL PILLAR

Stone 45

The impressive, notably large, and tall (pillar-like) stone that juts high above all the other

BMB Lost City Two — Main Central Pillar

BMB Lost City Two — Talus northern portion. Panorama looking north from the main central pillar stone.

stones in this portion of the south talus boulder field. This particular stone is a good logical spot to begin your bouldering adventure.

V1-2 [?] ☐
North tall aspect as a sit start.

V2 Uncommon Ground ☐
The hung west-facing side has incut holds that make for a unique moderate fun run boulder problem (sit start).

V4 Common Ground ☐
The rightmost part of this stone has a hung bulge to it. Sit start below it, and power crimp over the bulge, onto the angled upper slab.

VB Descent ☐
The upper side is the descent.

Stone 46

V_ _____ ☐
Short north face.

Stone 47

V_ _____ ☐
Short overhung prow.

Stone 48

A large flat-topped stone with a plethora of tall problems on the outer tall northern aspects of the stone. Beta is described left to right.

V_ _____ ☐
NE face problem.

V_ _____ ☐
NE face problem.

V_ _____ ☐
Ascend the north prow.

V_ _____ ☐
NW face problem.

Stone 49

LOW TRAVERSE STONE

V_ _____ ☐
At the top of the talus field next to the meadow is this double stone traverse problem on a flat short vertical face. Traverse both stones.

Stone 50

Tucked in the forest is this isolated stone.

Boulder Mtn Boulders ✦ PB 79

V1ss Porcelain
Sits start on smooth rounded prow (at the lower western end of this stone).

V2ss Wonder Why
Climb the short scoop at the central part of the same stone.

Stone 51

V_ _____

Stone 52

V_ _____

Stone 53

V_ _____

Stone 54

V_ _____

Stone 55

V0 Short Thing
Minor nothingness.

Stone 56

V_ _____

Stone 57

V2ss Hot Chip
The sunny south side of the block has a cool vertical crimps face. Sit start. Crimp start several moves to catch the high left prow, then go up right along that lip to the top.

V3ss Ruffles
Sit start, and climb the overhung outer part of the prow of the same stone.

Stone 57b

V0 Easy block
A small round block immediately right of #57.

Stone 58

V_ _____
Tall vertical slightly leaning stone with crimps. Leftmost problem.

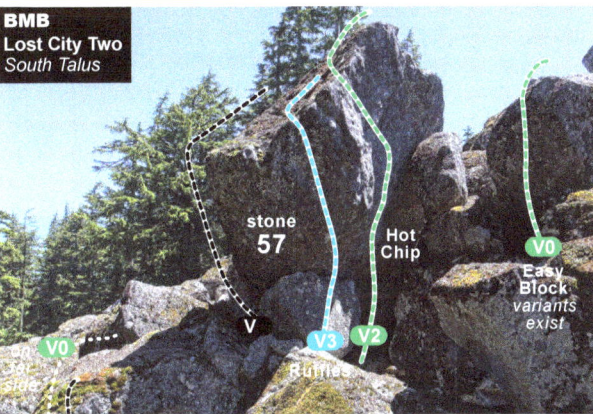

80 MT HOOD ZONE (SOUTH) ✦

V_ _____
The rightmost problem. Begin as sit start, crimp small holds on a slightly hung face.

Stone 59

V0ss Short Thang
Very short small problem adjacent to the Moonwalk area.

Stone 60

V0ss _____
Minor short face (crack on left).

Stone 61

V_ _____
A short overhung pig.

Stone 62

V_ _____
Possible short problem on a bulge.

Stone 63

V0 The Slab
Easy face on a slab left of Moonwalk roof.

V_ _____
Sit start the outer lower short brief bulge.

V_ _____
Sit start vertical face on north side.

Stone 64

V3 (V7) Moonwalk
Sit start under a roof in a low cave-*ish* nook using small features to gain good holds at the lip, then continue up left side of boulder to top out. The standing start is V3.

V7ss Chilly Willy
Same start as previous route but angle up slightly right to top out.

V8 Bark at the Moon
Toe hook high on the next route, crimps on face, and travel directly left to Moonwalk.

BMB Lost City Two
Moonwalk zone Two Trees area

BMB Lost City Two
Moonwalk zone Two Trees

V_ _____
The rightmost line, a short direct up hung sit start problem.

Stone 65

V2ss _____
Sit start in a low pit.

Stone 66 (Lone Stone)

A large stone in the meadow above the talus zone a short walk east of Moonwalk stone; only the north face, NE prow, east face, and SE prow are viable.

VB _____
The north face.

VB (V0ss) _____
The NE prow.

VB (V0ss) _____
The east face.

VB (V0ss) _____
The SE prow.

TOP MEADOW

This large open logged area (regrowth of new trees will eventually making navigating to each cluster a bit more tricky) offers 3-4 compact clusters of boulders that are well separated from each other. Be exploratory savvy because it takes a bit of sixth sense to trapse cross-country to reach each locale. The problems range in difficulty from VB to V7. Many of the boulders are short, thus sit starts are the name of the game, but a few gems do beckon.

To reach the **Top Meadow**: from the road split (on NF220) just east of the campsite (at the Bluebox trailhead), drive south on the rough NF221 road (AWD recommended) for about ½ mile until the road opens at a logged zone (which now has new tree regrowth). This entire broad old logged zone is referred to as Top Meadow and is situated around Blue Box Peak, a minor wooded knoll that the Blue Box Trail goes through.

TOP MEADOW NORTH

To reach **Top Meadow North** zone, you can park on NF221 where the logged zone first becomes apparent. Hike uphill west (past an initial mossy roadside cluster) along the northern perimeter of the logged zone for about 200' to reach **Top Meadow North 1 (TM1)** cluster, and about 200' west further is **Top Meadow North 2 (TM2)** cluster.

TOP MEADOW SOUTH

To reach the **Top Meadow South** cluster, continue driving south on NF221 road to its very end and park there. Hike uphill southwest for 400' to reach the main core zone (**TMS Core**). A smaller group (**TMS West**) offers a few more minor problems (*see topo map*).

TM3 thru TM8 (*see topo map*) are additional random scattered options (some single stones, and some minor clusters of stones) though none are detailed here.

GPS LOCALE FOR THE PRIMARY CLUSTERS:
UTM 10t 601213 5007230 (TM1)
UTM 10t 601134 5007230 (TM2)
UTM 10t 601055 5006955 (TMS Core)
UTM 10t 601008 5006957 (TMS West)

TOP MEADOW NORTH #1

TMN #1 ZONE

This is a cool zone to explore and climb at. It includes a unique low powerful cave-crawl problem, including the locally famous Flux stone, and the Airplane Tail stone, all of which combine to make a worthy quality combination of stones.

Stone 1

THE FLUX BOULDER

This boulder is the ultimate reason to visit this quality haven at Top Meadow.

V1ss Smog   ☐
This is the leftmost problem. Sit start and power out the hung bulge.

V2ss Flux Capacitor   ☐
Sit start and power straight out the huge bulge.

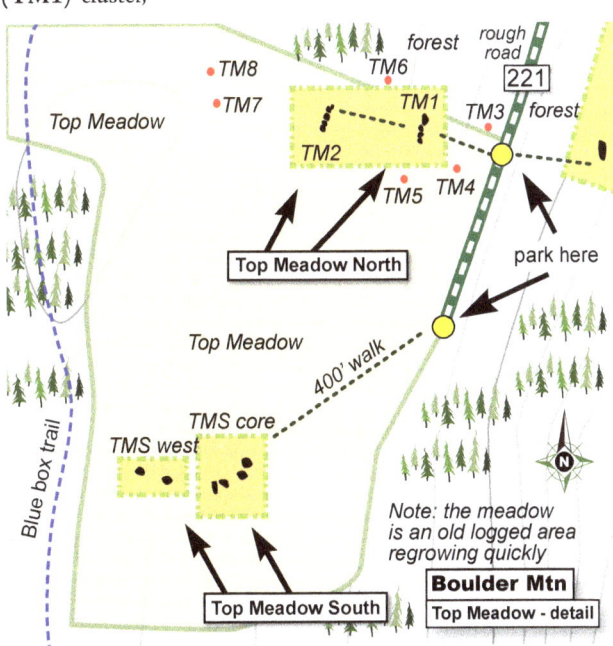

Note: the meadow is an old logged area regrowing quickly

Boulder Mtn
Top Meadow - detail

82 MT HOOD ZONE (SOUTH)

Boulder Mtn
Topo F: Top Meadow
Section One (TMN1)
The Cave & Airplane Tail

V3ss Smug
Sit start low on right at small hung crack, and run lip left to the outermost point then over it.

V4ss _____
Begin same as previous, but power straight up the crack onto the top.

V6ss _____
Begin on the farthest north side and traverse entire eastside of boulder to the big bulge at the south end.

Stone 2

Sam's cave-crawl problem is one of the other great reasons to hit this little haven.

V6 (and V9) Sam's Cave
Crawl deep under this flat topped stone deep into the cave craw. The easier option skips two moves, but the harder option tackles all the moves.

Stone 3

V_ss _____
Sit start low on left and pump the juggy overhung stuff up right to the top. Short but cool problem.

Stone 4

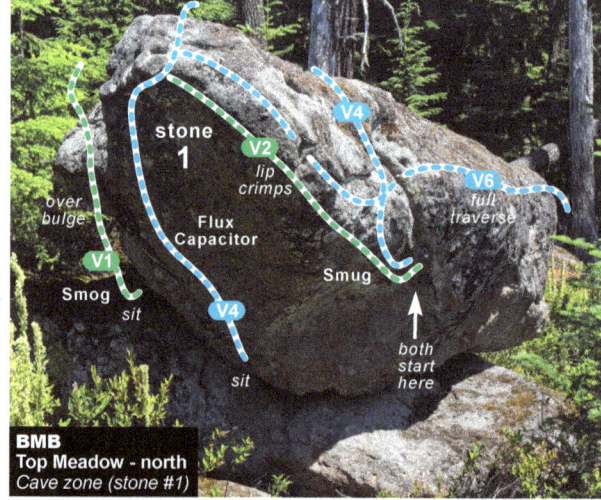

BMB
Top Meadow - north
Cave zone (stone #1)

BMB
Top Meadow - north
The Cave (Stone #2)

V_ss ____
A short problem.

Stone 5

V_ss ____
A short problem.

Stone 6

V_ss ____
A short problem.

Stone 7

A quite short boulder but with three very decent problems [TA].

V_ss ____
Leftmost problem.

V_ss ____
Short center problem.

V_ss ____
Rightmost problem.

Stone 8 (Airplane Tail)

This is the other cool reason to visit here - the uniquely shaped Airplane Tail boulder.

V1ss Airplane Tail
Sit start and crimp several thin seams, the top, and over it.

V1ss Tailspin
Sit start, crimp the slight bulge at center of stone and go over it.

V0ss Winger
Sit start, crimp the same bulge (further right) and go over it.

V2ss Wingman Traverse
Entire lip traverse (in either direction).

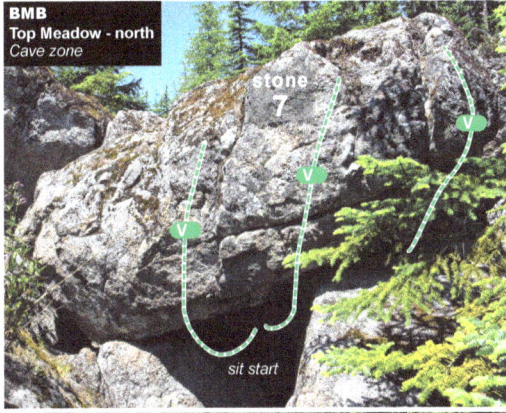
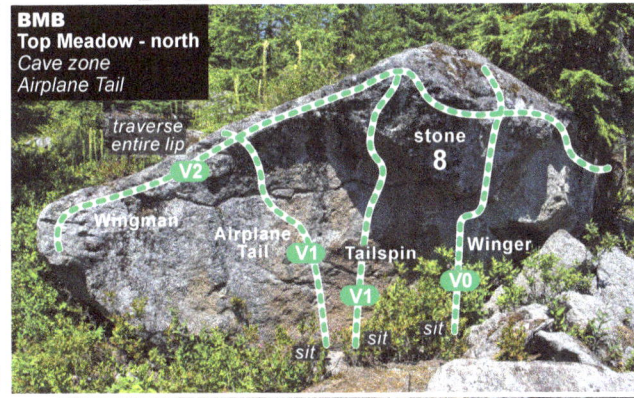

84 MT HOOD ZONE (SOUTH)

TOP MEADOW NORTH #2

FROGLAND ZONE (TMN #2 ZONE)

Another unique zone of quite short boulder problems, mostly in the lower easier grades. Located about 200' west of TMN1 zone (or 400' west of the parking spot on NF221 road).

Stone 9

V_ss _____ (minor short face) ☐

Stone 10

V_ss _____ ☐
Tucked in a narrow slot.

Stone 11

This is the core set of stones that make this little cluster unique. Plenty of fun time stuff. All are sit start problem.s

V_ss _____ ☐
Right sloped hung rail. This is the rightmost sit start route.

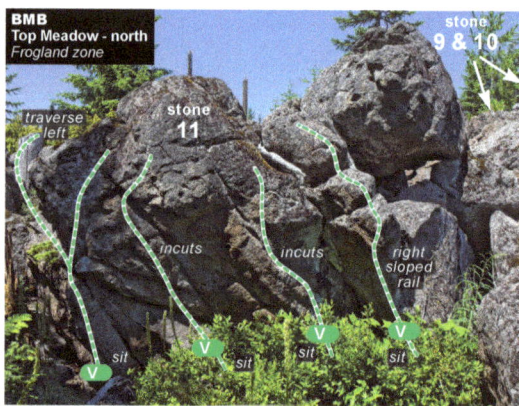

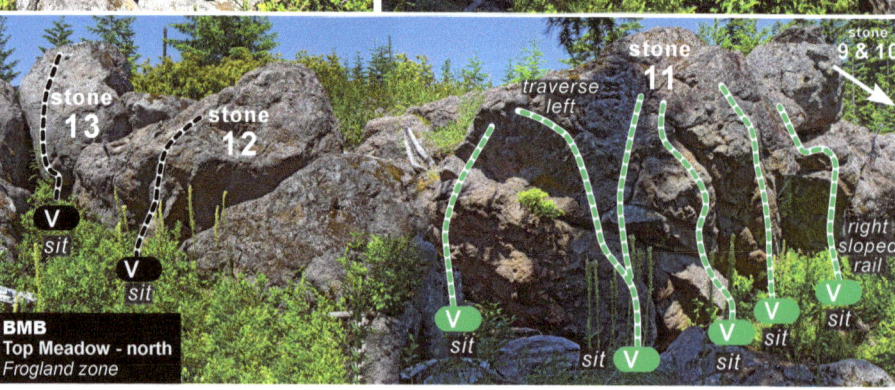

V_ss _____

Sit start and grab the incut jugs on an overhung section of stone.

V_ss _____

Sit start, grab incut holds, and power up the slightly overhung face angling up leftward.

VBss _____

Sit start; and power a bunch of easy jugs and edges, exiting either directly up, or traverse left a bit, then go up.

Stone 12

V_ss _____ (short low face)

Stone 13

V_ss _____ (short round stone)

Stone 14

V_ss _____

A brief low traverse.

TOP MEADOW - SOUTH

This zone has about thirty boulder problems (most already done). This pack is the southernmost zone at **Top Meadow** (see topo map). The zone is composed of two clusters of stones; the larger main **TMS Core**, and the **TMS Western** which are separated by about 100-feet distance from the other.

All problems at the Top Meadow South zone are sit start problems due to the vast majority of stones being quite short in height (though there are a few large sized units).

TMS - CORE ZONE

Stone 1

V_ _____

Stone 2

V_ _____

Sit start a short crimpy face.

VB _____

Stone 3

V_ _____

Stone 4

V_ _____

Sit start under the very rounded stone, and crimp the tiny features on the face. This is a unique little stone.

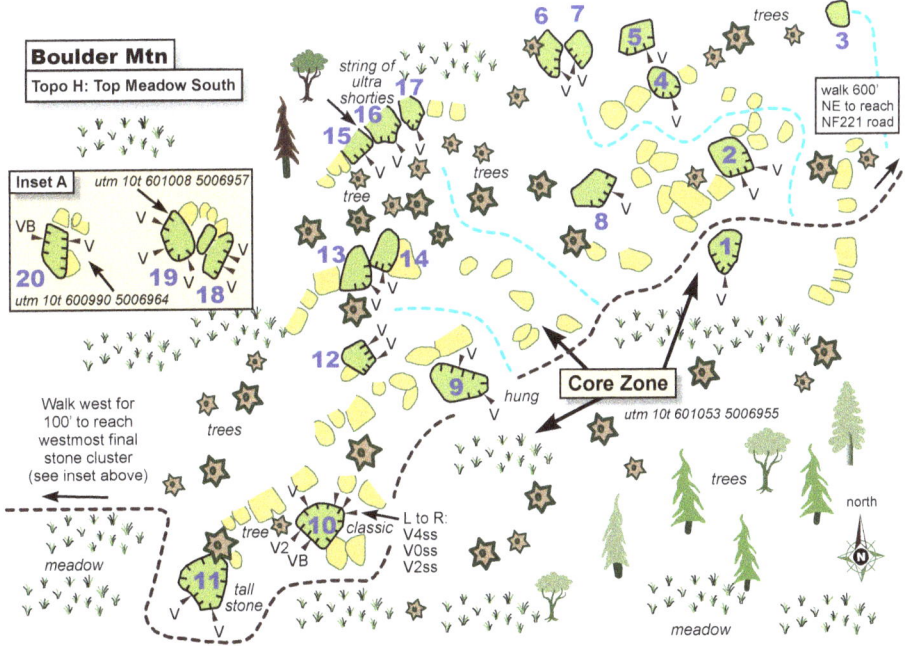

86 MT HOOD ZONE (SOUTH)

Stone 5

V_ _____ ☐

Stone 6

V_ _____ ☐

Sit start in a low trough (between two stones), and crimp the vertical face of this stone.

Stone 7

V_ _____ ☐

Sit in the same low trough (same as the previous stone problem does) and crimp up a slightly rounded bulge onto a short face.

Stone 8

V_ _____ ☐

Stone 9

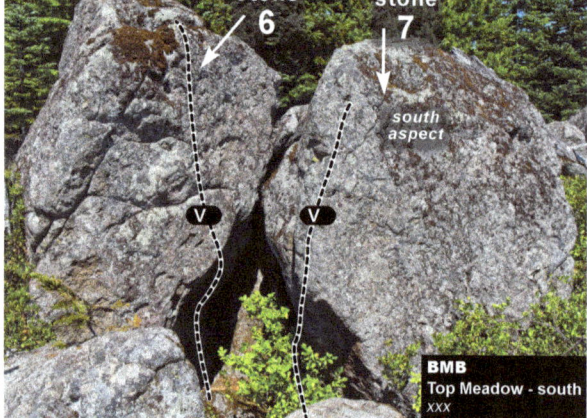

Boulder Mtn Boulders ✦ PB 87

V_ _____ ☐
V_ _____ ☐

Stone 10

Beta is described left to right, beginning on the southernmost problem next to the tree.

South Aspect:

V2ss Alpine Street Biscuit ☐
Sit start, crimps on face.

VBss _____ ☐

North Aspect:

All three of the next problems all begin using the exact same sit start hand holds in a low landing

V4ss Kona Blue ☐
One of the better problems on this stone. Sit start, crimp leftward along thin holds, surmount top lip on the far left.

V0ss Fetch ☐
Sit start, and climb up slightly left-ish using big holds.

V3ss Island Girl ☐
Sit start and climb crimpy holds up slightly right, then onto the low angled top. Another fine tricky pig.

Stone 11

This is the somewhat large stone that has several square-*ish* sliced aspects to it.

V_ _____ ☐
West aspect sit start problem using interesting knobby features and incuts.

V_ _____ ☐
Sit start and climb a rounded section of stone, while keeping your right hand on the right square sharper prow.

VB _____ ☐
South side walk up.

Stone 12

V_ _____ ☐
Very short sit start crimpy problem.

V_ _____ ☐
Begin as sit start under the slight overhang, and crimp the face, then angle up left.

MT HOOD ZONE (SOUTH)

Stone 13
V_ _____

Stone 14
V_ _____

Stone 15
V_ _____

Stone 16
V_ _____

Stone 17
V_ _____

TMS - WESTMOST GROUP

Stone 18

Both problems are on the under side of the sunny south aspect of the stone.

V_ _____

V_ _____

Stone 19

West Aspect:

V_ _____

Sit start, ascend a series of thin crimps on the west aspect of the stone.

South Aspect:

V_ _____

A slight bulge creates a short sit start problem.

V_ _____

Same slight overhung bulge for this one last minor shorty problem.

Stone 20

Several minor short problems on a flat face. This is the westmost stone (see topo).

V_ _____

V_ _____

BMB Top Meadow - south *Stone #19*

BMB Top Meadow - south *Stone #18 & #19*

Mt Hood Bouldering Areas (Northern)

This section details bouldering sites in the Hood River valleys, on both the Hood Fork and the West Fork river drainages, essentially areas found on the northern slopes or valleys of Mt Hood.

COOPER SPUR BOULDERS

For those who relish the invigorating nature of high-altitude bouldering, the stellar Cooper Spur Boulders provide a scenic, quality bouldering site just a short hike from the Cooper Spur trailhead (5,800') on the windswept northeastern alpine slopes of Mt Hood. The Cooper Spur Boulders are an idyllic little wonderland of rock, scoured impeccably clean by wind, snow and rain. The alpine scenery around the Cooper Spur Stone Shelter is a captivating, photographic blend of whitebark pine trees, numerous andesite and dacite boulders, jet blue sky, and the rugged north face of Mt Hood as a backdrop.

The 1.1 mile uphill hike begins at the Cloud Cap parking site, nestled in a hemlock forest. Just beyond the wilderness signage post, the hikers trail splits into several directions. The right trail fork goes up to Eliot Glacier along a windswept moraine ridge crest. This right trail fork also leads to the Eliot Cluster, a set of three boulders in a compact locale protected from the winds, a mere ¼ mile from the trailhead. The left trail fork is the primary trail (#600 Timberline trail) that leads up to the junction with the Tilly Jane trail (#600a) at the Cooper Spur stone shelter. From the stone shelter, the hikers trail braids uphill through the very midst of a vast cluster of boulders. There are a number of camping spots at the base of some boulders, some of which may be in use (more likely on weekends). Also, en route to the stone hut, but ¼ mile from the trailhead you will encounter an impressively large boulder 20' wide and 15' tall.

The Stone Hut Cluster of boulders begins near the metal roofed Cooper Spur stone shelter, and continues uphill for about 300' (from 6,800' to 7,100'). The entire area is littered with small stones (2'-6'), but of the larger 25 stones you will find 75+ boulder problems (VB-V5), with heights ranging from 9' to 12' (a few reach 14') tall.

The Eliot Cluster is a set of three stellar andesite stones (about 12' tall) with overhanging aspects, and a total of 17 problems (VB-V4) and several traverse lines. These stones are very likely to have been climbed upon eons ago. Historical bouldering data is non-existent. High altitude day hikers (and various mountaineers) who naturally boulder/scramble a bit are very likely to be first on many basic lines. Mr O did a virtual complete send of the entire site in approximately 2009.

The surface texture nuances of the stones show considerable weathering from rain, wind, and snow. This has softened the typical sharpness of the crystalline phenocrysts. With a softened textured surface friendly to bouldering, it is quite feasible to climb 40+ problems in one outing without wearing the fingertip pads thin. This weathering factor creates a challenge though, by giving the

On Tilly Jane Boulder

surface a slick greasy feel (less noticeable on shaded aspects). Expect cool morning temperatures (colder in October), so plan your trip according to your V-fix favorites. Rock surficial variances range from low jug rails, a plethora of traverses, some pockety features, glassy slopers, rounded crimpers; all the typical variables that entice, yet situated at the 6700' elevation in full sunlight. One crashpad is recommended for this site. The vast majority of the problems are short, and the landings gravelly or sandy.

Brief summer seasonal access is from about July 15th (or when the road opens to the Cooper Spur trailhead) until late October or early November. Check with the Forest Service to determine if the gates have been closed at the end of the season. Very warm daytime temperatures may occur in July-August, but you can attain colder sending conditions from mid-September onward. If a 2½ hour drive from Portland may seem excessive, if so, consider car-camping at the trailhead, or in the general vicinity. The nearest town with some amenities is Parkdale (about 15 miles), and Hood River (about 30 miles) to the north. The Northwest Forest Pass is required when parking at this site. The graveled portion of the road is 9.5 miles from the ski area (paved up to the ski center) to the trailhead (good 2WD vehicle road).

ELIOT CLUSTER

From the parking site, walk up the trail past the registration sign (past the Tilly Jane trail) to a "Y" in the trail. The left trail is #600, but let's take the right trail to the Eliot Cluster of boulders. It ascends up a steep sandy slope, enters a small grove of trees, and shortly reaches the first large boulder alongside the trail.

Barrett (CSB-EC)

A 12' tall (on the long side) block. Most of the lines are great on perfect stone.

V1 East Rib ☐
Tackle the rib starting low on the right and angling up left to top.

V3 North Rib ☐
Initial smear low on the right, crimp the rib, power the tricky moves onto a steep slab. Techy and committing moves. Ultra-classic.

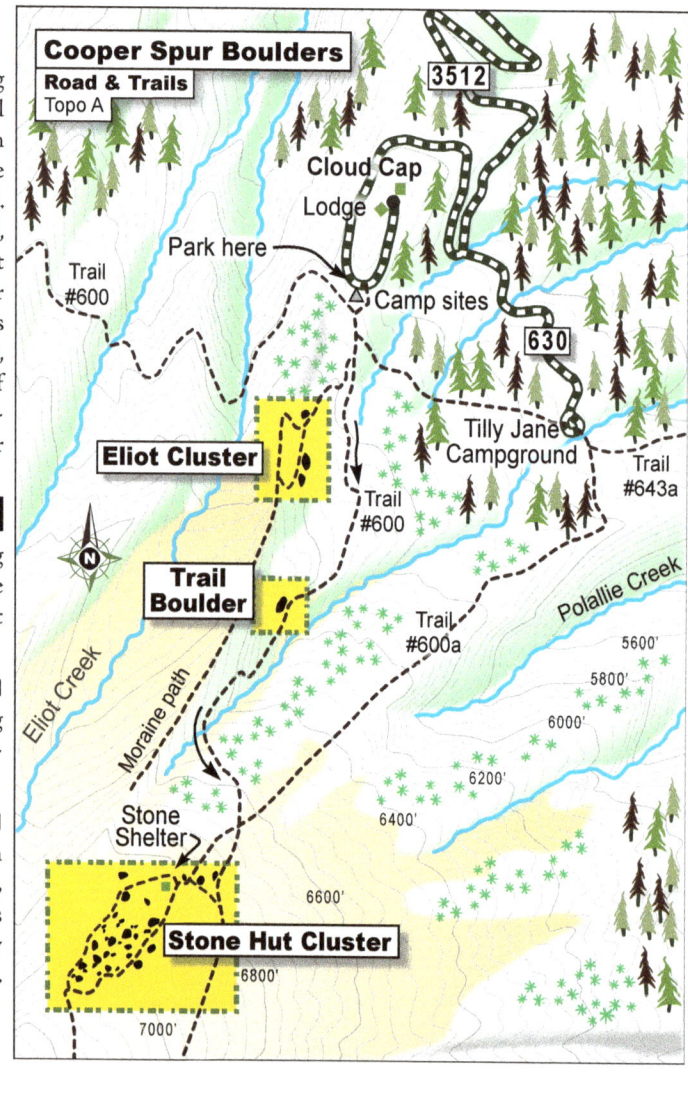

Cooper Spur Boulders Road & Trails — Topo A

Cooper Spur Boulders ✦ PB 91

V2 West Rib
Great moves with small edges and smears on the tallest section of stone.

V1 Shorty face
Shorty face on south aspect.

Walk southward up the trail 50' and when it splits, go left, and walk 150' to reach two more massive stones.

Eliot (CSB-EC)

The largest andesite stone in this cluster (25' long by 12' tall).
Beta is counter clockwise:

V0 North slope

V1 NW Face
An overhung start with rounded features for palming onto the slab.

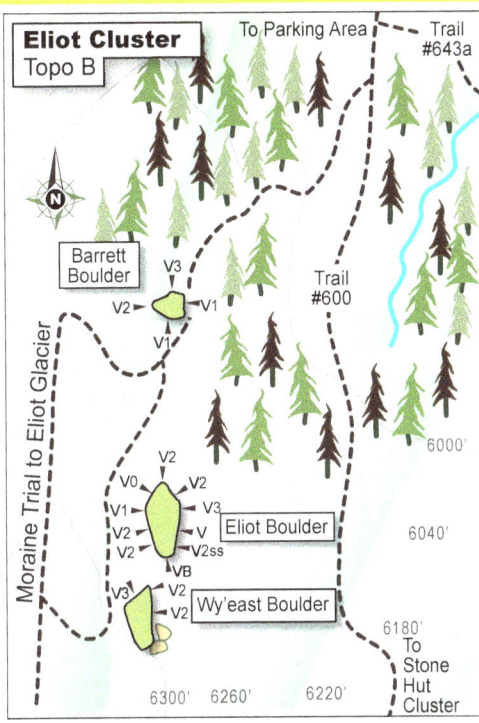

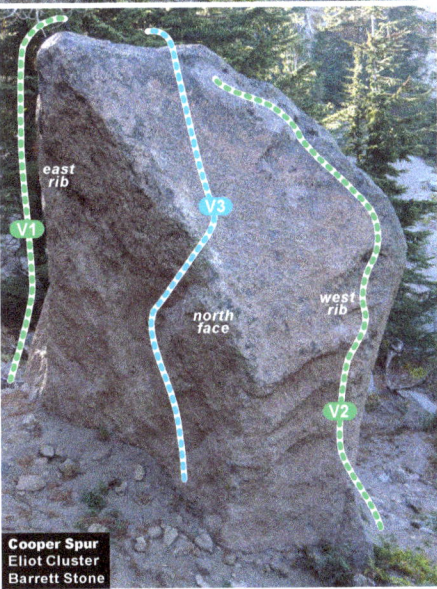

V2 West Face Direct
Use crimps and slaps to make a direct run up over the rounded lip. Great line.

V2 West Ramp
Start low on the right using rounded slopers, and waltz your feet up the obvious ramp leftward to top up. Classic line on this block.

VB South down climb

V1/V2ss
Sit start mantle up left, or up right (2 var).

V4/5ss
A possible stout line on the smooth overhung

Tymun on Jane's Folly V4

92 MT HOOD ZONE (NORTH)

central east face.

V3 East Point
A nice delicate set up with a high right foot on a small wafer edge to start.

V2 Corner Groove
Corner groove that is surprisingly stouter than it appears.

V2 North Nose
Starts on rounded feature and moves up right to top up.

Wy'east (CSB-EC)

This stone is 12' tall, and offers several high quality lines.

V3 Northwest Face
A classic. Start low on small holds with your right foot down on the obvious sloper foot hold. Slap up and catch the better edges, then keep pulling over the lip to the slab top out.

V2 North Fin
An ultra classic. Start on the east side and pinch and smear your way up.

V2 East Face
This is a short side pull maneuver on the east side.

We're all done here, so going back to #600 trail, start hiking uphill toward the stone hut.

TRAIL STONE

En route to the stone hut, but about ¼ mile up trail #600 you will encounter a massive

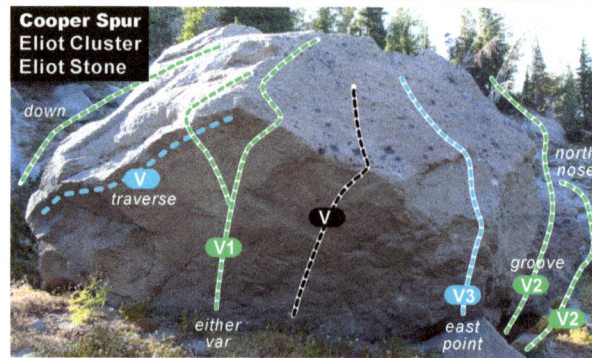

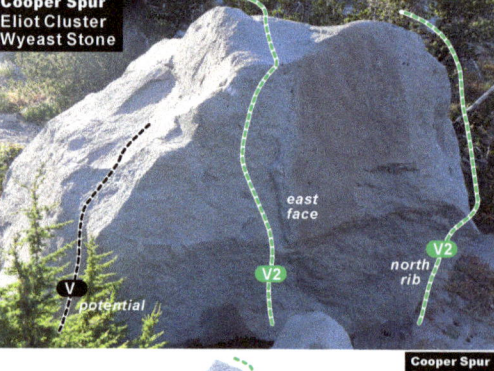

20' wide by 15' tall stone, with an impressive steep overhanging aspect.

STONE HUT

Continue up trail #600 until it junctions with the Tilly Jane trail #600a. Another 150' on the main trail you will encounter the first large stones.

Split Block

A nicely cleaved minor stone 11' tall with some minor warmup lines.

VB Perky Sidekick
Traverse the entire rim from right to left on the larger stone.

Cooper Spur — The Trail Stone

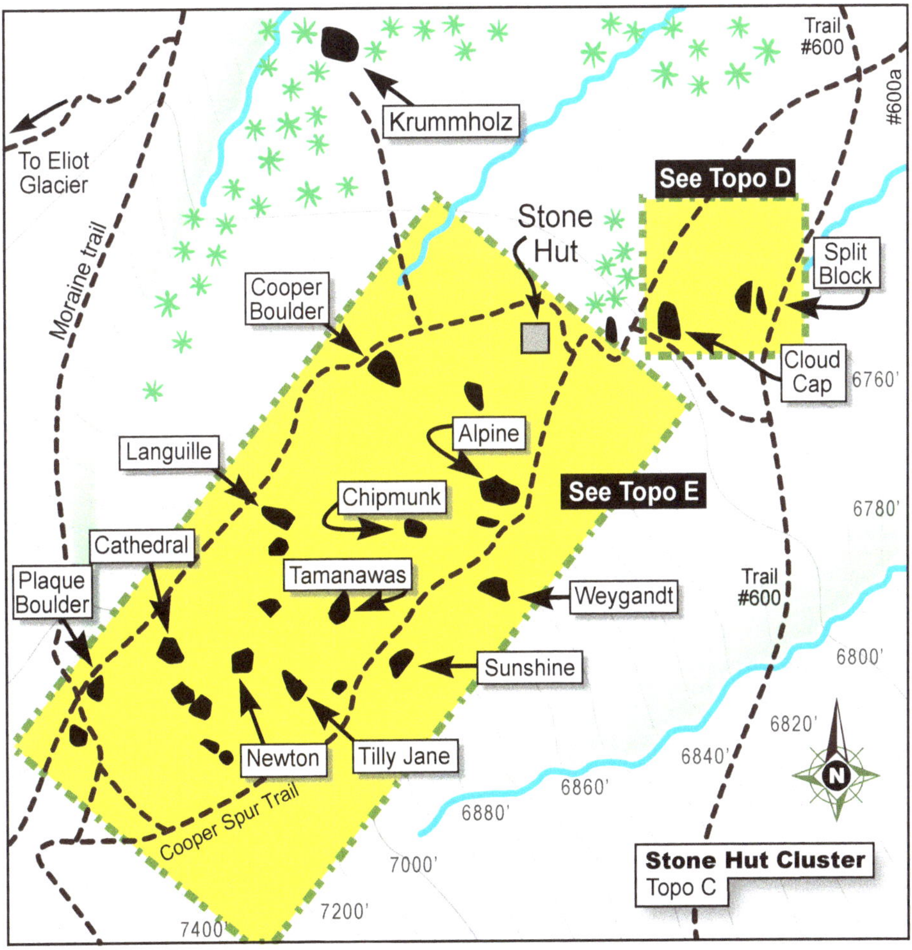

94 MT HOOD ZONE (NORTH)

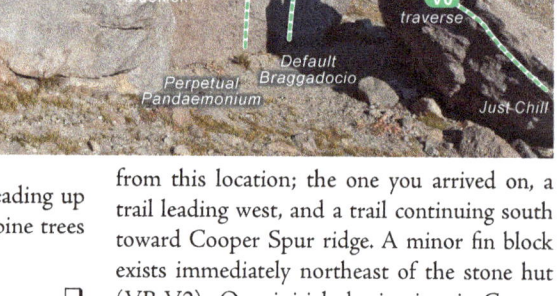

V0 Default Braggadocio
Center right face.

V1 Perpetual Pandaemonium
Center left face, thin feet smears to catch inset rock knob.

V0 Just Chill
The other boulder rail starting low on the right.

Cloud Cap

The prominent large stone located between #600 trail and the trail leading up to the stone hut. Several Whitebark pine trees grow along its northeast side.

V2 Drunken Sailor
A sit start using the obvious low jug hold, feet under the overhang. Aim up the minor corner.

V1 (V3ss) Ocean Blue
The fine quality east nose using various small edges.

V3 Buzzsaw Politics
Challenging techy flat face just left of pine tree.

V2ss Xenophobia
A face to a crack between the two pine trees.

Coordinate your bearings at the stone hut shelter with the diagram. Three trails lead away from this location; the one you arrived on, a trail leading west, and a trail continuing south toward Cooper Spur ridge. A minor fin block exists immediately northeast of the stone hut (VB-V2). Our initial destination is Cooper Boulder, the obvious large stone one-hundred feet from the hut along the west trail.

Cooper

An 11' tall by 18' wide block with 360° of quality problems on excellent rock with overhang-

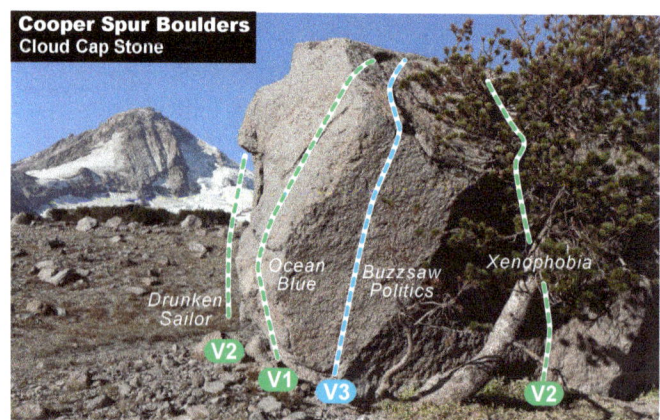

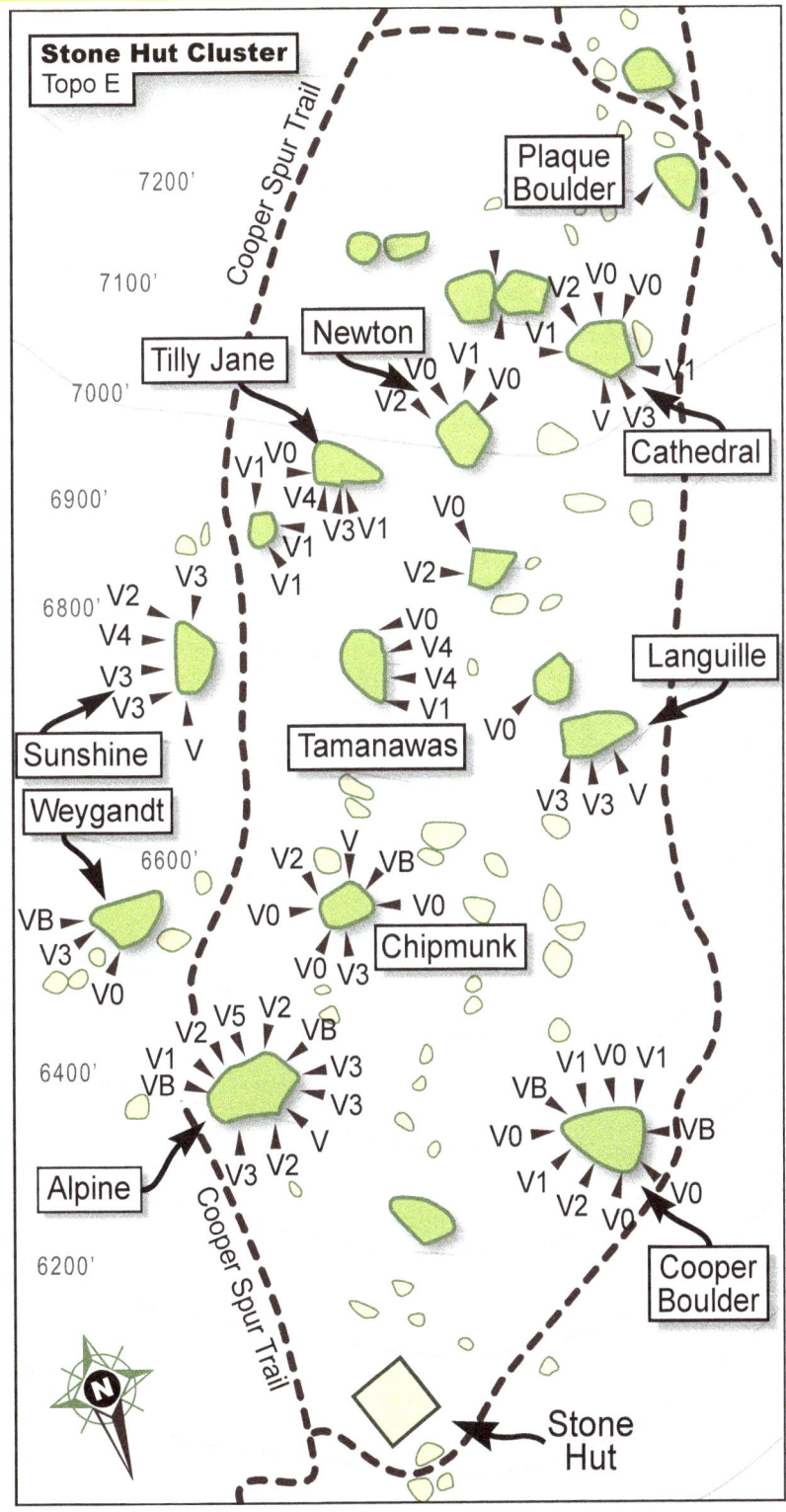

ing starts on most lines.

V0ss Cooper Classic
This is an cool overhung sit start upside-down jug run on the SE side.

V1ss Cooper's Folly
This tackles the overhung east face.

V2ss Noble Savage
Tackle the overhung face.

V0 Jackanape Whippersnapper

The NE arête.

V0 Solipsistic Sloth
Minor face.

VB Nothing Be

V1 Champagne Campaign
The west nose.

V0 Udder Codswallop
Brief foot smears on a steep face, then reaching up left.

V1 Myopic Pink Unicorns
Transcend up left on delicate face moves to a deep corner (avoid the easy holds on the down climb).

VB Down climb south nose

Krummholz

A quality stone. From the Cooper stone hike northwest downhill for about 150' into the cluster of stunted whitebark pine trees. Beta is listed R to L:

VB East face basic

V0 Topaz
This is a big hueco.

VB Down climb

V1 Agatized
This is a great problem. Merely grab the large knob and continue up to the top using more knobs and pockets.

V1 Amber
Yep, a classic. Start on north side, smear and pinch the arête.

V3 Turquoise
This is the steep north face.

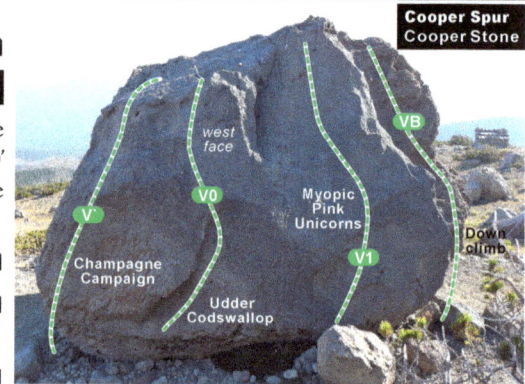

South of Stone Hut

From the stone hut, walk south uphill on the Cooper Spur trail. Approximately 100' up the trail on the immediate right is the famous Alpine Boulder, perhaps the finest massive block in the upper park. Beta is clockwise starting with VB on SE side.

Alpine

VB Down climb ☐

V1 Turning Point ☐
Dance up into the scoop.

V2 Unobtainium ☐
Stellar line that tackles the rounded rib.

V5 Asteroid Wrangling ☐
Wide flat overhung face with sit start using long reaches on crimps. The ultra classic test-piece at CSB. Faces the sunshine but can be slick as glass if the sunshine is baking it on a warm day.

V2 Grand Alliance ☐
A leaning arête that starts low on great holds and moves up to reach a big pocket, then up the arête rightward (Rules: stay on the overhung side of the rock).

VB Down climb ☐

V3 Let's Get Cirrus ☐
Start on the obvious knob, run the rail edges up left and top out on problem to the left.

V3ss Olive Branch ☐
Start low and send the crimps up the overhang and top up.

V5ss Vision Within ☐
Crimps on overhung scoop.

V2ss Merchants of Deception ☐
Pocketed fin with numerous holds on the overhung aspect (and a terrific line).

V3 Snowjob ☐
North scoop is a delicate smooth face with a single high starting hold.

On Tamanawas Boulder

From the Alpine stone, walk uphill along the trail. Within 50' is a minor shorty block to the west that has two feasible lines on pockets and a crack. Just uphill and to the immediate east of the trail is the Weygandt Boulder (11' tall), a cluster of three blocks, one of which is large enough to warrant interest.

Weygandt

V0 Natural Regress ☐
Layback seam is a good set of balance moves up

a seam.

V3 Multipolarity
Mono pocket face is a delicate quality line.

VB Thingamabob
East arête is simple.

Chipmunk

Chipmunk stone is a set of two boulders, one of which has good power lines.

V0 Seamingly Cirrus
Stellar line that sends east slab face prancing up using rounded texture of the seam.

V2ss Utopian
East Face starts low on the left and moves up using a series of small divots and merges into the seam.

V5 Deep State
Round rail starts between the two boulders. Cruise up right on round rail using the overhung portion of the face.

VB down climb

V0 Illiquidaceaous
West nose.

V3 Pretzel Logic
North Rail runs the north side sloping rail up right across face and top out on West Nose.

V0 Borealis
Step up left onto the slab.

Tamanawas

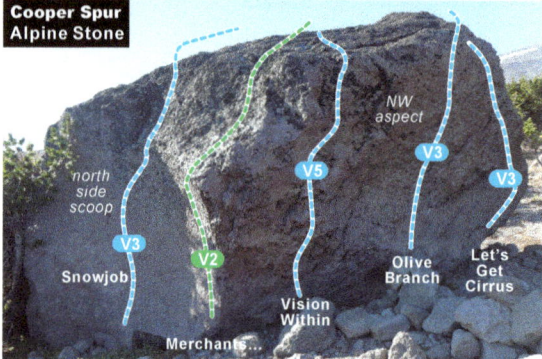

One of the ultra cool stones with a very flat west face that overhangs a little and a lot.

V1ss Jane's Arête
is one of the best arêtes here. Climb mostly on the west side of arête.

V4ss Go Crack
Start low on the vertical crack on jug, smear on small foot edges under the big overhang. Leap

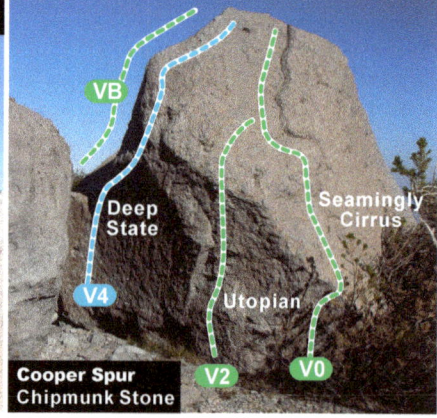

for the flat hold way up high and left. Reset, match, and finish. Wow!

V4ss Go Bust ❏
Using left hand on pinch jug, and slap up right to catch the arête, then catch the better flat edge, and finish.

V0 (V3ss) Illusion & Fallacy ❏
Begin the sit start on slopers, move up left, catch the layback corner crack, layback up one move to top.

Languille

Immediately west of Tamanawas about 40'. It's a combo set of stones, a larger and a smaller block.

V3 Fresh Crow ❏
Start with feet in the obvious pockets and move directly up the face.

V3 Flesch 'n Fisshe Alle Raughe ❏
Tackles the rounded north nose straight on.

V5 (?) ___ ❏
Thin face.

V0 The Circuit ❏
The other block is a short 7' tall boulder that is totally flat on top, so traverse the entire stone.

Minor Block

Approximately 50' southwest uphill from Tamanawas Boulder is this minor block with a flat east face to it.

V0ss Rocksters & Hucksters ❏
Left fin from low sit start.

V2ss Reef & Riptide ❏
Right rail using a right foot heel hook, run the entire rail up left and top up on the other line. Cool line!

Sunshine

On the east side of the trail is this low stone offering well overhung 'ss' style cool traversing.

V0 (V3ss) Mere Mortal ❏
Sit start on jugs left of Alpenglow, run jug rail to

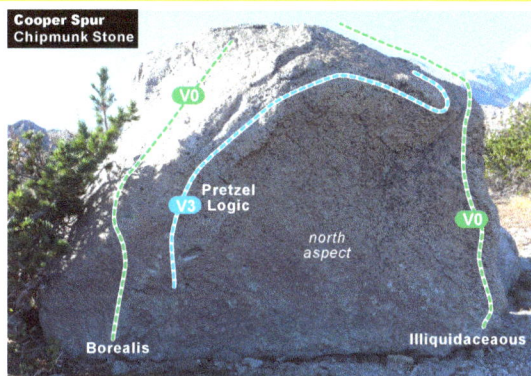

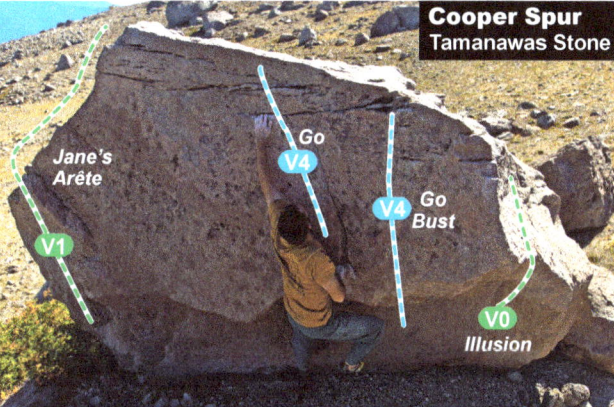

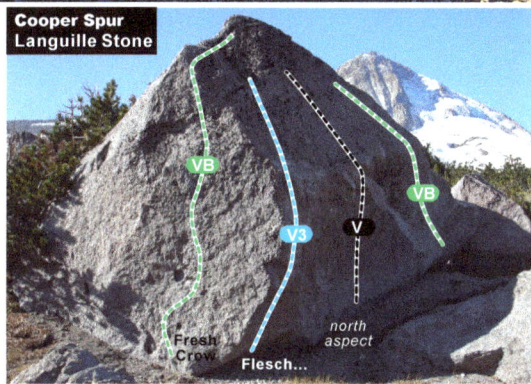

the very overhung nose, then over it.

V2ss Alpenglow ❏
Do sit start on incut jugs underneath, powering over the most overhung part of the nose.

V4ss Thought Czar ❏
East face thin crimps; sit start.

V3ss Broken Arrow ❏
On NE face on tiny crimps, bump to catch tooth (side pull); sit start.

V3ss ___ **(North Point)**
A delicate matter on thin smears and crimps.

V5ss (?) ___ **(North Side)**

Tilly Jane

An ultra classic stone that offers several cool lines. Located just west of the trail past another round unnamed block (has three short sit start V1-V2 lines on 8' tall round block). Tilly Jane is readily identifiable by the vertical right-facing ramp on its north aspect.

V1 (V3ss) Tilly Jane
The reason to be. The initial method is to smear the foot inside the ramp, left hand pinching the outer edge of the ramp, catch lip, run lip left. Cool! Now move it up a notch to V3 sit (the outer edge). Begin on the outer left side of the same vertical ramp (right pinch), move delicately up to catch top rail, run left to tag summit. Yeowza!

V4 Jane's Folly
The superb flat face on this block. Starts with a slight overhang for the feet, and powers up a series of sloped crimp holds on the face.

V0 Willful Blindness
East face using portion closer to the rounded rib. Low 'ss' bumps grade.

Newton

Unique 10' tall block that seems minor until you reach the uphill side and spot the high quality arête. Beta (R to L) east to west:

V2ss Fig Newton
Foot in low pocket on right, power up left over rounded east nose.

V0ss Agent Provacateur
Several variants on low face.

V1ss Sir Newton
Ultra short arête sit start on smaller holds, bump up using arête and prominent flat holds to top up.

V0ss Passions Forged in Fetters
Low using jugs, run short jug rail on west side.

Cathedral

Located uphill southwest of Newton Boulder 100'. It's the obvious black lichen covered stone offering a nearly 360° set of problems to climb, though some need a bit of dusting off the gnarly black lichen first if you need that one key hold.

V_ (?) ____ ☐
Just right of the pine tree on the black lichen covered north face is a potential line.

V3 (?) ____ ☐
Tackles the outer side overhung north side of the following problem. Initial easy moves (black lichen masks holds).

V1 Figaro's Folly ☐
Start between two large stones on upside down face where it calved off. Move up left on smears, limited crimps, casual reach over upper lip, dance up left over the top.

V0ss Campfire ☐
This is a low sit start oddity one mover.

V0 Huckypuk ☐
Tackle the face into a groovy dish on south side.

V2 Gothic Cathedral ☐
Rounded delicate face, yet quality movement.

V1ss Bishop ☐
Using slopers, bump up to slopers, finish with slopers.

A short distance southeast uphill from Cathedral Boulder is a double set of boulders that offer some minor 'ss' problems (VB to V0). Nearby is the Plaque Boulder, which has an obvious steep glassy smooth aspect, and is the general upper limit of interest in this wonderland of rock boulders. Bring a camera to capture a scenic moment in time.

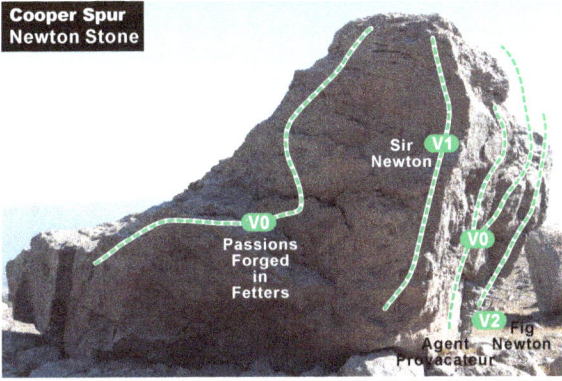

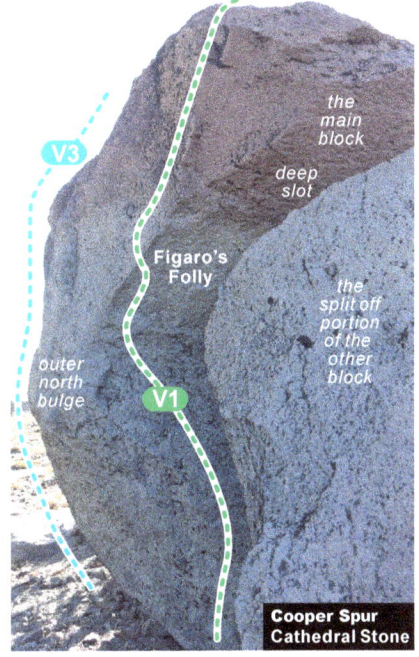

TAMANAWAS BOULDERS

A minor site of limited appeal because of the small number of problems and awkward landings all accumulated from a recent massive collapsed cliff. The site is creekside so it has well moderated cool temperatures even on a hot day in summer. The popular hikers trail travels right through the boulder field. The entire talus field is of recent history, in that the entire boulder field originated from a very recent collapse from a tall cliff band just uphill. Some of the rock is still very fractured so caution is wise. Most grades range from VB-V3 (up to V5), but has seen only minimal exploratory bouldering to date. Potential for about 30 problems.

Rock composition is dark basalt with tiny quartz crystal mineral (1-2mm) and black feldspar (1mm) infrequently distributed throughout the matrix. Surface nuances reveal plenty of crimps and smooth aspects all slightly slick feeling. Crashpads recommended (1-2). Boulder height range from short to hi-ball lines (9'-13'). The setting is a scenic mixed alder, cottonwood, hemlock and fir forest environ next to a refreshing cold stream.

Seasonal access is viable from mid-May through October, and is located at the 3,300' elevation. The site is just prior to Tamanawas Falls on the Tamanawas Falls trail #650, which starts immediately north of Sherwood Campground on Highway 35, about 20 minutes south of Hood River, Oregon. Hike distance is about 1.4 miles to the site. A few minor stones exist along the hiking trail, but are generally small VB oriented. See diagram for beta (some landings are).

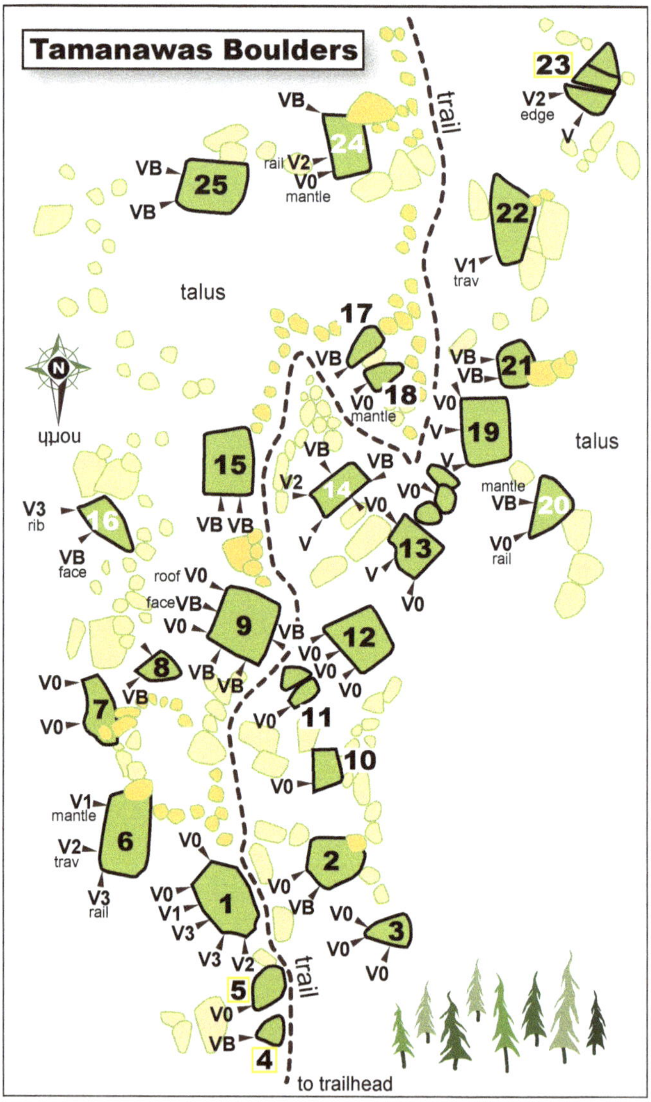

Tamanawas Boulders ✦ PB 103

104   MT HOOD ZONE (NORTH)

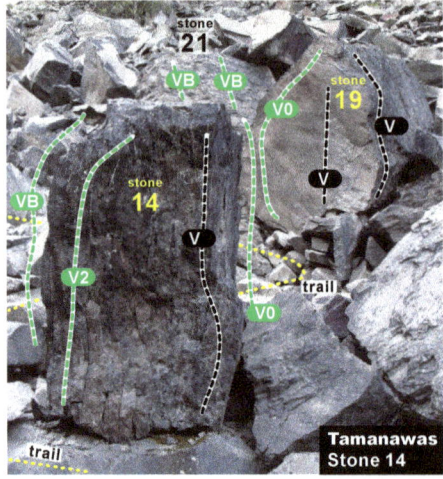

LOLO BOULDERS

A small site, roadside accessible (first big stone is 20' from the road) with a southwest facing aspect, perched high on a forested ridge overlooking the upper West Fork Hood River basin. Accessible from mid-May through October, but quite hot on non-breezy days in summer. Bouldering is limited in scope to about 40+ problems. Some persistent minor moss, and some welded lichen (which gives some holds a slick feel), but surface features offer numerous crimps and smears. The site has several quality problems, a 12' roof under a big block, all on stones that range in height from 8'-9' (up to 15' hi-ball lines on a few stones). A minimum of 1-2 crashpads is recommended.

The rock composition is a gray matrix loaded with minute (1-3mm) gaseous pockets, basaltic-andesitic but lacking prominent crystals, with noticeable surfice texture enhanced or etched from weathering processes. Good quality rock at moderate altitude. The main formation is about 100' tall, though little of it is viable for bouldering or tope-roping (oddly broken). Ideal for Spring or Fall season bouldering. *General history*: This site was initially tapped (select VB-V6) by Mr A and Mr O in the summer of 2013, yet there are plenty of stout V-lines yet to conquer. Beta will be expanded in future editions if a greater quantity of problems are established.

Directions

Drive over Lolo Pass (on NF18) from Zigzag, Oregon (U.S. Hwy 26 corridor). Or drive from Hood River via the tiny community of Dee Flat, then southwest on NF13, then NF18. At the junction of NF16 go uphill on this paved road (NF16) for 6.25 miles to the site.

Roadside Stones

This set of two stones offer cool power lines. Beta is listed left to right.

Stone 1

This is the taller left stone (of the roadside stones).

VB YurEgo ☐
Brief short face on left.

V4 Banana Ball ☐
Powerful crimps on a steep tall face. Quality.

V3 Short-game shot ☐
The tall west facing prow. Quality problem.

V2ss Apparatchiks
On the east side in a low gap between both stones.

Stone 2

This is the low slab stone.

VB Willie
Low angle slab.

VB Chillie
Low angle slab.

V0 Hillbillie
Steeper slab moves.

Short Slab (3)

This is located about 20' further uphill from the Roadside Blocks. Beta is detailed left to right.

VB Naval Lint Gazing
Leftmost problem utilizing a midway edge.

V3 Civil War
Thin crimp moves on steep face.

V0 All the tea in China
Crimp moves on steep face.

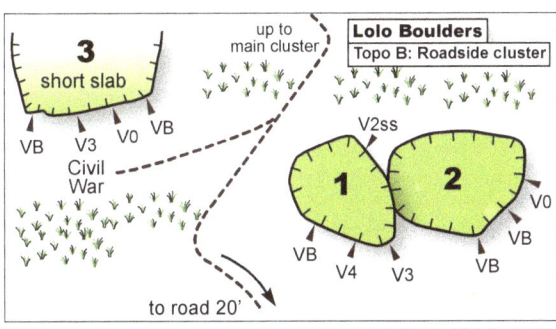

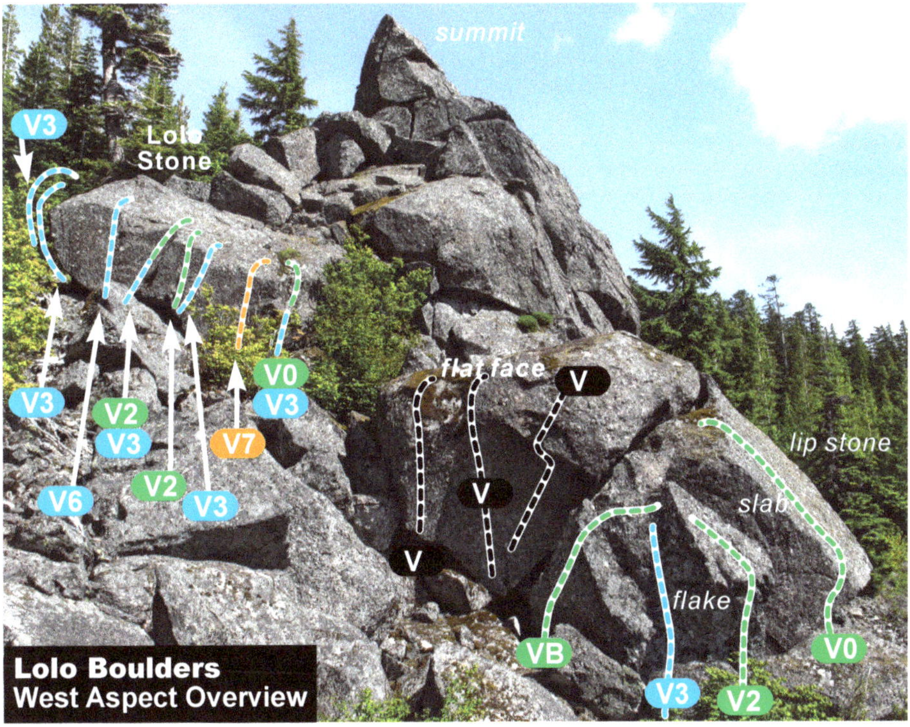

106 MT HOOD ZONE (NORTH)

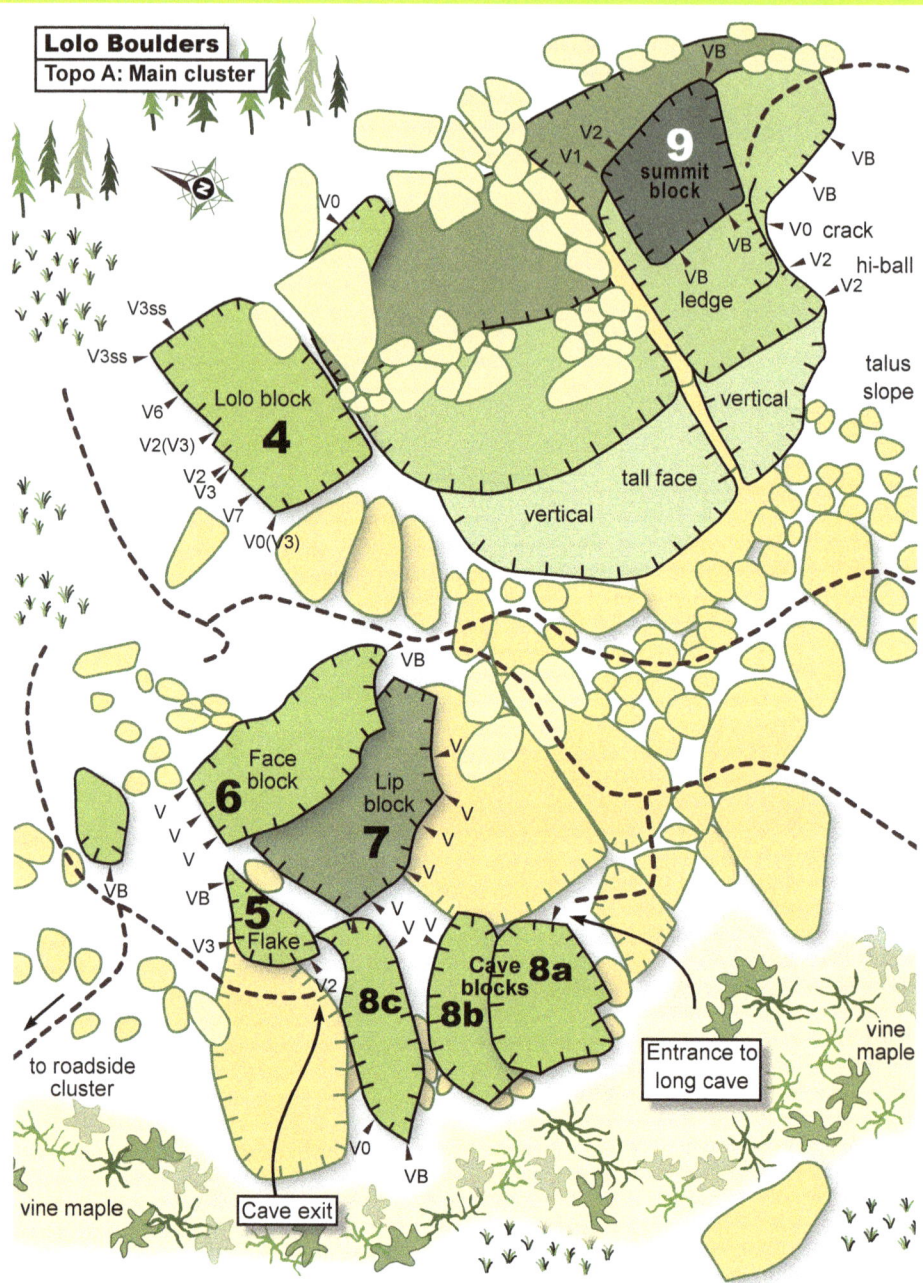

VB Dirty Laundry ❏
Rightmost problem at a seam.

Lolo Block (4)

This has short aspects loaded with quality power problems. Beta is described from left to right.

V3ss Wannabe Fly Bum ❏
Faces north. Punch out an overhung series of moves (left hand using left prow). See photo of climber on it.

V3ss Charlatan Salesman ❏
Faces north. Punch out a series of overhung moves (right hand on right prow).

Lolo Boulders ✦ PB 107

V6 Dreamcatcher ☐
Stay just left of the slight jog in the boulder where it juts out. See climber photo.

V2 (V3ss) Noble Cause ☐
Standing is V2. Use a slight jog in the boulder where it juts out. Left hand uses all of it.

V2 Eco-apocalypse ☐
Slightly right of the slight jog in the stone; begin on a low key hold.

V3 Killin' Time ☐
Slightly right of the previous problem.

V7 Viper's Nest ☐
Powerful short face.

V0 (V3ss) Short Put ☐
The southernmost problem at the prow. Standing is easy.

The Flake (5)

VB Left Rib ☐
Climb up the left edge of the flake.

V3ss Center Face ☐
Sit start and climb the center face of the flake.

V2 Right Rib ☐
Begin down in the hole at the right lower part of the flake. Climb the outer right rib of the entire flake.

Flat Face Stone (6)
This has 2-3 untapped overhung short power lines facing west.

V_ _____ ☐

Lip Stone (7)
This has about five steep short futuristic potential problems on its south aspect, most of which are overhung to start.

V_ _____ ☐

Cave Stones (8)
Offers several enticing futuristic untapped V-hard problems, all inside a large roomy gap underneath three giant boulders.

V_ _____ ☐

V_ _____ ☐

Summit Block (9)
Other potential exists on the tall south aspect of the summit formation, though it's all very hi-ball solo terrain. The uppermost brief summit problems are quite short.

VB Sun Dance ☐
On the south aspect; a brief series of moves on a face (+1 variation).

VB Moon Dance ☐
On the east point is a brief 1-2 moves.

108 MT HOOD ZONE (NORTH) ✦

ELIOT BOULDERS

A quality site (relatively new block party arrival) created after late Fall season heavy rain storm flash flood conditions abruptly stripped the site of all trees and brush for several miles along Eliot Creek, ripping out a concrete bridge in the process. The clean sweep gave boulderers a wide open (until the trees regrow) sunny area with a string of fun andesite gems, from a mega monster stone (18' tall and 360° circuit of problems) including a selection of smaller boulders. Most landings are naturally groomed flat. Summer days can be warm (choose Spring or Fall season [or cloudy days] if V-power is your game. Existing lines range from VB-V5.

Due to its notably active stream re-channeling efforts Eliot creek tends to wipe out various smaller stones in just 1-4 years, so to date (2022) only the largest stones still survive intact. The updated topo map provides the presently available options (mainly the southernmost giant stones). Anticipate future stream re-channeling that will effect the smaller stones. Brush and tree regrowth will eventually require of you more effort to locate and use the stones. Cell phone reception is good. Site is suitable for 1-2 crashpads.

Andesite rock type nuances are tumbled and rounded edges, light sandpaper-like crystalline surface texture, techy powerful footwork friction smears that utilize tiny nuances, small crimps, slopers, and palm slapping festivities on dicey steep lines. The ultimate gem is certainly the massive Eliot stone, a must-do for anyone touring the site.

This site was barely explored (on Eliot stone) on a few problems in about 2009 by a few locals. Later, an extensive site analysis was attained by Mr O who tapped 50% of the lines in one day, followed immediately after by Mr A who tapped an additional string of stout lines.

A few minor boulders may still exist to the north of the gravel road (NF2810) where it crosses the creek (though the active stream will alter availability there, too). But quality (some crumbly stuff), quantity (3-4 viable stones), and orientation are limiting factors.

Directions

Drive south from Hood River 12 miles on Hwy 35 and turn SW onto Hwy 281 (Hood River Hwy) driving 1½ miles to Parkdale. From the center of town (at the general store) drive south on Clear Creek Road for 2¾ miles, then turn right onto NF2810 and drive 2¼ miles till it crosses Eliot Creek. Park just west of the bridge at a wide pullout. Walk south ¼ mile to reach the primary area, the Eliot Boulder being the furthest stone in the group. Paved roads to the site (its a primary road to Lawrence Lake).

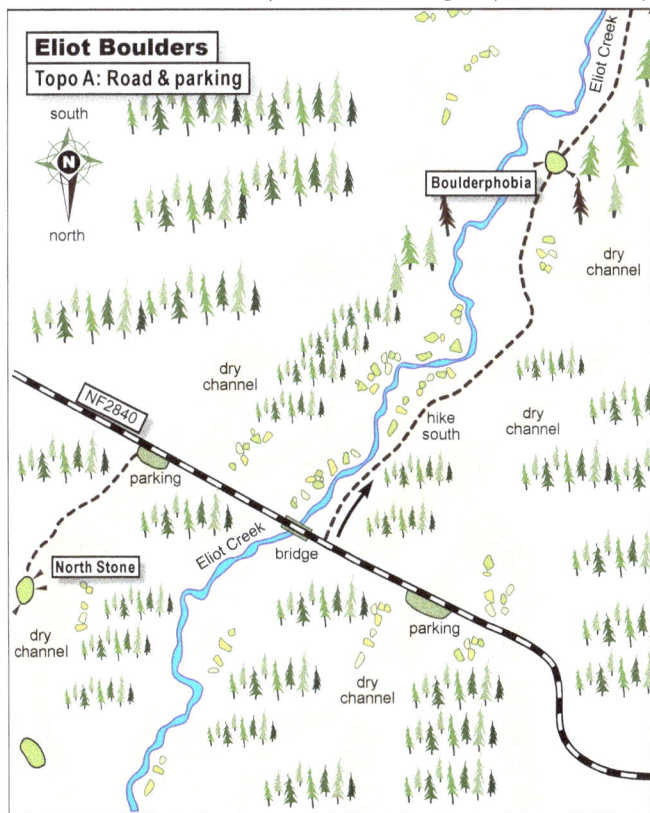

Boulderphobia

Boulderphobia is the first prominent stone about 300' hike south from the road. The creek has altered the gravelly base landings, so some of the problems are taller and some are shorter.

VB North side ☐
North side descent next to a tree.

V1ss Hung face ☐
Short overhung aspect on the west side.

V4ss Pillage the Village ☐
Pockets problem on the west side.

V4ss Head above Water ☐
Crimps on a rounded sligthly hung nose.

V0 Spendthrift ☐
Rounded short minor nose.

V0 Race to the Bottom ☐
Just a short face on the south side.

V4 Monkey Business ☐
A short face with nothing to start, gastons to rounded top out.

V2 (V3ss) One Arm Monkey ☐
The quality line. Left hand uses pockets.

V4 Blowout ☐
Shorty on the east face.

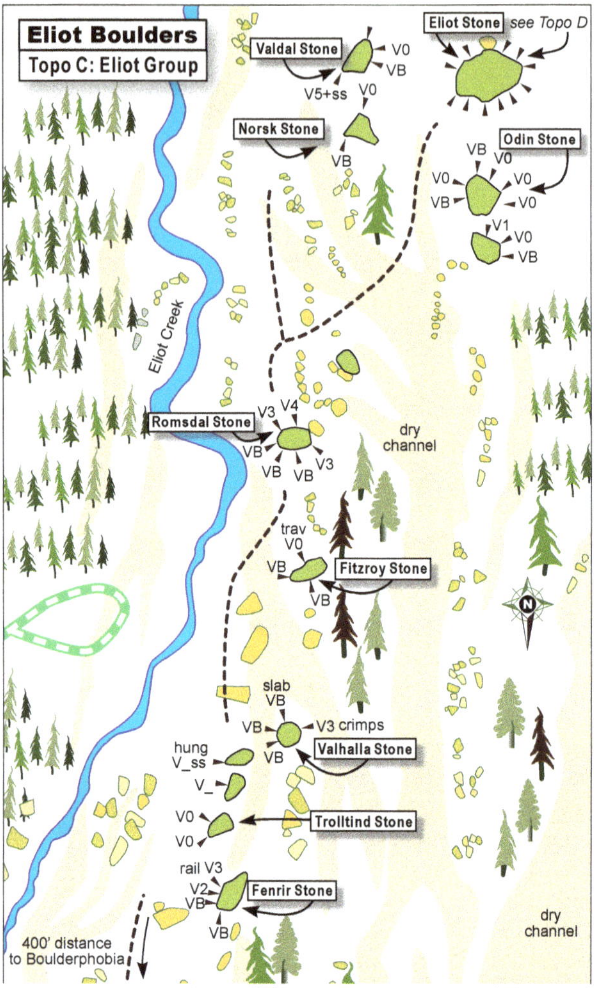

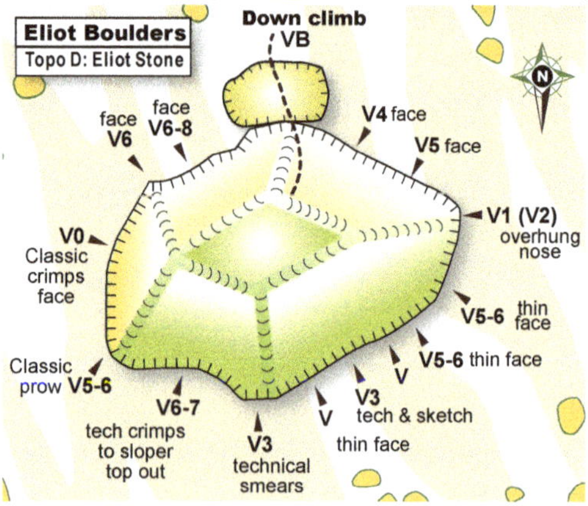

Eliot Boulders ✦ PB 111

V2 Washout
Slight groove near the top.

Wolf Stone (aka Fenrir)

A short 10' high stone. This particular stone got slightly shifted (by recent stream erosion activity) so the grades will vary a bit. Beta is listed left to right.

V3ss Wolf
The cool overhung rail; sit start.

V2 Mutato Nomime
Thin smears on east side slab.

VB Droolius Caesar
Climb the east face slab.

VB Particularly Stupid
Climb the north side slab.

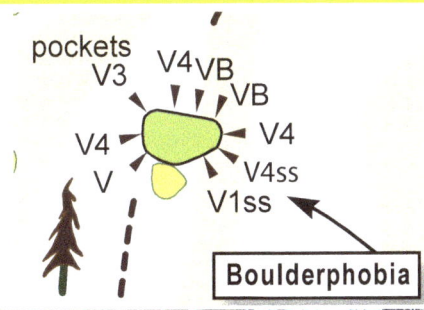

On Wolf Stone at Eliot

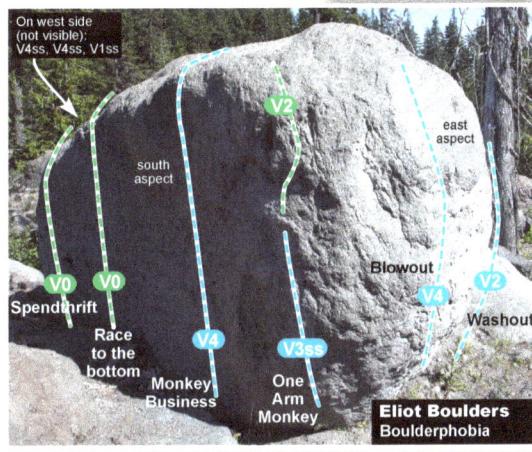

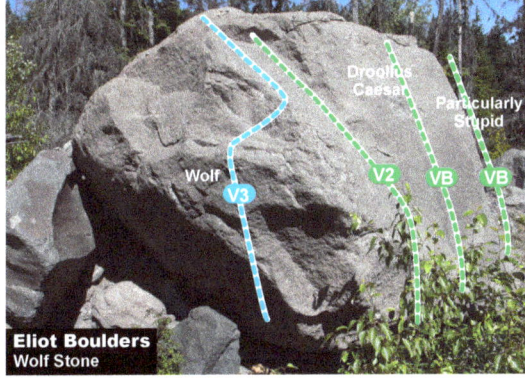

112 MT HOOD ZONE (NORTH)

MINOR SETS OF STONES

Trolltind Stone

V0 Shrouded in Secrecy ☐

V0 Cross-pollinator ☐

X Stones

On two minor low stones are the following.

V_ss (?) ___ ☐

V_ss (?) ___ ☐
Hung low nose.

Valhalla Stone

An 11' tall stone that is quite round. There is only one dominant problem.

V3 Midnight Poker Game ☐
The high crimps on west side.

VB, VB, VB ___ ☐
The rest are basic, all on the east side, all well-baked cookies.

Fitzroy Stone

Large flat stone with a minor circuit traverse.

VB ___ ☐
Minor moves on north side.

VB ___ ☐
A minor blunt east prow.

V0 Till The Nadir... ☐
South side (traverse included).

Romsdal Stone

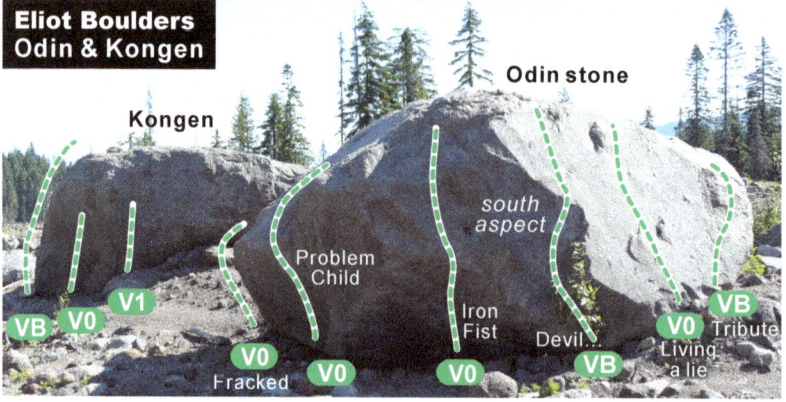

A 10' tall big fat stone with rounded slightly hung aspects on most sides. Beta is described left to right.

V4ss Need for Speed
On the south side.

V3ss Useful Idiots
On the south aspect.

VB, VB, & VB _____
Three basic problems all in a row.

V3ss Whirlwind of Change
Shorty in the north nook.

Norsk Stone

A brief slick basalt unit.

V0ss Hollow Dreams
The very short south prow face.

Valdal Stone

A long laying stone about 40' east of the giant Eliot stone.

V_ ss+ (?)
A super hung low round prow.

VB Mere Stone's Throw
Brief crimps on NW side.

V0 Parsiminous Pipsqueak
Brief crimp moves on west side.

V_ (?) _____ (on south aspect)

TWO STONES

Two 8' tall fat low laying stones just north of Eliot stone (beta is left to right).

Odin Stone

V0 Fracked
The leftmost shorty problem.

V0 Problem Child
Bulge start, landing on a low angle slab.

V0 Iron Fist
Scoops on a short face, ending on round top.

VB Devil in the Details

V0 Living a Lie
Smears on south face slab.

VB Tribute & Bribary
The rightmost shorty problem.

Kongen Stone

VB Duopic Antidote
The leftmost round nose.

V0 Essence of Power
The middle problem, starting at two minor hand edges at chest level.

V1 Essence of Truth
Smears and crimp edges getting up onto a short steep slab. No free cookies.

Eliot Boulder

The Eliot boulder is a mega-gem 18' tall beast with 360° circuit and about 12+ problems. Beta is clockwise starting with the south face descent line.

VB Get Down
Descent using a smaller stone on the south side.

V4 Dyno
Catch good hold, mantle to top. Start lower

Eliot Boulders – Norsk stone

Eliot Boulders – Valdal stone

bumps the V-grade.

V5ss Day of Reckoning
Line up a tough compression sequence and dyno for jug, then mantle.

V1 (V2ss) Maelstrom
Cool west nose, finish as a mantle.

V5-6 ____
Thin, overhung, yet feasible.

V5-6 ____
Also quite thin, overhung, yet feasible.

V_ (?) ____ *(maybe not)*

V3 Rules for Fools
Standing start with thin tech holds, and sketchy top out. On the NW side.

V_ (?) ____ *(maybe not)*

V3 Yggdrasil
North prow starts at odd side pull, catch a sloper, sketchy mantle.

V6-7 Royal Standard
Crimps and sequential moves reaching up left to catch the lip; palm mantle onto slick slab. Hi-ball on northeast aspect. Project still?

V4 Eliot Arête ⚠
The mega gem hi-ball prow that beckons, but few actually do it. On the east face.

V0 The Viking
The obvious east face hi-ball classic. Crimp crux sequence to a stance, then a fat jug up high at the top. On the east face.

V6 Crimp City
Southeast side on a series of thin crimps.

V6-8 (?) ____
A tough looking potential pig (on SE aspect).

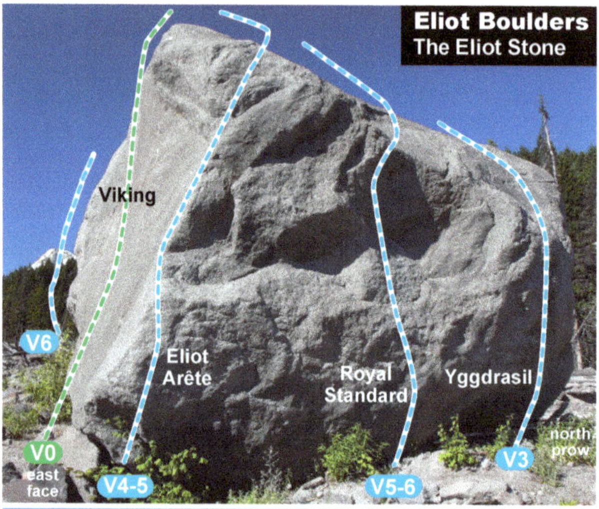

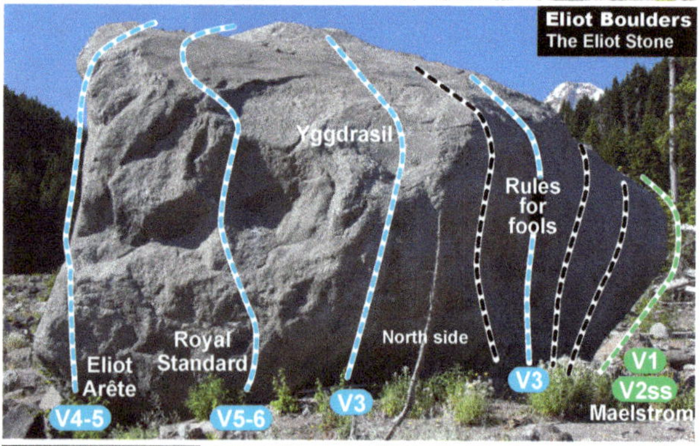

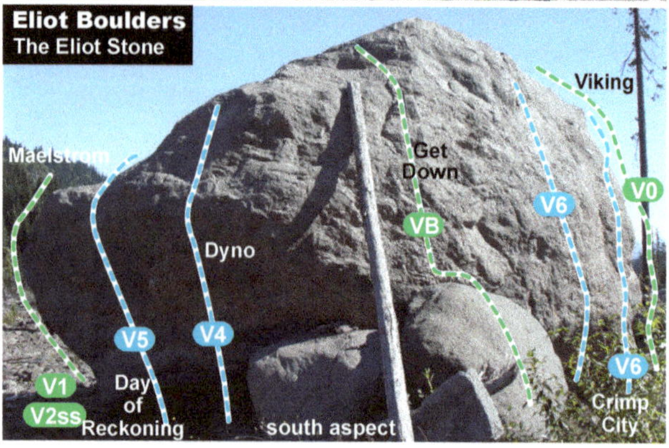

WEST FORK BOULDERS

Situated on the outskirts of the idyllic Hood River valley in a rain-shadow zone of the Cascade Mountain range, this site offers good bouldering for folks seeking sunnier climes. Good paved road access the entire distance to the site (via I-84, then through Dee Flat), and a mere 200' walk to the first boulder. The entire boulder field is quite extensive (¼ mile long), yet there are a limited number of giant stones worth sending (all the best stuff is packed at the North Cluster).

Season ranges from mid-May through October, and is a scorcher in mid-summer due to its sunny southeasterly aspect. Generally protected from the brunt of the western Oregon rain storms, its elevation (1,900') may have showers on high percentage days, but a 5%-40% rain forecast west of Cascade Mtn range is unlikely to effect the West Fork site.

Broad sweeping scenic views of the valley and Mt Hood yield great photo qualities. The andesite stones have a dark phenocryst matrix, but a remarkable subtle gritty texture that provides effective hand or foot smear friction. Rock textural nuances are unique edges, waves, and jugs to suit your scream. Size of stones are massive (11'-25' diameter) though the tallest stone is only about 16'. Several stones offer 360° worth of problems. Bring 1-2 crashpads minimum. No cell phone reception beyond Dee Flat.

History: Tapped primarily by Mr A and Mr O (about 75% of the problems), though several other notable persons also did a few high quality meaty lines as well (on the Illusion, Hood and Scoop Stone).

Directions

Drive time from Portland is about 1.5 hours (approach via Lolo Pass is feasible). Take I-84 to exit #62 at Hood River, then drive south on 12th Street zigzagging south into the country on State Hwy #281 (Dee Hwy). At about 8 miles, turn right, cross the river bridge, and drive through Dee, continuing on NF13 (this splits so take the [left] south main road) to the junction of NF18 (Lolo Pass road). Turn south onto NF18 and drive ½ mile. The boulders are plainly visible above the road. Park along the roadside below the boulder site.

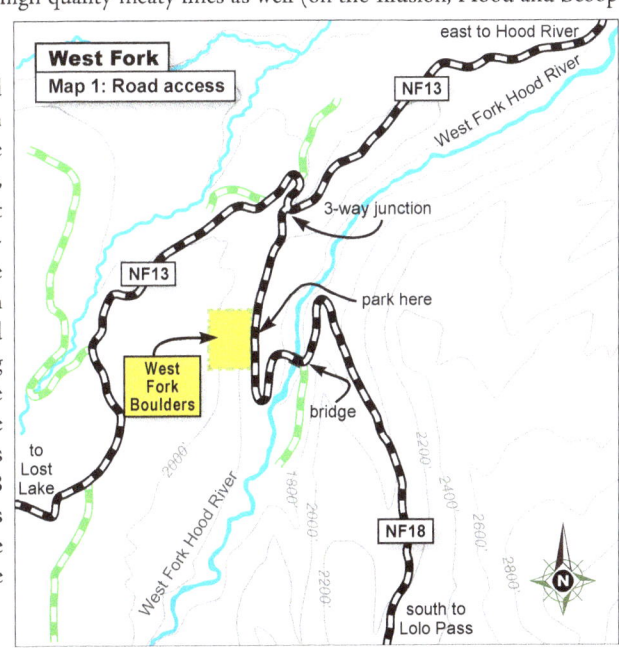

West Fork
Map 1: Road access

Illusion Dweller Boulder

This is the noble giant stone closest to the road.

VB Descent ☐
One move on the SW side; the descent.

V0 South side ☐
One move and mantle up on the south aspect.

116 MT HOOD ZONE (NORTH)

On Algorythm

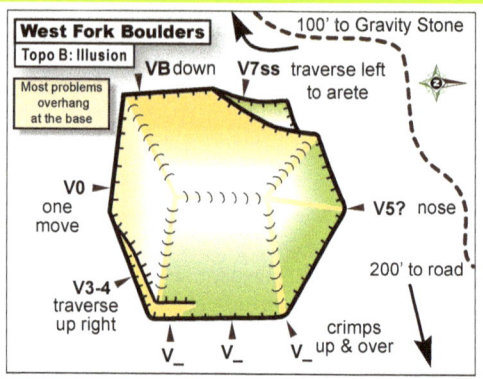

V3/V4 ____
Run a series of thin crimps up right to the top lip, pull over to land on the top angled slab.

V_ ____
On the east aspect. Sit start, crimps on the overhang (crimp the rail), and thin crimps past the hung bulge lip, landing on the topside slab.

Option: same start crimps, but cruise left along a thin crimps rail to merge into the previous problem.

V_ (?) ____
Sit start, then go over the short hung bulge using thin crimps, landing on the topside slab.

V_ (?) **North prow**
Sit start, and just get over the overhung bulge.

V7ss **Rip Tide**
The lip traverse, starts quite low (sit start) and runs left to the north prow and up a few final top holds to the summit.

Gravity Boulder

Beta is from right to left.

V3 **Gravitational Pull**
Ascend the hung nose.

V4 **Rip Cord**
Overhung move then up to the top point.

V1 (V2ss) **Gravity**
Starts at the east corner at a small foot notch.

V3 **Newton**
Mantle over the hang onto the face.

V6 **Sir Isaac**
Run entire rail left then up the arête.

West Fork Boulders ✦ PB 117

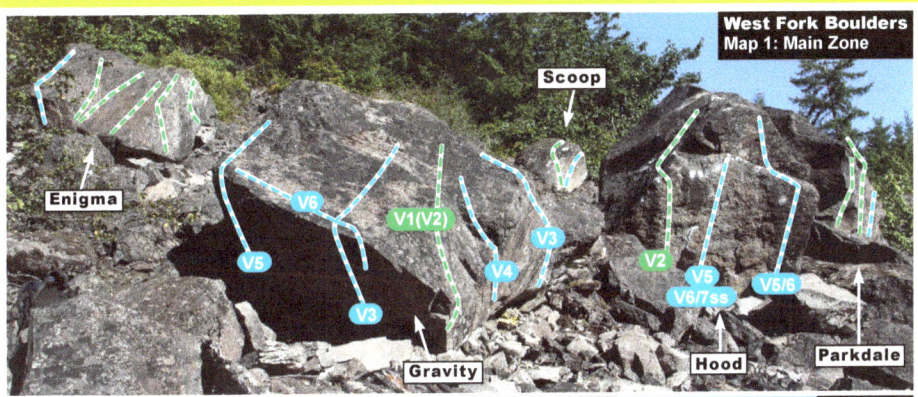

V5 Gravitron
Tackle the arête (on south side).

V_ (?)
Thin short face on uphill side.

Enigma Boulder

Beta starts at descent, then counter clock-wise.

VB Descent
Descent on the west (uphill) side.

VB Conspiracy
Short problem, with nice holds.

V5 Lupus Non Mordet
Traverse the thin face leftward.

V2ss Enigma Arête
Low sit start using overhanging arête for right hand, small side crimp for left hand, punch up to catch the arête, and finish to top.

V5ss Algorithm
Tackle the arête by a sit start underneath, going up and over the entire overhang.

V3ss Filthy Rich Me
Face up a minor scoop, reaching for arête soon.

V0 Cyber Warfare
Tackle the low angle slab with a slight kink on it. A nice series of smears.

V0 Cryptic Void
Dicey, long angled run that uses only the slab smears going from the lowest point to the top.

VB Cryptanalysis
Fun rib to jugs using arête and slab.

V1ss Rain Shadow
Overhung a few punchy moves to easier top out.

V2ss Rain Dance
Sit start, then out to the lip and over it.

V_ss (?) ____
One more potential next to descent line.

Hood Boulder

This is a 16' tall boulder (on the east side). Beta is listed right to left, starting on the north side.

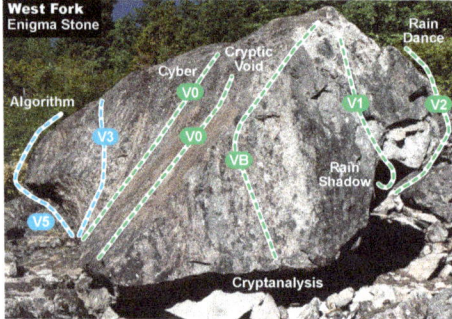

V3ss Lux Aeterna
Thin techy line (the rightmost line).

VB Sheer Wishful Dreams
Basic fun face on the north aspect.

V0
A nothing dance up onto the top slab.

V5-6 (?)
On lower east side overhang, power up the right arête (with right hand on that arête), then move left, and merge with the next route to top out.

V5 (V6/V7 ?)
Classic powerful problem using a series of thin seam crimps at a seam on the overhung east aspect. Well worth the visit.

V2
Left arête making one-two moves, then pull left onto a low angle slab and run the slab to top.

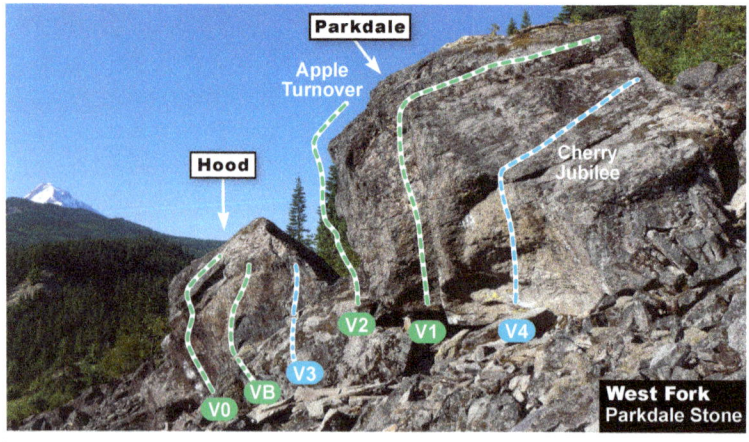

Parkdale Boulder

Beta is listed from right to left.

V4 Cherry Jubilee ☐
This is the cut loose swinger line out and over the overhang. The rightmost problem.

V1 Know your Enemy ☐
The overhung groove on the east face.

V2 Apple Turnover ☐
The slightly overhung east jutting nose with good small edges for hands and feet.

V2 Grapes of Wrath ☐
Use a tiny tips seam, reach up right to a top lip, and top out. Yep kinda short.

V3 Fine Wine ☐
Start at a thin crack-seam, but work up left on thin vertical terrain using key crimps.

V3 Stark Reality ☐
Sharp nose going up past a small hollow flake to reach the top lip.

V3 Ascendant Power ☐
Thin flat center face on the south aspect.

V1 Creampuff ☐
Short thin face just right of a rib (left hand using the rib).

VB Cookies ☐
Ascend a short vertical rib (west uphill side).

Scoop Boulder

Way uphill behind the Parkdale Boulder is this loner 11' tall stone, that has a prominent bright east facing aspect with a notable scooped out shape to it.

V4ss ☐
Sit start, use several thin crimps on a vertical scooped face, reach up right to an angled rail, bump over left to grab holds on the left angled rail, then mantle over onto the top sharp rib.

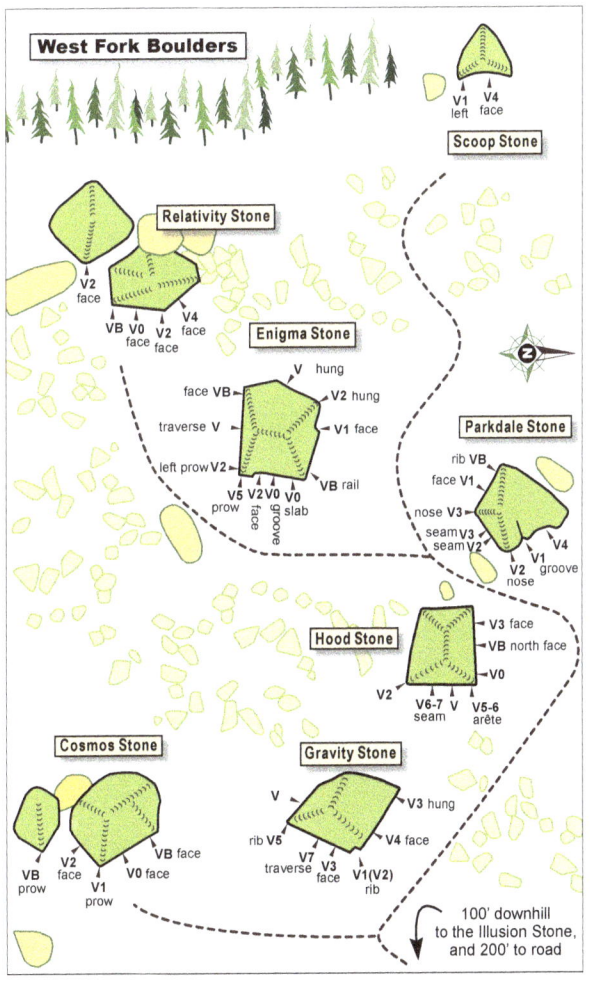

120 MT HOOD ZONE (NORTH)

V1ss _____
A brief series of crimps getting over the left rail.

Cosmos Boulder

An 11' tall stone (part of a set of two southern-most boulders at the West Fork group).

VB Shark Hunter
Basic short face on the right, starting low.

V0 Slaves
The center thin face (north aspect).

V2ss Marathon Man
Pinch arête, then step onto ramp, then up (on the east aspect of this stone).

V2ss Bondage
Bulge and pockets on steep face (east aspect).

Lipstick Boulder

VBss Lipstick Ranch
A short jug run on a double stacked block to the left of the previous boulder.

Relativity Boulder

This is a set of 2 boulders way up at the upper leftmost area of this site (just below the forest).

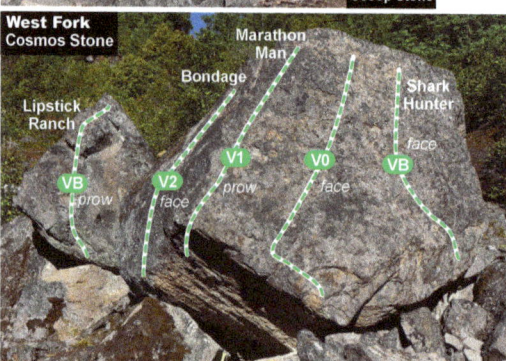

V4 Relativity
Overhung tricky reach, mantle over bulge onto slab (this is the rightmost line).

V2 Cosmic Waltz
Crimp a delicate balancey starting move up and catch the incut on the arête, then dash to the top lip.

V0 Minor Waltz
Smears and edges on the steep east slab.

VB Step Waltz
Steps on leftmost part of this stone.

V2 Nothing Boiger
Thin shorty on nearby block to the left.

Next Door Boulder

V2ss Nothing Boiger
Sloped crimps get you a brief move or two on the next door stone.

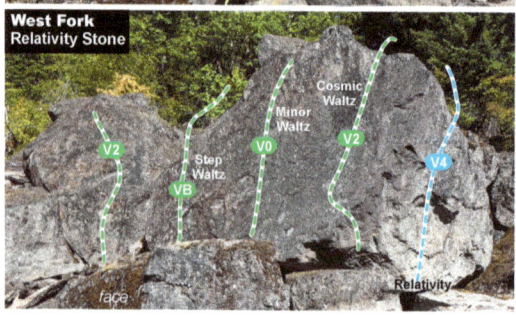

PINN BOULDERS

Pinnacle Trail Boulders (aka Pinn Boulders) is located alongside a hiker's trail on the northern slope of Mt Hood. A seldom visited minor site. Only a dozen or so stones are large enough to tap, yielding as a whole perhaps 25+ boulder problems. Site has two talus fields (East and West Talus), VB-V4 is common, and the boulders range in height from 8-11' tall. Rock type is platey smooth fine-grained basalt with numerous crimp features, and often black lichen. The site was privy to a recent forest fire that zapped that entire region crisp, so it has no tree canopy to keep it cool (you get full sunshine). One crashpad suitable site.

Directions: Drive to Parkdale, OR, then go south on Clear Creek road for 2.7 miles, then SW on Laurence Lake road (4.2 miles). From the campground junction drive uphill south on NF2840 gravel road for 2.8 miles. Park at roads end. Hike trail #630 for 1.1 miles to reach the East Talus Cluster (after crossing a minor stream). Walk trail 350' more to the West Talus Cluster. **History:** Mr O tapped select lines in about 2016 on various boulders.

Pinn Trail Boulders
East Talus Bluff

EAST TALUS CLUSTER

King Cool Boulder

V0 Tangibility ☐
Ascend the tall north nose on spooky moves.

V0 King Cool ☐
The tall west nose is a fun spook run.

V5-7 (?) _____ ☐
A slightly overhung powerful crimps problem that certainly beckons.

V1 Logobabble ☐
Brief steep series of thin holds on a slab on the southeast face.

Burn Boulder

One main cool problem on this stone.

V1ss (V4ss+) Hypocrites ☐
Cool sit start going left to the outer point and then up to the top.

Pinn Trail Boulders
King Cool Stone

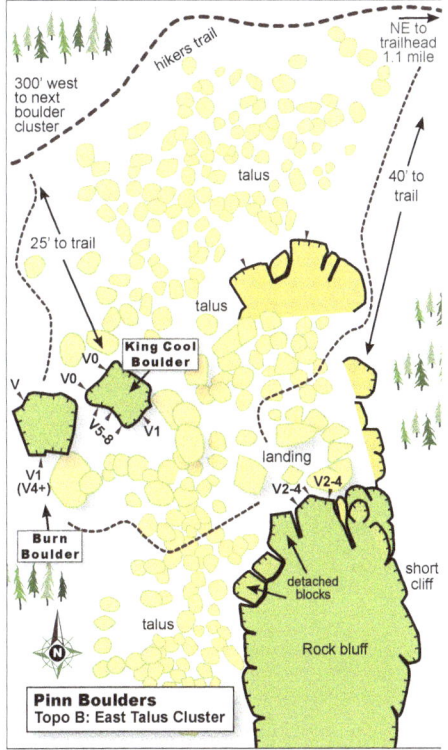
Pinn Boulders
Topo B: East Talus Cluster

East Talus Bluff

About six possible problems can be tapped on the tall north-facing aspect of this minor bluff (V0-V3 range projects).

V_ ____ ☐

West Talus Cluster

Blaze Boulder

Beta is listed left to right.

V1 Tinkered ☐
On the immediate NE side of the prow.

V1 Tampered ☐
Climb the north prow.

V1 Tainted ☐
Thin crimps on the west side.

V1 Tango ☐
Thin crimp; west side (center).

V0 Taco ☐
The rightmost problem (on west side).

Frog stone

VB _____

Lip stone

V0ss _____
A traverse that starts at the right prow and go

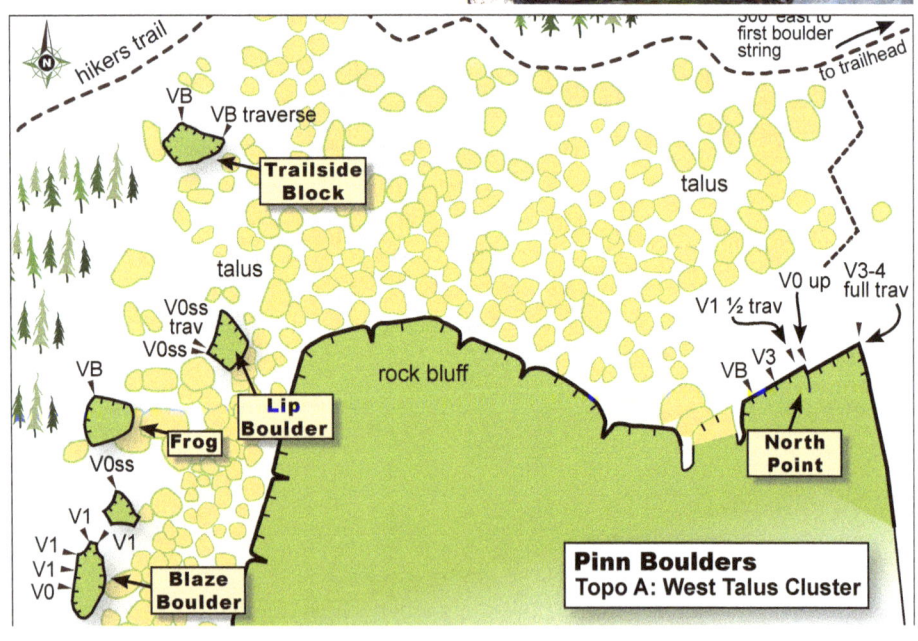

Pinn Boulders
Topo A: West Talus Cluster

left, then up to the top.

V0ss _____
Ascend the right prow straight up.

Trailside stone

VB & VB _____ (minor)

North Point

This clean overhung short rock bluff is one of the best reasons to visit here. It offers an excellent string of cool quality problems. Beta is listed right to left.

VB Minor Cut ☐
The blocky easy vertical problem on the right.

V3 Razor ☐
A cool quality thin seam. Climb the seam up left to join into the Razorblade route, then use its jugs to the top lip, then traverse all the way to the right, stepping to the walk off descent.

V0/V1 Razorblade ☐
The classic half traverse. Climb the prominent vertical hung crack to the top lip (V0). Include the traverse rightward all the way to exit off bumps it to V1.

V3-4 Full Razorblade ☐
The full traverse (project). Climb the well hung prow to the top lip, then traverse all the way to the right and exit off.

DEE FLAT BOULDERS

Not a particularly fancy musical tune, nor a unique site, but it has suitable andesite stones (12' girth on the big mother), and offers about 3-4 stones immediately alongside a gravel road. Hot (too hot?) in summer; better in spring or fall season; VB-V4 is common; as a whole perhaps 20+ viable problems (only the Dee Block is tapped at present). Brief entertaining stuff if you like low grade problems, and if you live nearby. About 20 minutes from Hood River. Crashpad recommended (one), cell phone reception (yes), low altitude site, season from April-November, and possible year-round. **History**: Site was tapped by Mr O and Mr A in about 2016.

Directions: From Hood River drive south on 12th street on State Road 281 (aka Dee highway) for 10.2 miles to a junction. Turn right downhill onto Lost Lake Road, cross bridge, turn right onto Punchbowl Road, and drive 1.3 miles (to West Fork River bridge). Just .1 mile after the bridge turn left on Green Point gravel road and drive south 1 mile. Two stones are on the left and 1-3 stones are uphill on the right.

Dee Boulder

Starting with the obvious west nose (beta going clockwise):

V0 Change Agent ☐
Cool moves on the flat nosed west prow.

V0 D'form ☐
Brief series of smears on the NW side.

VB Dee Best ☐
Fun run on the steep north face slab.

V4 D'fender ☐
Eastside problem at slight overhung bulge face.

V3ss D'interlude ☐
Thin crimp moves on the SE rib.

V0 Chubster ☐
Minor one move problem (on south side).

VB We Wuz Robbed ☐
Enjoyable fun run on the south side.

V3ss D'ception ☐
Brief powerful crimps on the SW side (and near the west prow).

124 MT HOOD ZONE (NORTH)

Dee Flat
The Dee Stone

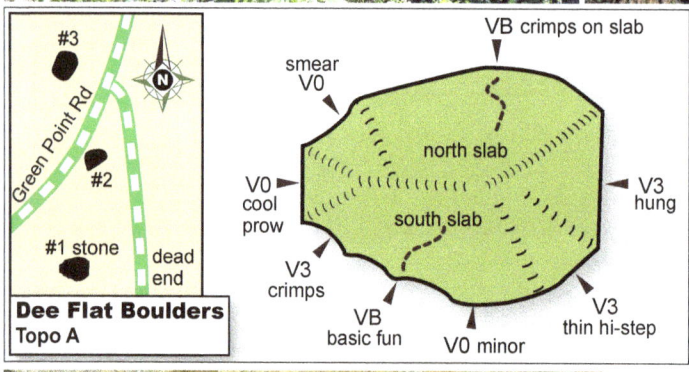

Dee Flat Boulders
Topo A

LOST LAKE BOULDERS

An extensive haven with a substantial concentration of bouldering opportunities, certainly one of northwestern Oregon's most extensive bouldering sites, with a potential for over 1,000 boulder problems, all within an extensive, all-encompassing talus field zone. In terms of quality and quantity this highly rated site offers a great variety of bouldering problems at all levels (VB-V10 and higher). From numerous basic fun run VB-V3 routes, to desperate hi-ball powerhouse lines, to fine selection of overhung lines, Lost Lake Boulders has it everything a boulderer could seek, all in a scenic forested setting.

Many stones range in size from 7' to 14' tall, with a number of stones reach 15'-20' tall or long, including a few rare beastly stones that stretch upwards to 35' long, yielding a surprising number of problems on just one stone (think 10+ lines).

The full extent of the boulder field (roughly 932,800 sq ft) covers an area from an initial bluff (near Buck Peak) above the road, down a gentle slope for a thousand feet northward. On hot days you will find delving into several of the cooler pits (15° cooler) agreeable. A single crashpad will suffice for the short lines, but 2-4 crashpads are optimal if you plan to tackle any of the really big beasts. Some of the formations (e.g. Tall Wall) easily qualify as roped climbing terrain. Of surface nuance features (ribs, rails, arêtes, overhangs, traverses) LLB has it all. The stone is composed of sticky textured andesite rock with minor amounts of moss/lichen.

The LLB bouldering site is situated about 1¼ miles from Lost Lake. The final USFS paved road to the site has been closed due to a small landslide washout (but you can easily walk the paved road down to the bouldering site). The talus fields are challenging to negotiate on foot because of angular blocky landings and pits (not exactly kid friendly) so use caution when visiting here.

The Upper South Talus Field is the most popular because of two easy access paths and the concentrated quantity of problems. The Middle Talus Field has a lesser quantity of problems (but one of the best boulders [Full House]. The Lower North Talus Field is the furthest from the road, the most time consuming to get to, and its talus field is a bit trickier to negotiate.

Camping options

Lost Lake Resort and campground is a quality and popular lakeside camping facility (that means you can attach your camper unit to your pickup, rack up a canoe, bring a mountain bike, and stay for a week if you want to mix it all into the outing). The lake is Day Use/Overnight accessible, and has a general store, 148 campsites, a public boat launch, lodge rooms for rent, RV's spaces, etc. The store has plenty of basic amenities of groceries, beer/wine, fishing tackle & license, prepared foods, etc. Wow! Let's go camping. The Lost Lake Resort web link is www.lostlakeresort.org.

Attractions / Detractions

Though a single crashpad will suffice for many shorter problems, multiple crashpads are needed for the taller/longer lines. The site is at the 3,000-ft elevation and buried in snow during the winter months, while the summer temperature can get quite hot, especially during the mid-day in July and August. Seasonal access exists from mid-May to late October. The nearest town (Hood River) is about 35 minutes drive, so having an ankle twister here would be a slow process to reach a doctor.

No cell phone service at the site.

History

The site was likely explored minimally on several roadside stones by unknown locals (probably hikers) before 2012. The site attained some activity in 2013 when a local person tagged a string of new problems in one day. The site development phase really kicked into high gear during the summer of 2014. Various associates and other teams stepped up to the plate early in summer of that year to tag a smart string of cutting edge problems. By the following year new problems reached into the elusive V10+ range. Within short time a broad array of folks from Portland to Bend were catching the wave at LLB.

Today certain parts of LLB are well tapped (the Upper Talus), but the bouldering refinement phase as a whole (especially for the North Talus) will take years or decades to fully tap (including the VB stuff).

Rock Type

The rock compositional structure has a strong surficial texture, definitive gray groundmass of miocene tertiary Andesite rock with a mineral matrix ranging from plagioclase platy feldspar, hornblende, pyroxine, biotite, and a considerable imprint of platy hexagonally shaped quartz (3-4mm in size). The unusual size of certain crystal minerals (e.g. quartz) provides considerable friction-*ability* for smears and power

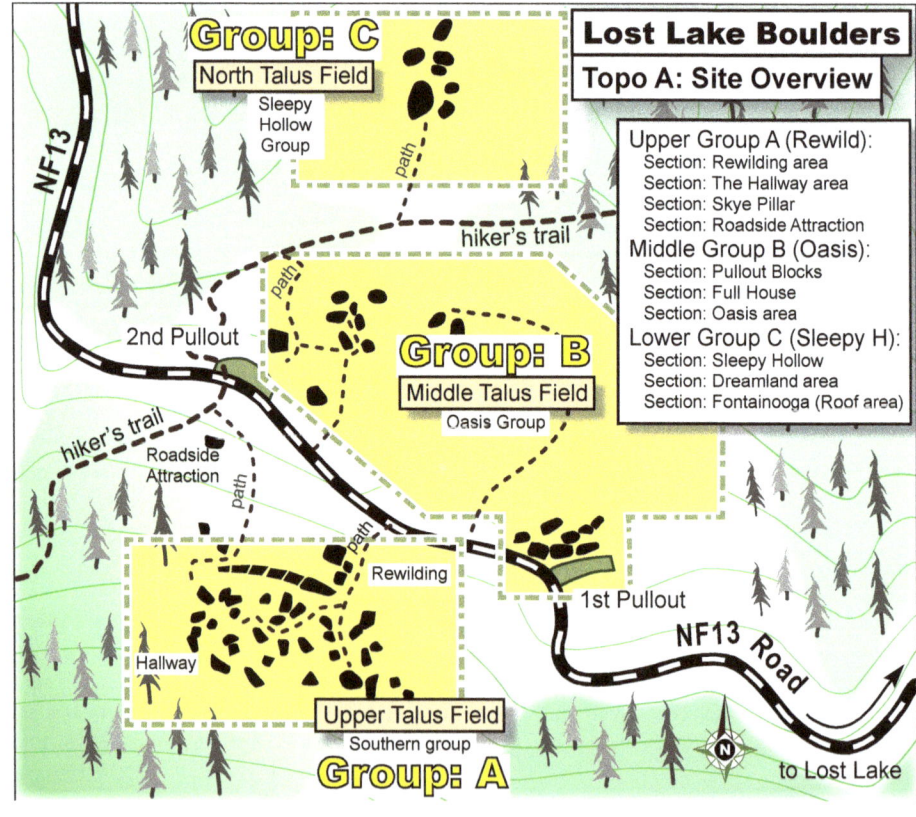

crimps. Many boulders show parallel jointing resulting in giant cleaved cubes and prominent rectangular shapes.

Directions

Drive time from Portland is two hours. Take I-84 to exit #62 at Hood River, then drive south on 12th Street zigzagging south into the country on State Hwy #281 (Dee Hwy). At about 8 miles, turn right (at the old lumber mill site), cross a river, and drive through Dee, continuing on NF13 (this splits so take the left south main road) and drive NF13 (past the junction of NF18 Lolo Pass road) to Lost Lake. When you reach the 3-way road junction at Lost Lake, park at the concrete barrier. Walk the closed paved NF13 (Lake Branch Road) road for 1¼ miles downhill to the site.

If you opt to drive the less travelled northern Lake Branch Road, it's even less maintained, and from a road blockade concrete barrier you will need to hike about 2¼ miles to reach the site. Access from either direction, beyond the barriers, is walking only, due to washout and erosion factors.

GPS coordinates

UTM 10t 590476 5038887, Elevation 3,000-ft.

The Three Main Zones

- Upper Talus Field (Rewilding, Roadside Attraction, Extra Crispy, etc) - located above the paved road. The Upper South Talus Field is the most popular zone because of two easy access paths and the concentrated quantity of problems.
- Middle Talus Field (Oasis with its various subdivided zones such as House Boulder zone, Dynosaurus zone, Grass Knoll zone, etc). The Middle Talus Field has the plenty of problems, some of which tend to be scattered liberally, yet this zone has one of the most popular boulders of all (the Full House boulder).
- Lower North Talus Field (Sleepy Hollow, Dreamland, Fontainooga (i.e. Roof area), Pocket Group, etc). The Lower North Talus Field is the furthest from the road, the most time consuming to hike down to, and its talus field is a bit trickier to negotiate (awkward pits and other obstacles), yet it has some ultimate gems like the Dreamland Stone.

The diagrams describe an entire group first (striving to give a guided tour of each zone) following a path of least resistance through the tangle of boulders. Our highly detailed diagrams are very specifically effective visual overview representations of the LLB site utilizing concise at-the-site creatively designed maps. These diagrams are not GE specific, nor intended to match any space-based photography. The boulder shapes shown on the diagrams may not always be exact; the diagrams are not exact science, but stylized artistry. For key visual beta, see the photo of that particular problem you are seeking to ascend.

The V-grade star rating system for LLB is simple; one star (for worthy lines), or no star (for ordinary lines).

In summation, by all means have an enjoyable day at LLB; many climbers have already realized its value!

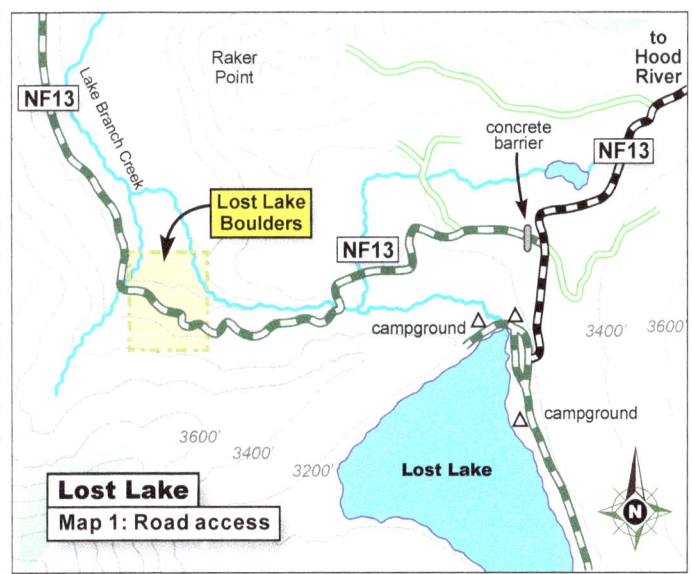

Lost Lake
Map 1: Road access

UPPER TALUS GROUP

REWILDING AREA

The **Rewilding Area** is a popular area with a unique concentration of problems. It has a plethora of unique lines from minor to moderate, to powerful crimp-fests, to sketchy hi-ball affairs. Access this by walking west along the paved road from the first pullout spot for several hundred feet, then go up a path into the Rewilding Area. Some grades on the diagram are mere raw estimates. This section starts with the famous "Keystone/Rewilding boulders", then encompasses beta on the various smaller stones alongside the path.

Keystone Boulder (#1)

Keystone Boulder has a short east facing aspect. Beta is described left to right.

V4 Diving Board ★ ☐
Sit start, ascend a short face; when you're tucked underneath the top jutting block, muscle your way over it.

VB Chubsteroni ☐
Sit start a short offwidth, then exit right.

V4 Endangered Species ★ ☐
Sit start by crimping in from left or right to the center of face, then go up to top.

VB ____ ☐
Turbulent short misfit on the right.

Boulder #2

V_ ____ ☐
Minor short slabby problem with a bulge.

Rewilding Stone (#3)

V5 Rewilding ★ ☐
Sit start. Start on sloper and move up slightly right to top. Alternate V4 begins the same but moves up slightly left to top out.

V4 Extinct Species ★ ☐
Ascend the slightly overhung arête (the left part of the arête). Also known as Apex Predator V3/V4.

V_ ____ ☐
A face problem to the right of the previous line, on north facing aspect (is this done?).

Boulder #4

To the right of Rewilding stone; it's got a north facing aspect.

V_ ____ ☐
The wide jam crack.

V_ ____ ☐
Face to the right of the crack.

FIRST PATH CLUSTER

The "First Path Cluster" has six stones, all very short, and all minor problems.

Boulder #5

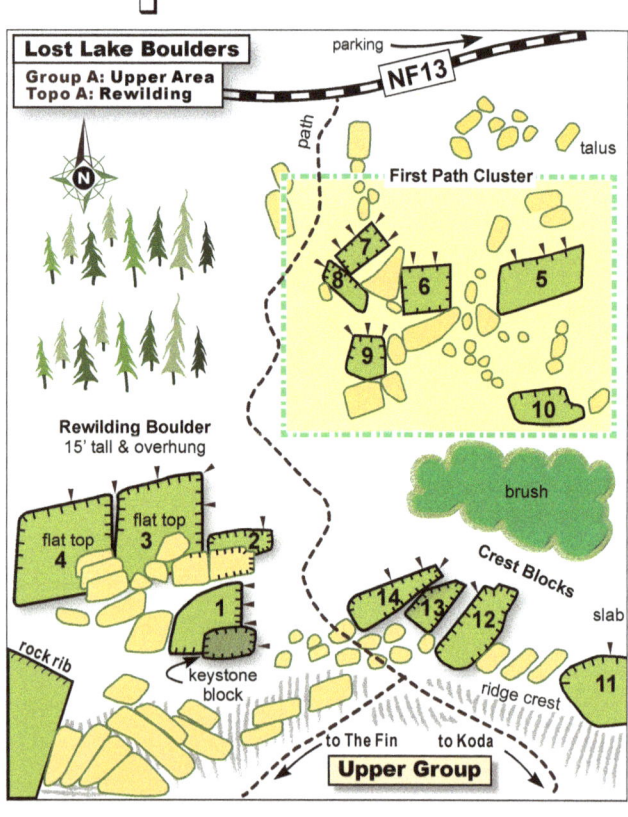

Lost Lake Boulders
Group A: Upper Area
Topo A: Rewilding

Lost Lake Boulders ✦ PB 129

V_ _____	V_ _____
V_ _____	V_ _____
Boulder #6	**Boulder #8**
V2 [?] _____	V_ _____
Boulder #7	**Boulder #9**

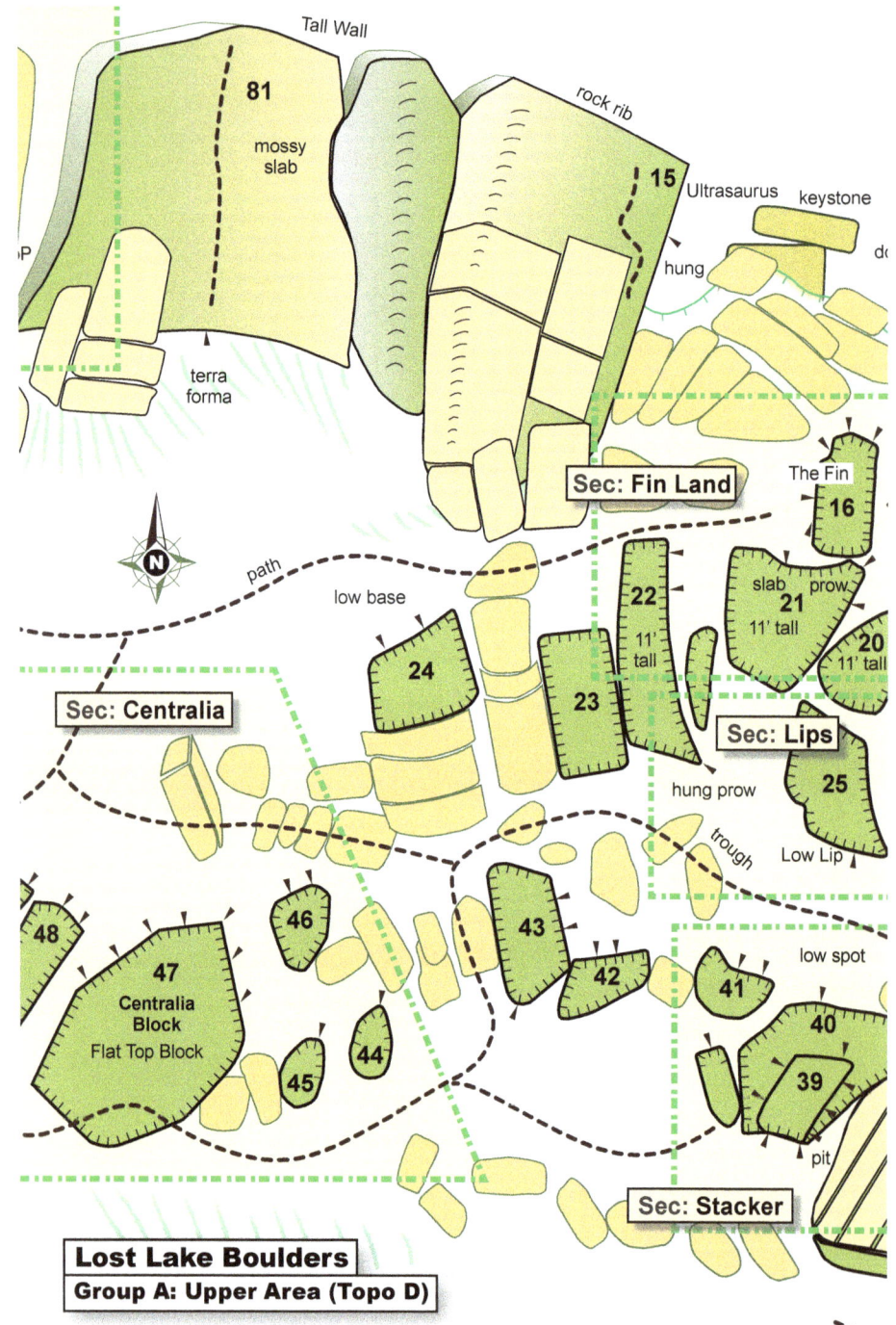

Lost Lake Boulders
Group A: Upper Area (Topo E)

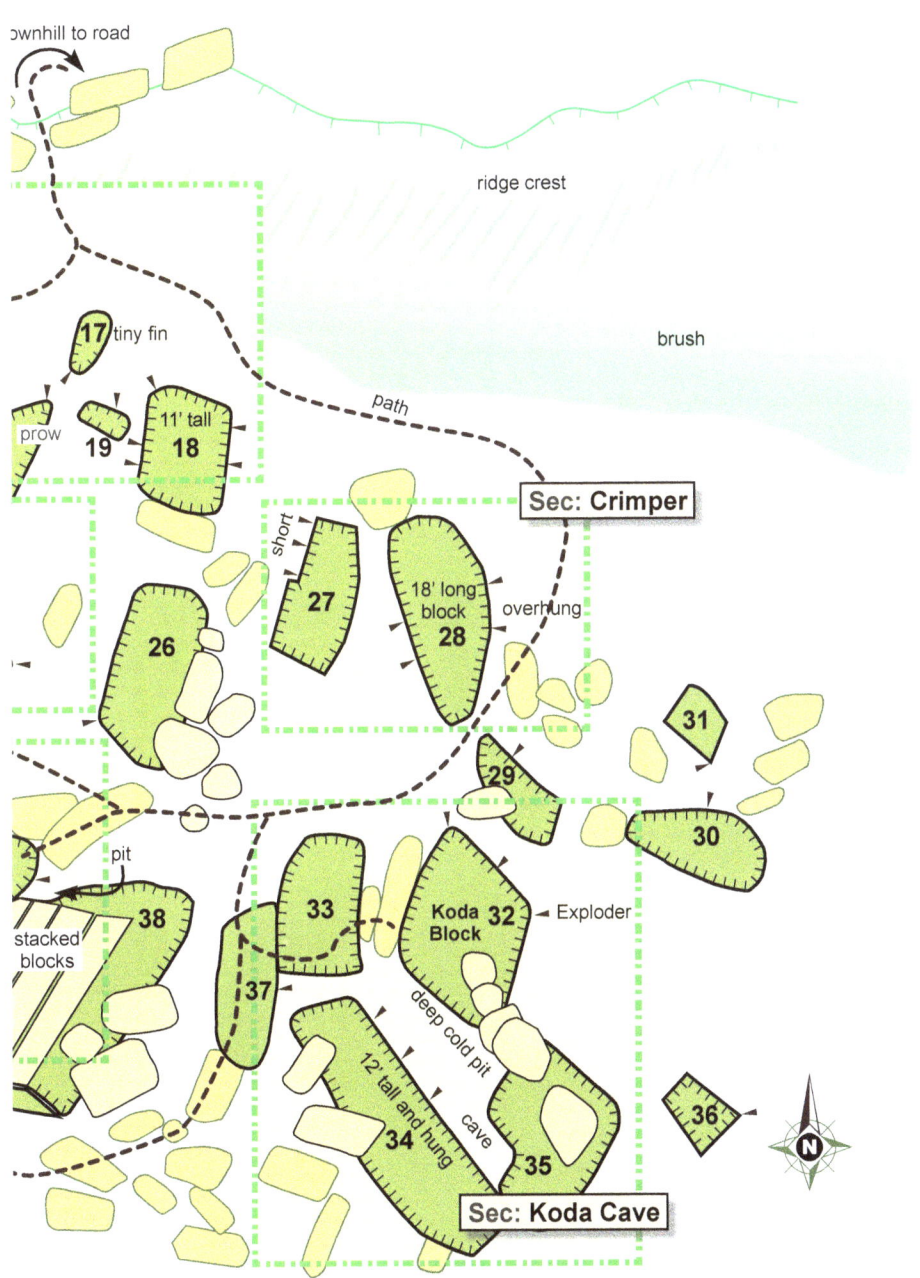

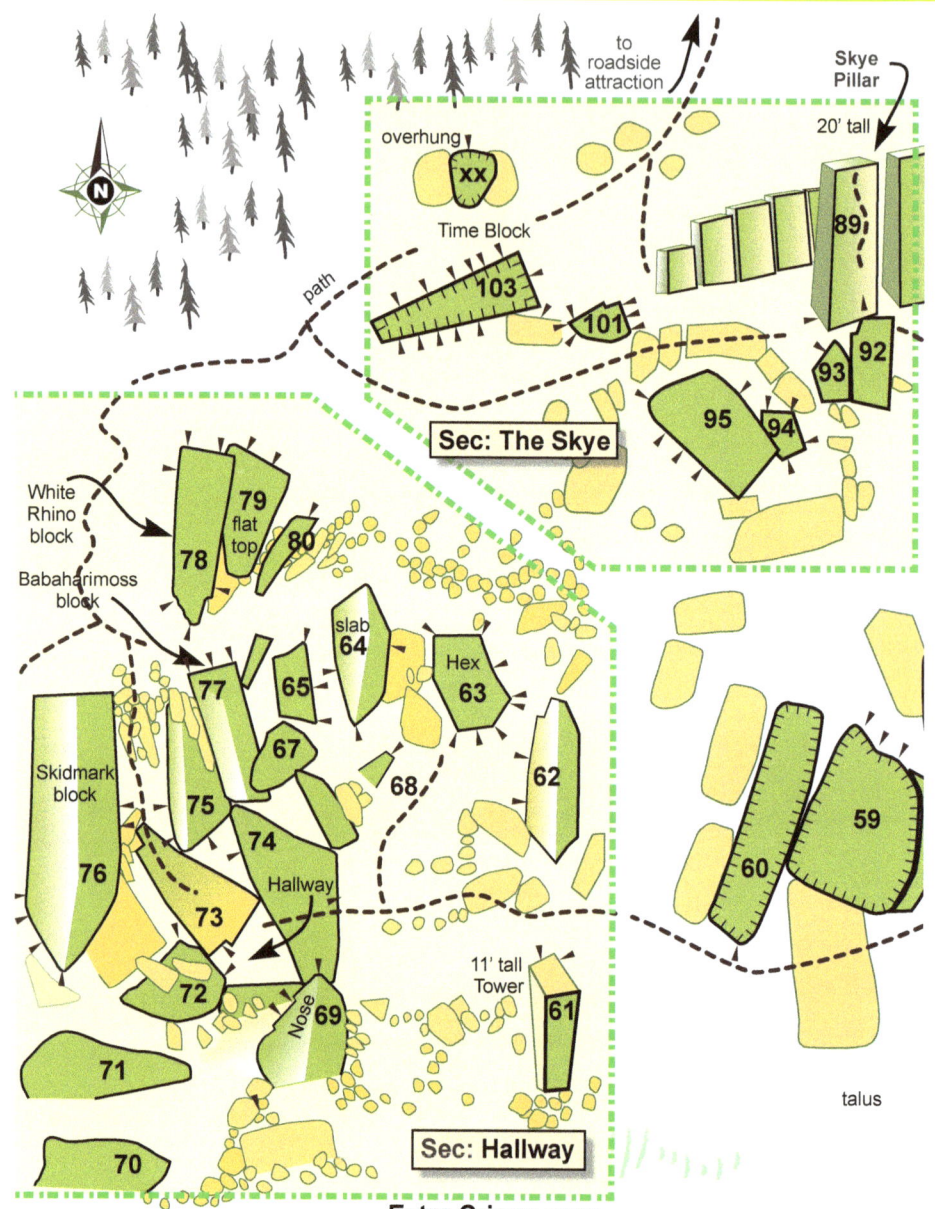

Lost Lake Boulders
Group A: Upper Area (Topo B)

134 MT HOOD ZONE (NORTH SIDE)

V_ _____ ☐
V_ _____ ☐
V_ _____ ☐

Boulder #10

V_ _____ ☐

CREST CLUSTER

Minor stuff on the crest of the hill (most are done). Situated along the same ridge crest to the immediate west of this cluster just a few yards is Ultrasaurus problem on a slight overhung section of the utter east end of Tall Moss Wall.

Boulder #11

VB _____ ☐

Boulder #12

VB _____ ☐

Boulder #13

V_ _____ ☐

Boulder #14

VB _____ ☐
V1 _____ ☐
V0 _____ ☐

Ultrasaurus Boulder (#15)

V7 Ultrasaurus ★ ☐

This is a powerful crimp line on a slight hung face. Sit start low on left and work up rightward.

V_ _____ ☐

A minor line to the left on the less low angled slabby aspect.

FIN BOULDER SECTION

A common spot to warmup on various minor short prows. This stone is tucked down in a low draw to the south of Ultrasaurus about eighty feet.

The Fin (#16)

Beta is described from left to right (NE

around to west side); most are sit starts.

VB Head Fake ☐
Basic NE face, though as a sit start it's slightly harder.

V3 Where the Sidewalks ★ ☐
North side on the prow; do it as a sit start.

V4 Light in the Attic ★ ☐
Climb directly up the slightly hung prow on crimps; sit start.

V3 Ziggurat ★ ☐
Crimps on the flat west face; sit start; very short.

V1 Cover your Eyes ☐
Lip traverse going at angle up left.

Tiny Fin Boulder (#17)

V2ss Archaeopteryx ★ ☐
Low sit start little minor problem.

Boulder #18

This may yield about 4-5 short lines.

V_ _____ ☐
V_ _____ ☐
V_ _____ ☐
V_ _____ ☐

Boulder #19

V_ _____ ☐
A possible shorty on north aspect.

Boulder #20

LL Boulders South Talus Stone 17-20-21

LL Boulders South Talus Stone 25

LL Boulders South Talus Pano of upper zone

136   MT HOOD ZONE (NORTH SIDE)

V3 Creeper ★ ☐
Prow on the next block.

Boulder #21

V1 Dorito ★ ☐

Broad sloped end prow as a sit start (VB if doing it in standing mode).

V_ _____ ☐
Short flat face on east side of stone.

Boulder #22

This stone may yield about 2-3 lines.

V_ _____ ☐

V_ _____ ☐

Boulder #23

Nothing here.

Boulder #24

This stone may yield about 2-3 short lines.

V_ _____ ☐

V_ _____ ☐

LIPS SECTION

Cube Boulder (#25)

V4 The Cube ★ ☐

A cool, well undercut stone. Begin on left, traverse along lip, then surmount

Lost Lake Boulders ✦ PB 137

it at the outermost point while using the right side aspect of the stone. Several variations to the main line can be done too.

Boulder #26

V_ _____ ☐

Boulder #27

May offer several very short mantle problems.

V_ _____ ☐
V_ _____ ☐

CRIMPER SECTION

Crimper Boulder (#28)

The east face of this boulder yields several power lines mostly sit start on a low, but long east facing aspect.

V7ss (?) _____ ★ ☐
The left of two powerful problems using slopers. Exact rating anyone?

V9ss _____ ★ ☐
Powerful hung problem using sloped crimps.

Boulder #29

This little stone is smack between Crimper and Koda stones.

V0 _____ ☐
Sit start and muscle a few moves with right hand on the better holds. Exact rating?

Boulder #30

V2ss Archosaur ☐
Minor north facing block with a brief crack problem. Standing is V0.

138 MT HOOD ZONE (NORTH SIDE)

Boulder #31

V_ _____ ☐
A minor shorty problem.

Koda Boulder (#32)

V9ss Exploder ★ ☐
The cool looking overhung east face with a dyno or long reach to catch the top lip, then mantle over onto the flat top.

V_ _____ ☐
Another stout looking potential line on the overhang to the right of the previous line.

VBss Yixian ☐
Basic north nose; sit start.

Koda Cave (#33-34-35)

This is a deep pit, where the wafting temperature coming out of the nook cave-like hole keeps the deep pit quite cool in the summer. All problems are on the south wall in the pit. Beta is left to right.

V2 Kibbles ★ ☐
Left part of the pit, on a slight overhang going up a bunch of jug holds.

V1 Bow Wow ★ ☐
Center part of the wall, going up a series of jugs.

V0 Wo-of ☐
The right face of the wall, going up several nice jug holds.

Boulder #36

To the east of Koda Cave is this isolated minor stone with a slight overhang to it.

V_ _____ ☐

Boulder #37

V0 _____ ☐
Minor short crack at the far west end of the Koda's Cave group (situated in the low draw).

STACKED SECTION

Boulder #38

NORTH SIDE PIT:

V3 _____ ☐
This is a sit start problem tucked in a narrow deep north facing pit. The problem ascends the

vertical and slightly hung parts of the cave-like nook, starting on small crimps, then some juggy holds, then exits rightward near the top. Technically, it starts upon the inner cave-like nook on stone #40 and finishes upon the slightly hung part of stone #38.

Boulder #39

This is the upper smaller stone sitting on a bigger lower stone. Certain problems were done as standing starts, then various lines were done as sit starts, plus now there's a cool traverse. This block is a rectangular cube shape. Beta starts with the leftmost west side lines described counter-clockwise.

VB _____ *(west side)* ☐
VB _____ *(west side)* ☐
V2 _____ ☐
Sit start for the western of two outermost points of rock.

V3 _____ ★ ☐
Do a sit start for this interesting outer point.

VB **Rum Run** ☐
The standing start method on same outer point.

V3 **Blonde's Traverse** ★ ☐
Begin on flat face, and traverse rightward and top out near the north hung point.

V2 **Tarball** ★ ☐
The brief north overhung point.

Boulder #40

LOWER MAIN STONE - NORTH FACE

This is the lower larger stone, on its outermost flat north facing aspect.

V7 **Seduction** ★ ☐
Sit start, and climb thin crimps upward. Located to the immediate left of a wide gap.

Boulder #41

V2ss **Gondwana** ★ ☐
Straight up the round nose (just right of wide gap between the stones). Sit start.

V2ss **Pangaea** ★ ☐
Sit start using crimps on right face trending up left and merging onto same round nose of Gondwana. A boring VB variant exits off to the right after the first move.

CENTRALIA SECTION

Centralia Stone

This section describes stones 42, 43, 44, 45,

140 MT HOOD ZONE (NORTH SIDE)

46, 47, 48, and 49. Most of these stones are quite short and will yield brief sit start lines.

Boulder #42

V_ _____ ☐
V_ _____ ☐

Boulder #43

V_ _____ ☐
V_ _____ ☐

Boulder #44

V_ _____ ☐

Boulder #45

V_ _____ ☐

Boulder #46

V_ _____ ☐

Centralia Boulder (#47)

V_ _____ ☐
V_ _____ ☐
VB Centralia ☐
V_ _____ ☐

Boulder #48

V_ _____ ☐
V_ _____ ☐

Boulder #49

V_ _____ ☐
V_ _____ ☐

WOW SECTION

A worthy spot to visit that has a stellar notable stone with cool powerful lines on it, plus several other minor half-worthy stones of interest nearby.

Boulder #50

Lost Lake Boulders ✦ PB 141

V_ _____
V_ _____

Boulder #51

V0 _____
Sit start up ultra short crimpy face.

V2 (?) _____
Around on the north aspect of this stone on a flat clean block is this sit start short crimp problem ascending a seam on a slightly hung face (upper right holds are large).

V_ _____
V_ _____

Boulder #52

Impressive stone well worth the visit. Beta is listed from left to right. All are sit start lines. All problems are considered to be good quality.

V5 Image of Injustice ★
Climb up a hung prow to sloped lip, then traverse up the outermost left side of lip on rounded palmy holds till you reach the leftmost apex high point. Sit start. It's V4 standing.

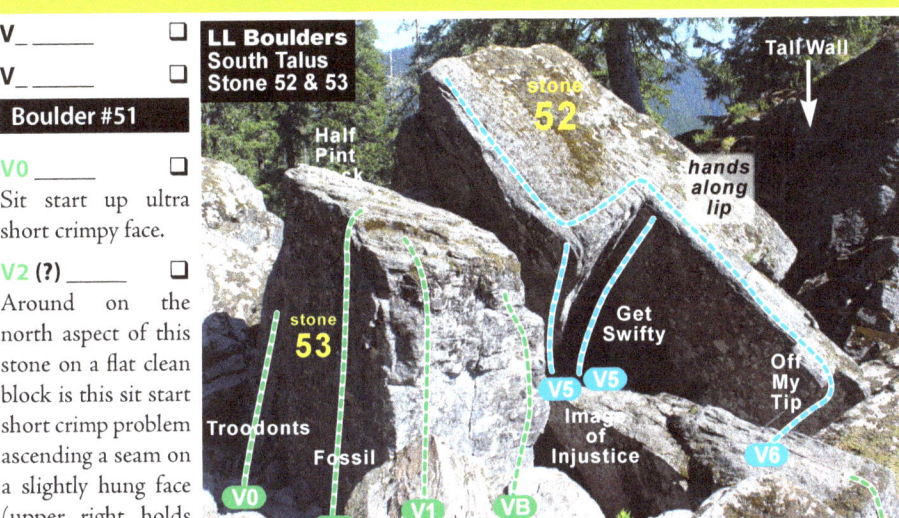

V5 Get Swifty ★
The inner overhung corner and go over the sloped lip onto the top slab. Sit start.

V6 Off My Tip ★
Begin as sit start, traverse right to outer low point, then cruise up the sloped rail traverse using hand palms on the rail, till you encounter the spot where the lip jogs left. Traverse left along the rising lip, and continue to palm up the outer leftmost part of the lip (as the first route) till you reach the apex summit point to top out. The standing start is V4.

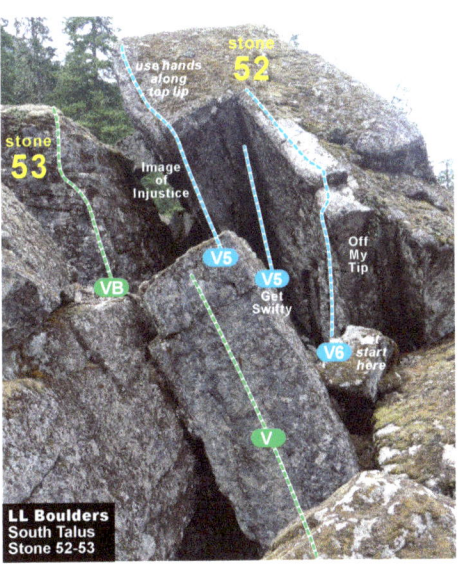

142 MT HOOD ZONE (NORTH SIDE)

Half Pint Block (#53)

This is the tiny boulder (aka Warmup) immediately south of Wow Boulder.

V0ss Troodonts ★ ☐
Sit start; left part on south face; crimps.

V1ss Fossil ★ ☐
Right part of south face; crimps; sit start.

V1 Petrified ★ ☐
East aspect; sit start.

VB _____ ☐
East aspect; rightmost line; sit start.

Boulder #84 [yep!]

V1 (?) _____
This is a short flat face in a low trough to the immediate east of stones #52 and #53.

Boulder #54

V_ _____ ☐

Boulder #55

V3-4 [?] _____ ★ ☐
The east face is a flat vertical short face, which offers a unique powerful crimpy sit start problem.

V_ _____ ☐

Boulder #56

V_ _____ ☐

Boulder #57

V_ _____ ☐
V_ _____ ☐

Boulder #58

V_ _____ ☐

Boulder #59

V_ _____ ☐
V_ _____ ☐

Boulder #60

V_ _____ ☐

Boulder #61 (Tall end)

This stone is visually tall-*ish* (only about 11-ft tall) on its northern vertical end, and it offers

two unique minor lines.

V2 ____ ★ ☐
The outer left slightly hung power line on this tall stone; has a midway sloped jug, and a nice top ending jug.

V3 ____ ★ ☐
The right problem on outer north facing aspect; thin crimps on flat face. Sit start.

Boulder #62
Several minor slabby problems on its west side aspect.

VB ____ ☐

VB ____ ☐

VB ____ ☐

Hex Boulder (#63)

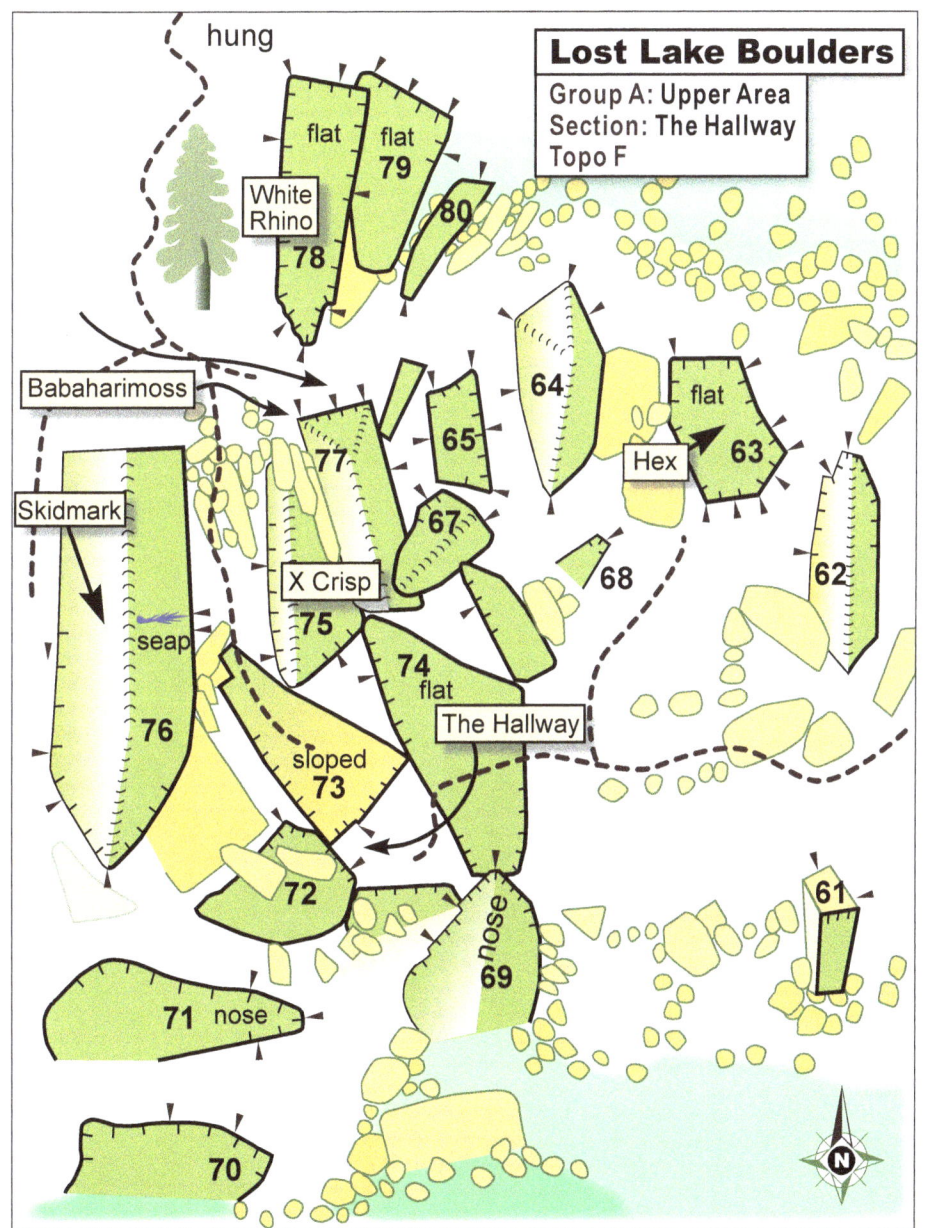

Lost Lake Boulders
Group A: Upper Area
Section: The Hallway
Topo F

The Hex Boulder is a quite short flat topped unit, all problems are ultra short sit starts. And there's a minor south lip traverse.

VBss Presstitutes ☐
The southwest nose.

VBss Regurtitation ☐
Short face in scoop.

VBss Blood ☐
The outer minor point.

V0ss Greed ☐
The southeast face.

VBss Freedom ☐
The southeast nose.

VBss Humid ☐

V0ss Rites ☐
The northeast nose.

VBss Ingrained Idiocy ☐

The northwest nose.

Boulder #64

VB _____ ☐
Low angled smears on slab.

V4 (?) Undertaker ★ ☐
This was dug out underneath of it to produce a quality powerful crawl under sit start problem. Sloped left lip holds, and once you reach the outermost overhung point, power over it.

VB _____ ☐
Minor shorty stuff on far back side.

Boulder #65

This stone is immediately east of Babaharimoss stone. Beta is described from left to right.

V2 (?) _____ ☐
Traverse the left lip rail going rightward.

V3ss Double Tap ★ ☐
Sit start and reach high to catch

All are sit start problems

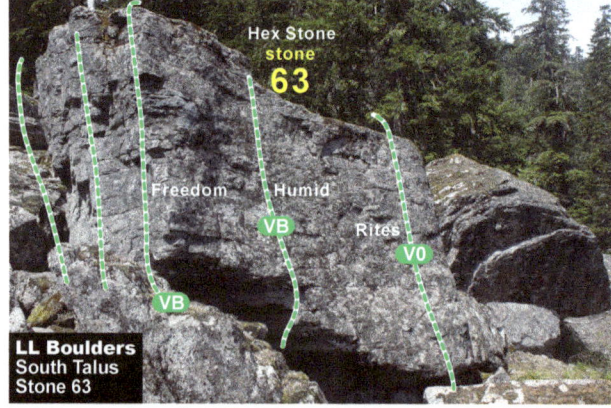

Lost Lake Boulders ✦ PB 145

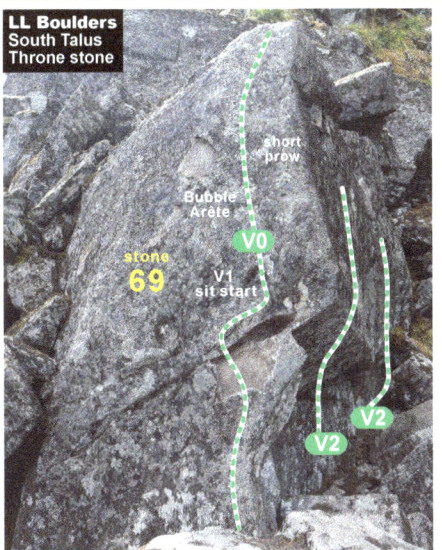
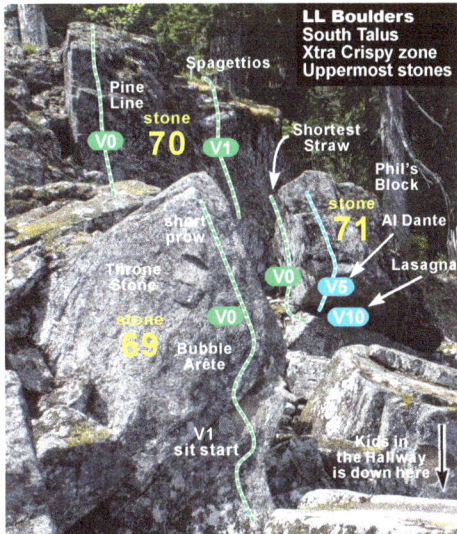

the midway pocket, then reach again to the top lip.

V0 _____ ☐
North rail run on an angled slab.

Boulder #66

V2 (?) _____ ☐
All dug out and now a fine entertaining sit start under it; power out a very brief short jutting block.

Boulder #67

V_ _____ ☐

Boulder #68

V_ _____ ☐

Throne Boulder (#69)

V1 Bubble Arête ★ ☐
Short outer nose starts from atop another block (up on flat rock bench just east of the Hallway). The standing method is V0.

V2 Pulling Teeth ☐
Right side of same block. It may start down on the lower stone (on stone #74).

V2 Whiplash ☐
Climb face right of previous line.

Pine Boulder (#70)

The is the uppermost stone in this entire group. Beta is described from left to right.

V0 Pine Line ☐
The obvious prow with a minor tree growing on it.

V1 Spagettios ☐
The tall face to the right of the previous line.

Phil's Boulder (#71)

Uphill south of Skidmark Block is a jutting hung prow. Beta is described left to right.

V0 Shortest Straw ☐
The upper side of the jutting prow.

V5 Al dante ★ ☐
The actual jutting prow.

V10 Lasagna ★ ☐
Thin line on the same jutting prow.

KIDS IN THE HALLWAY
One of the most fascinating spots to visit at LLB. Beta is described beginning on the north wall of this tunnel-like hallway. This "Hallway" beta section includes stones 72, 73, and 74.

Boulder #72

V4 Across the Hall ★ ☐
On the east side of the hallway going up a flat face.

V2 _____ ★ ☐
Climb the jam crack overhead of you up in the roof (on east side of the hallway).

V7 (?) _____ ★ ☐
A powerful thin traversing crimp problem cruises from the west side of the hallway, going through the hallway and out the east side of the hallway.

Boulder #73

V4 Kids in the Hallway ★ ☐
Start in hallway, using an arête, move right onto its outside face, then up to top.

V1/V2 (?) _____ ★ ☐
At the western end of this hallway boulder is an angled rail. Begin low on left, and cruise up right along the rail, with feet on the vertical south aspect that lacks foot holds.

Boulder #74

V4 Heart of Darkness ★ ☐
Begin deep in a snug low cave-like dark hole, power

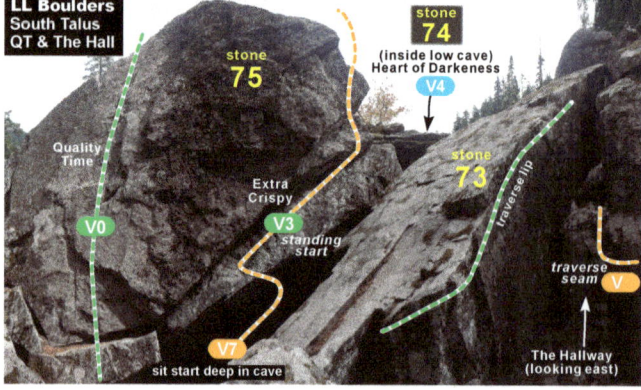

Lost Lake Boulders ✦ PB 147

out on overhung holds, then up the outside using better flat holds to the top of the stone.

Extra Crispy (#75)

V0 Quality Time ★ ☐

Climb the steeply angled face on the outside of this boulder. Sit start.

V3 (V7ss) Extra Crispy ★ ☐

Start in pit on roof edge, go up left on slopers, then up right along rails and up to top.

V_ (?) Fade to Black ★ ☐
Inside under the backside of same stone.

Skidmark Boulder (#76)

A popular long beast stone with problems on the west, south and east aspect. Beta is described beginning on the west side of the stone.

V2 Skidmark Traverse ★ ☐
A long west side traverse, going left to right, ending at the south point.

V0ss Sanity Gasp ☐

V1ss __ ☐
Just to the left of the prow.

V2ss (?) __ ★ ☐
The south hung prow as a sit start.

V1 Spineless Jellyfish ★ ☐
The slab smear problem immediately left of the water seepage stain on the east aspect.

V2 Skidmark ★ ☐
The other fine smear slab problem immediately right of the seepage stain.

Babaharimoss Boulder (#77)

Superb quality lines on a triangle shaped slightly hung north end of a large block.

V4 Babaharimoss ★ ☐
Ascend up the left arête.

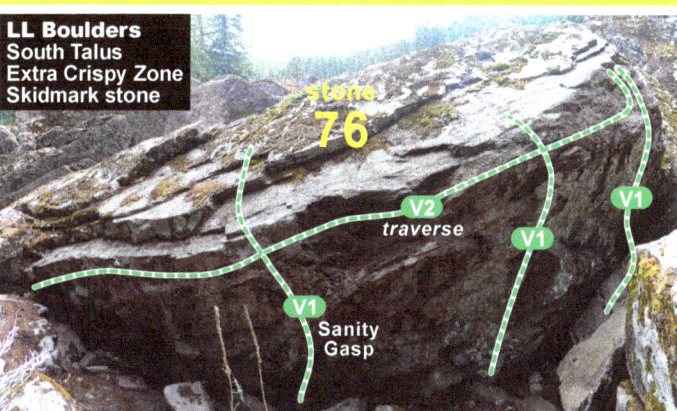

LL Boulders
South Talus
Extra Crispy Zone
Skidmark stone

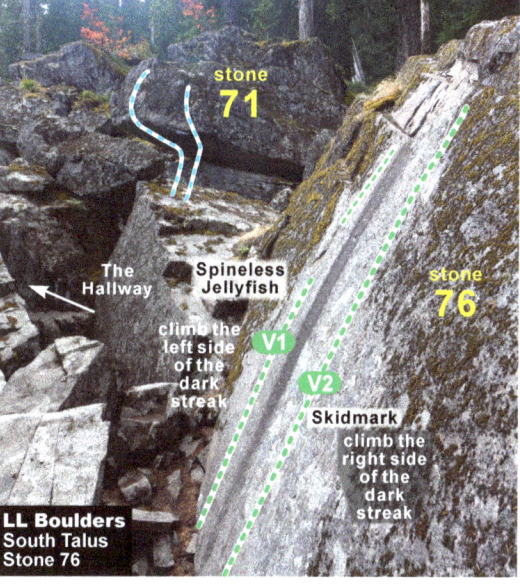

LL Boulders
South Talus
Stone 76

V5ss Morning Yoga ★ ☐
Sit start at center, bust up left to the arête (aka A.M Yoga).

V6ss Gyoza ★ ☐
Sit start at center face and go directly up

V8ss The Struggle Within ★ ☐
Sit start at center going up to right arête.

V3 Struggle Bus ★ ☐
Run the right arête to the top most point

White Rhino (#78)

The problems are described right to left, beginning on the short overhung lines on the south end tip point, then detailing the west side short problems, and finally the taller north as-

148 MT HOOD ZONE (NORTH SIDE) ✦

pect lines.

VB _____ ☐
Minor on the east face of this southern jutting point.

V1ss True Vitt ★ ☐
Crawl underneath it and power out the overhung prow and muscle over it.

V3ss Time n' Time Again ★ ☐
Traverse L to R all the way to the jutting out prow, then muscle over the prow.

V_ _____ ☐
Short face on west aspect of the stone.

V3 White Rhino ★ ☐
Overhung tall powerful crimpy prow that faces north with gently sloped terrain below it.

V_ (?) W.R. Face ☐
Just left of the regular White Rhino route. This is even more overhung, with notable difficulties:

Black Rhino (#79)

This is a short flat topped stone immediately east of White Rhino stone.

V_ _____

V_ _____

V_ _____

Boulder #80

V_ _____

V_ _____

TALL MOSS WALL ⚠

This is a moss-rich tall wall with a steeply angled south-facing slab. The rock formation travels for several hundred feet from Ultrasaurus (at its easternmost end) to the Skye Pillar

(at its westernmost end). The wall is all hi-ball, yet a few bold problems have been etched into existence.

Boulder #81

V0 Terra Firma ❑

A slab line on a steep slab on the eastern portion on the Tall Wall.

EGRESS SECTION ⚠

Boulder #82

Located at a large alcove with a superb vertical east facing aspect. Many crashpads are recommended for this hi-ball stuff.

V3ss Point of Egress ★ ❑

Start deep in a dark pit, climb up rightward on great hold out the 'window' slot, and stop at dirt landing. The route is virtually all underground. This is a very deep hole slot and requires extra crashpads and a spotter.

V8 Prince of Persia ★ ❑

This route climbs out of the pit and onto the overhanging face (above the sloped dirt landing). Climb up the face, reaching up left to a tips crack, then continue up the hi-ball crack to finish. The standing start on the dirt landing at the horizontal hold gets you V5. The full route is V8 (from the deep pit cave start up to top of bluff).

The following are several more lines on the outer portion of this tall rock formation.

V_ (?) _____ ❑

Climb the entire crack system (merging into the previous line).

V0-1 (?) _____ ❑

Outermost left crack system.

Boulder #83

VB Walk the Plank ❑

A tall slab problem on the western portion of

the long tall wall.

SKYE SECTION

This section is at the westernmost end of the Tall Wall rock formation.

Boulder #88

V_ _____

V_ _____

Skye Pillar (#89) ⚠

A 30' tall pillar with a prominent vertical west aspect. This is located at the far west end of the Tall Moss Wall.

VB Paleontology ★ ☐
The basic fun run jog up the south face slab to the summit of this tall pillar.

V2 Phoenix ★ ☐
The noble west face line (variations may exist). Hi-ball on sloping rails and good holds that moves right at mid-height onto an angled prow and continues up the south face to top.

V_ (?). _____ ☐
Immediately right of Phoenix on a rounded prow. Merges into the Phoenix route higher up.

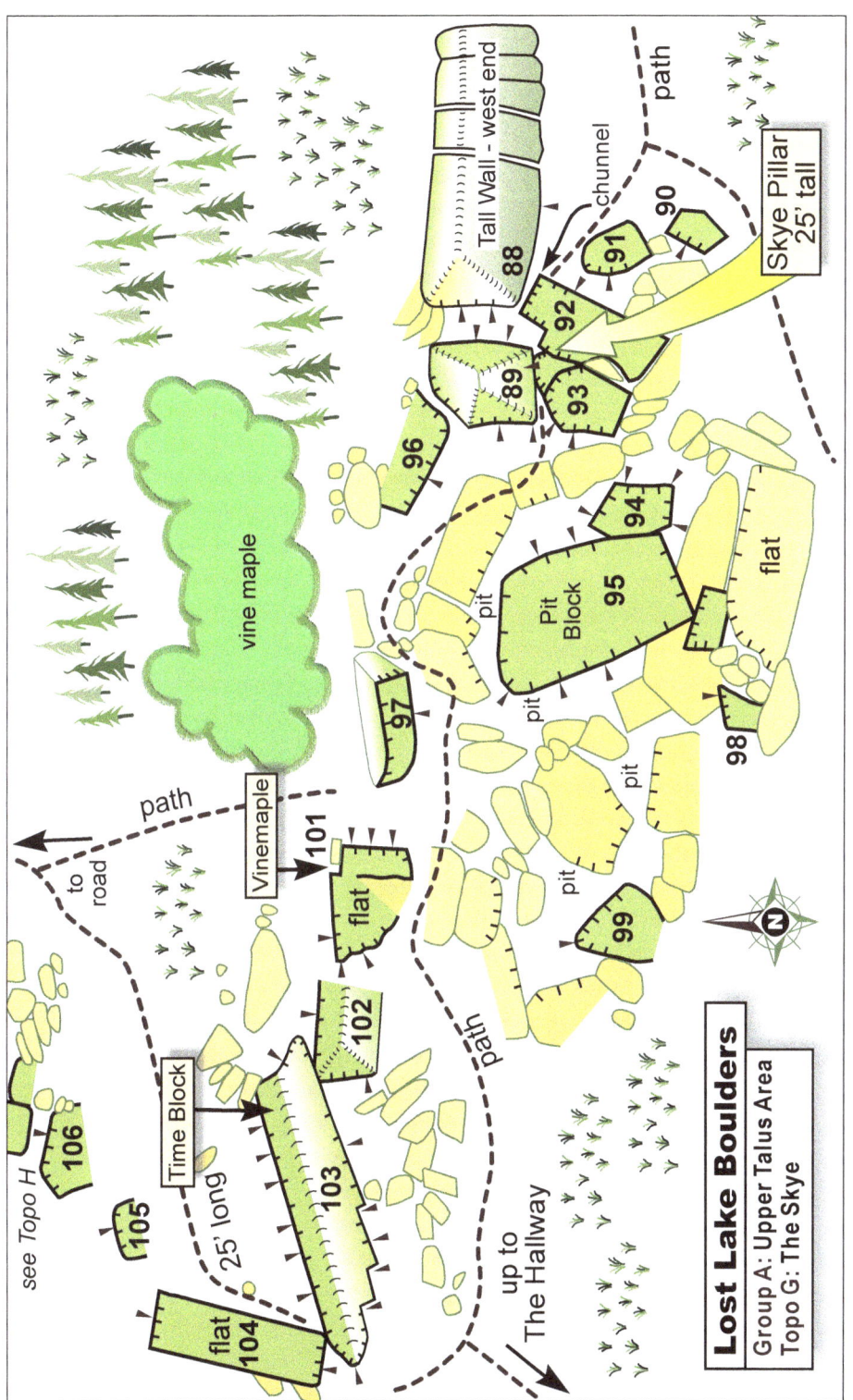

THE CHUNNEL

This low grotto section behind Skye Pillar exists because a big stone abuts up against the pillar and the end of the Tall Moss Wall, leaving a gaping crawl-way. This crawl zone yields a string of viable lines, some well done.

Boulder #90

V_ _____ ☐

Boulder #91

V_ _____ ☐

Boulder #92

V_ _____ ☐

Boulder #93

V5 For the Never ★ ☐
Short sit start crack on the stone to the immediate right of Skye Pillar.

Bump Boulder (#94)

Leans up against the Pit Block and yields all minor basic problems.

VB _____ ☐
The leftmost line, on south aspect.

Lost Lake Boulders ✦ PB 153

VB ____
The east line (left of two).

VB ____
The east line (right of two).

VB ____
The north line on the north aspect of stone. Rumored to have a V5 sit (say what?).

Pit Boulder (#95)

Cool stone in a low pit and overhung on east, north and west aspects.

V6 Seek and Destroy ★
This is on the slightly overhung east aspect of the flat topped stone, tucked down in a low trough. Sit start in this trough. There may be additional variants on this stone.

V_ (?) ____
North facing overhung problem.

V_ (?) ____
Sit start in low spot and power up thin crimpy face.

V_ (?) ____
Sit start in low spot and climb thin crimps on face.

Boulder #96
V_ ____

Boulder #97
V_ ____

Boulder #98
V_ ____

Boulder #99
V_ ____

Boulder #100
V_ ____

Vinemaple (#101)

Sit start problems on the west aspect.

V2ss Manus Unum
The left problem.

V3ss Mare Nostrum

V2ss Mare Liberum
The rightmost problem.
  Three sit start problems on the east aspect.

V1ss Manu Forte

V3ss Manu Propria
The center face.

V1ss Manu Militari
The rightmost problem.

Boulder #102

This boulder abuts up next to the south side of the classic "Time Warp Boulder."

V8 Slaytonian Physics
Blank crimpy thin steeply angled north slab.

154 MT HOOD ZONE (NORTH SIDE)

VB Belly Ache
A west end little minor.

TIME WARP SECTION

Time Warp Boulder (#103)

A stellar fun 35' long global ballistic missile with a fat string of quality problems, especially its north hung aspect. All totally cool. All are done as sit start lines. Beta is described from left to right (starting on the east aspect, then the popular north side problems). Then the beta describes the south side problems.

East aspect of the stone:

V5ss Block Party ★
Do the short east flat face.

North aspect of the stone:

V1ss Time Warp ★
On far left go up hung edges to lip & over. Also can start on sloped two-hander, bump left into the same route.

V3ss Anchors Away ★
Near previous fat sloper, start on crimps and cruise up over lip.

V6ss Born Free ★
Start low on right on crimps (near next route), move up left to join previous lines exit moves over the lip.

V3ss Enlightenment ★
The center rail straight up hung face.

V1ss Tattoo ★
On right start on incut rail jugs, punch over lip.

V2ss (?) _____ ★
A sit start crimper short problem tucked low on

far right.

WESTERN END OVERHUNG TIP:

V_ _____ ☐
This overhung thing looks intriguing.

SOUTH ASPECT OF THE STONE:

Southern aspect of this same long stone, Minor slab lines; beta is left to right; nothing special to see here

VB Bad Odor ☐
VB Dysfunction ☐
V2 Reactionary ☐
VB Grin Weaper ☐
VB Masochist ☐

Boulder #104
V_ _____ ☐

Boulder #105
V_ _____ ☐

Boulder #106
V_ _____ ☐

Boulder #107
V4+ (?) _____ ☐
This is a notable overhung stone perched atop to other stones, leaving a nice crawl underneath of it for a sit start line. Has it been sent yet?

Boulder #108
V_ _____ ☐

Boulder #109
V_ _____ ☐

Boulder #110
V_ _____ ☐

156 MT HOOD ZONE (NORTH SIDE)

Boulder #111

ROADSIDE ATTRACTION STONE

This is one of the most famous classic boulders at LLB. At the western parking pullout spot walk a few yards briefly up the hiker's trail, then cut left to this classic big stone. The super hung roof offers quality and popular power lines. The base flake broke off and the beginning moves on certain routes are stouter.

V4 Get Lost ★

Begin as a sit start at lowest spot under the boulder, climb up the face till you encounter the overhung roof, then go out to the outermost part of the hung lip, then mantle up over the lip onto easier terrain for the final few moves.

V8 Lost & Found ★

Same sit start as previous but at the big overhung lip, you will move right to the outermost nose, then go up to the top

V10 Roadside Attraction ★

Sit start (same as previous problem) under roof in middle at the base of the stone, go directly out the overhang to the outermost part of the lip, run lip leftward to the outer nose, then go up to the top.

V6 Mother Hucker ★

Far rightmost line. Make a few moves using high edges in a seam, and a dyno to the top.

V2 Not Lost

Traverse the entire top lip from the right to the left, exiting at the last move of the Roadside Attraction route.

LL Boulders
South Talus
Roadside Attraction
Stone 111

LOST LAKE BOULDERS
MIDDLE TALUS GROUP

OASIS AREA

This large talus field lays to the north of the road (down slope from the road). Though it's extensive the viable stones tend to be grouped in scattered clusters. Some stones are quite short (especially the stones in the eastern section), and the center part of the talus field offers minimal bouldering viability. This zone is more befitting of a desert as it can get blazing hot standing out in the middle of this talus field in mid-summer.

The better concentration of stones in this zone lay along its western and northern perimeter. So, from Runnel Stone in a grand sweeping arc eastward you can visit a string of cool packaged gems.

The stone numbering sequence system starts with the 'Pullout Boulder' cluster, then proceeds north as if you are traveling northward past the Family Boulder.

The next group of stones that are detailed in this section begin at 'Runnel Stone' encompassing a pack of stones just north of it, including House Boulder. You'll likely aim directly for this core group on your first or second visit since its holds one of the best stones at LLB.

PULLOUT CLUSTER

This minor area has about 9 stones with about twenty total problems; most are sit start problems. This spot is known as the 'Parking Lot' cluster, but till the road is reopened it's just a flat landing zone.

Foxglove Boulder (#1)

V1ss Wild Lily ★ ☐
Sit start and climb the center west face.

V2ss Foxglove ★ ☐
Sit start and ascend the right arête (same west face).

Mindbender Boulder (#2)

This is a smaller stone just west of Foxglove.

V_ _____ ☐

Boulder #3

VB _____ ☐
Minor sit start slab.

Distraction Boulder (#4)

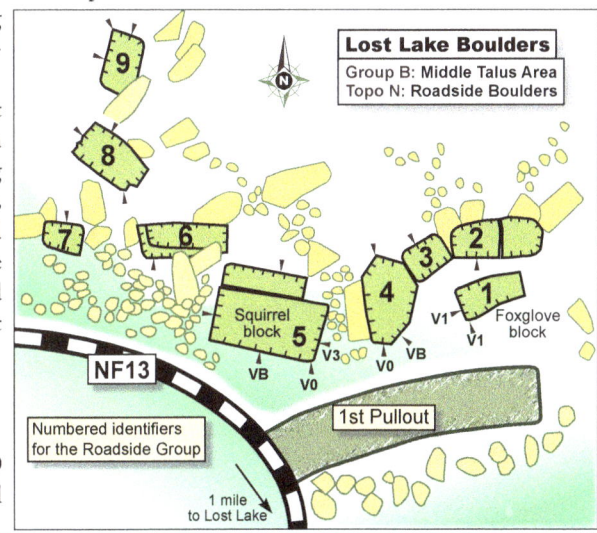

158   MT HOOD ZONE (NORTH)

V3 _____ ★
Sit start a fine short problem on the right portion of this stone.

VB _____ ★
The center problem using the outer point and all its holds.

VB _____ ★
Leftmost problem using both outer prows.

Squirrel Boulder (#5)

V3ss White Squirrel ★
The overhung east face of this stone.

V0 (V3) _____ ★
Power over an overhung bulge at the point.

VB _____
South face problem; standing start.

V0 _____
Sit start and climb the short west face.

Boulder #6

This is a smaller stone just west of the White Squirrel Boulder.

V1/2 Bender ★
Sit start, bump along the left arête, right on a small sloper.

V5ss Dr Mindbender ★
Sit start beginning with all hands on the sloper.

Boulder #7

V_ _____

Boulder #8

V_ _____
V_ _____

Boulder #9

V_ _____
V_ _____

Boulder #10

V_ _____

Boulder #11

VB [?] _____
V0 [?] _____

Boulder #12

V3 [?] _____
A notable overhung jutting prow tilting downhill.

Stone #13

V_ _____

Family Boulder (#14)

   A large fun stone with angled slabs on all sides. My family and I developed the entire boulder.

V3ss Mother-in-law ★
East aspect; slight bulge with a low squat sit start problem that quickly lands upon a slab.

VB Billy Joe ★
North side, left face.

VB SusyQ ★
North side, center steep face.

VB Uncle Bob ★
North side, right line (right hand along prow).

VB Auntie May ★
West side, left steep slab (left hand on prow).

V0ss Mother Jones ★
West side, center steep slab. Sit start.

VB Go Daddy ★
West side, right line.

V1ss Sweet Sister ★
Sit start, very short, south face problem.

Boulder #15

V_ _____

Boulder #16

V_ _____

Blur boulder (#17)

V1 Do It One More Time ★
On the south side is a very short sit start.

Boulder #18

Two short sit start lines.

V0 _____

VB _____

Boulder #19

V0 _____
Sit start, and layback the outer edge of the fat crck. Very short.

Boulder #20

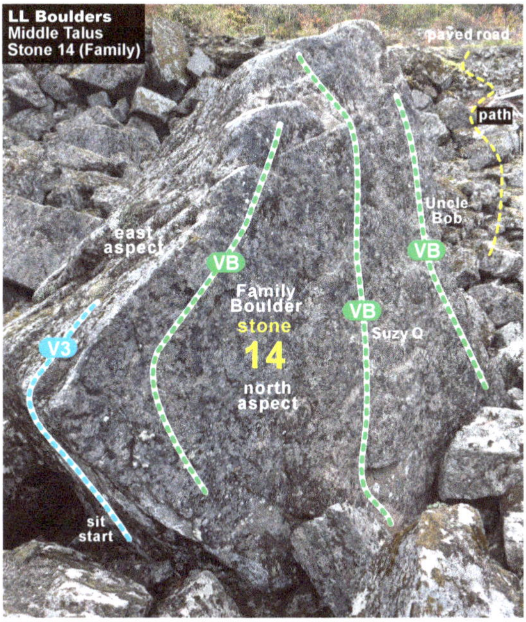

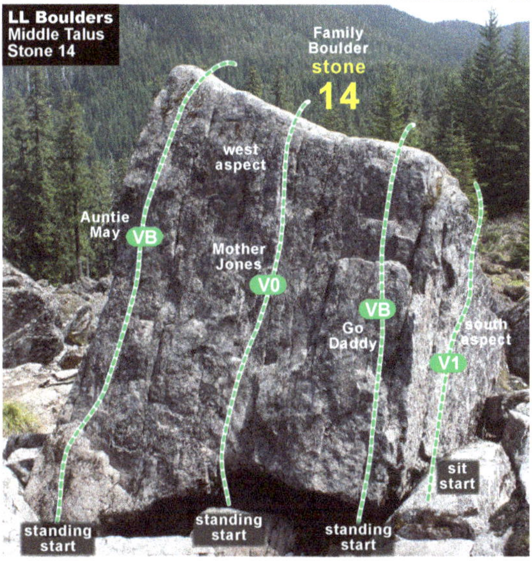

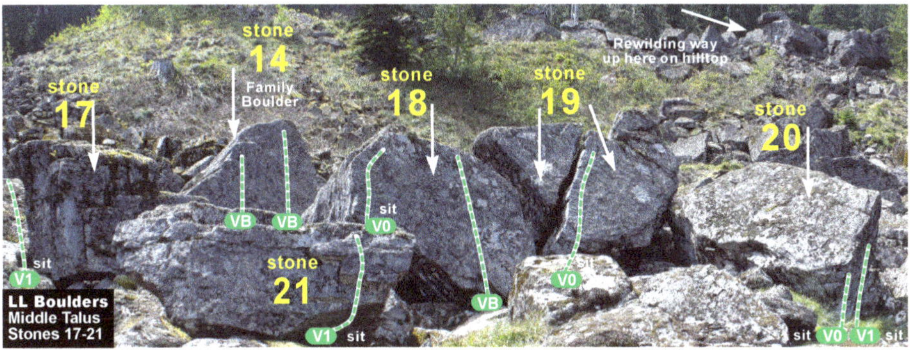

160 MT HOOD ZONE (NORTH)

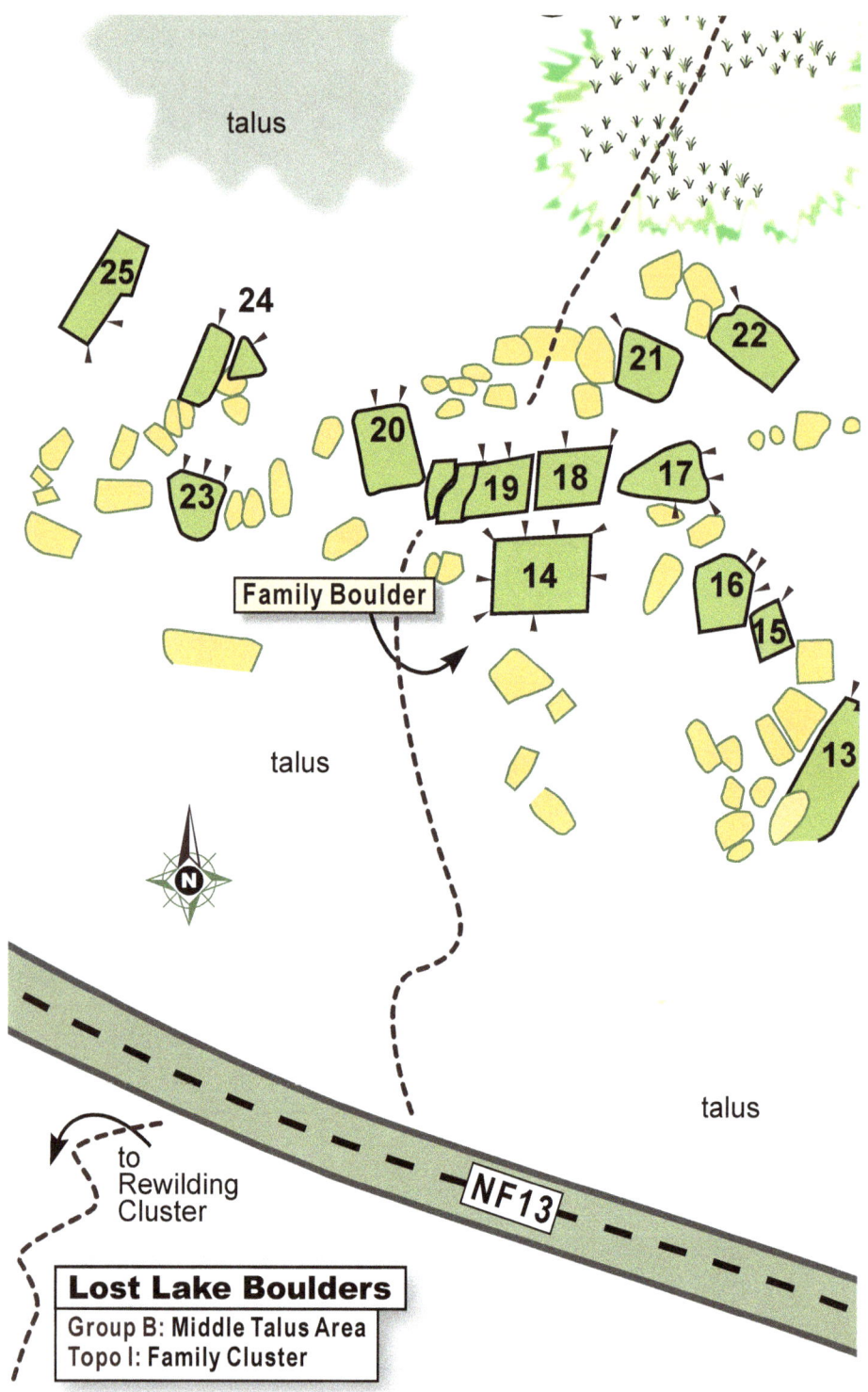

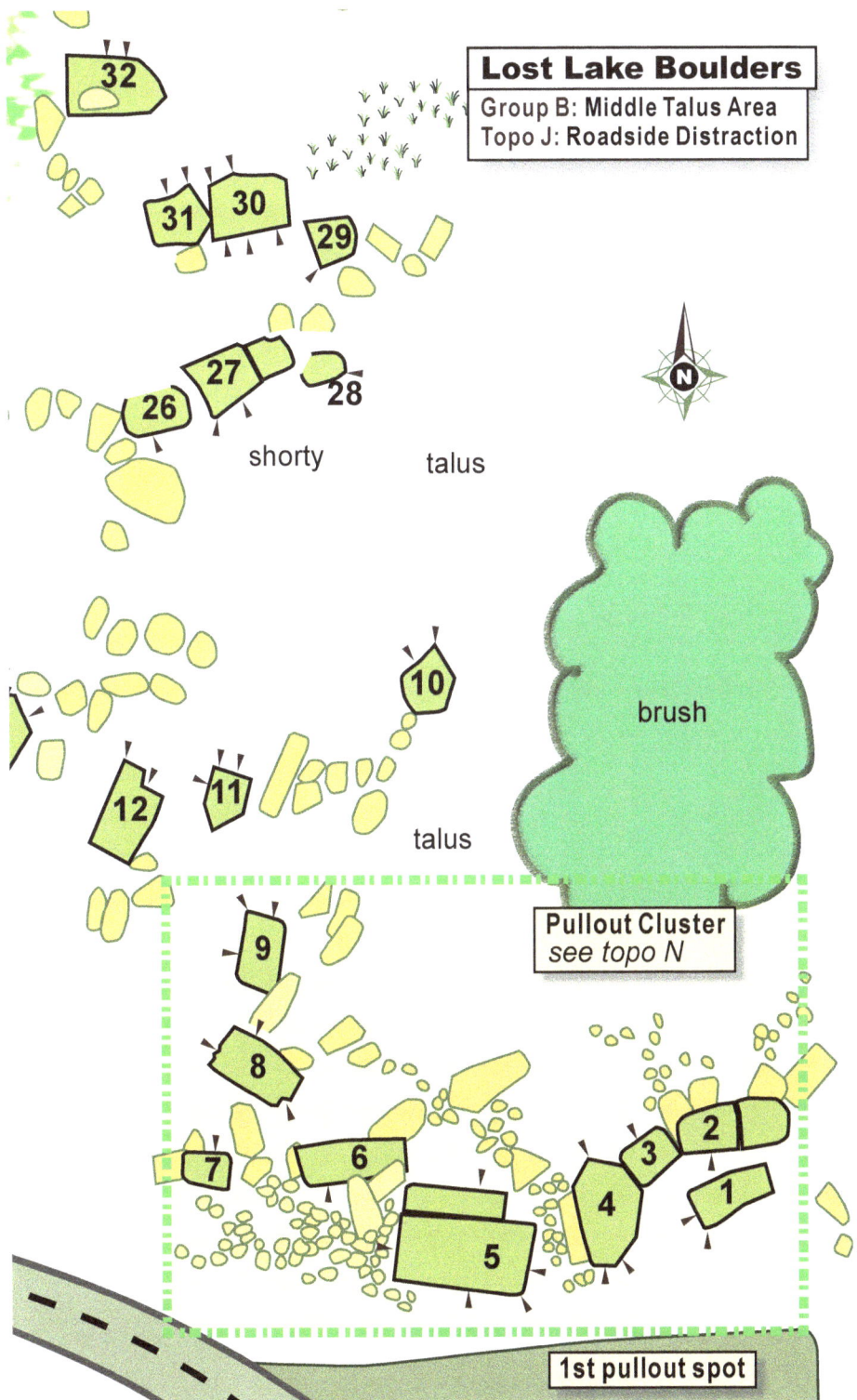

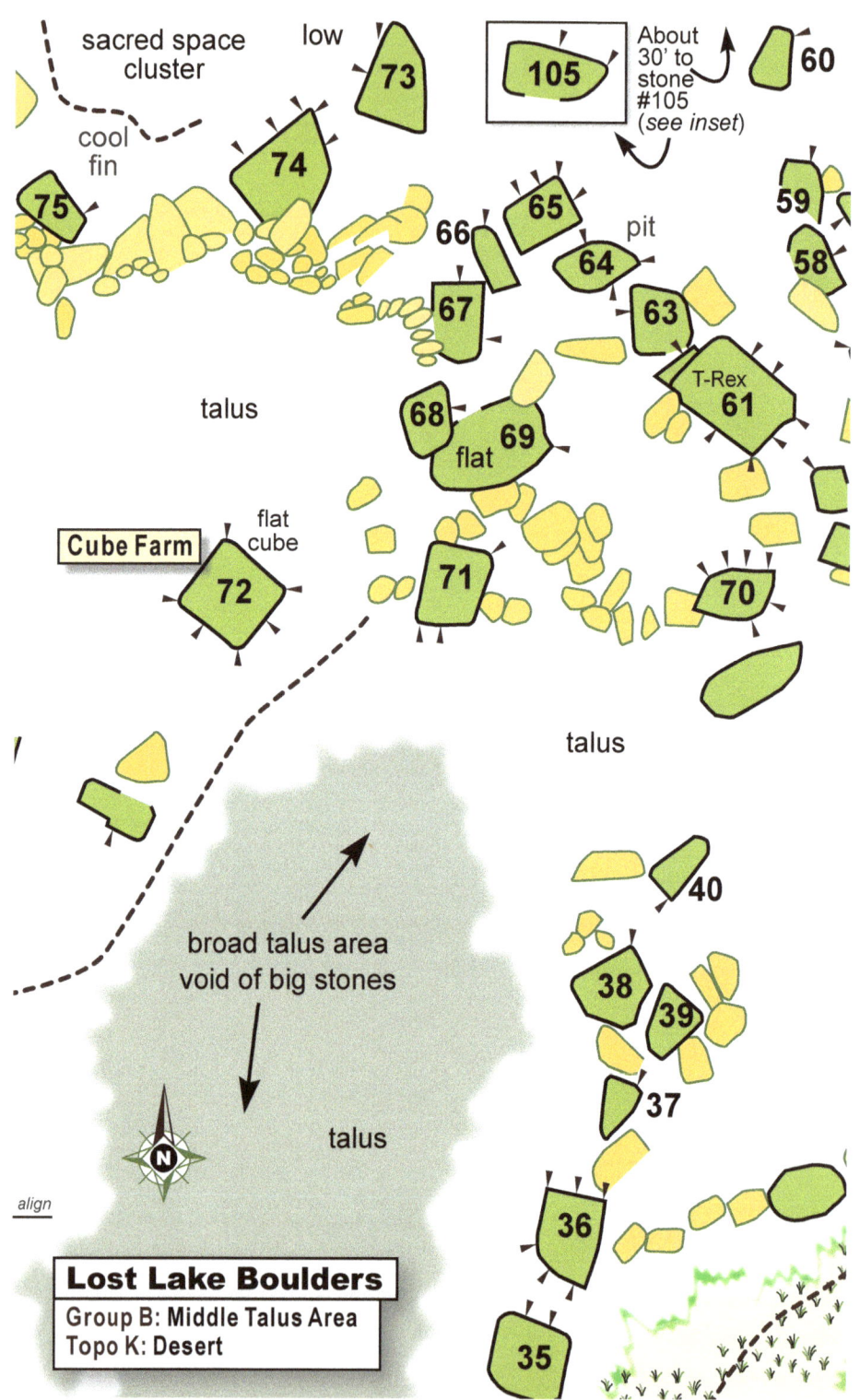

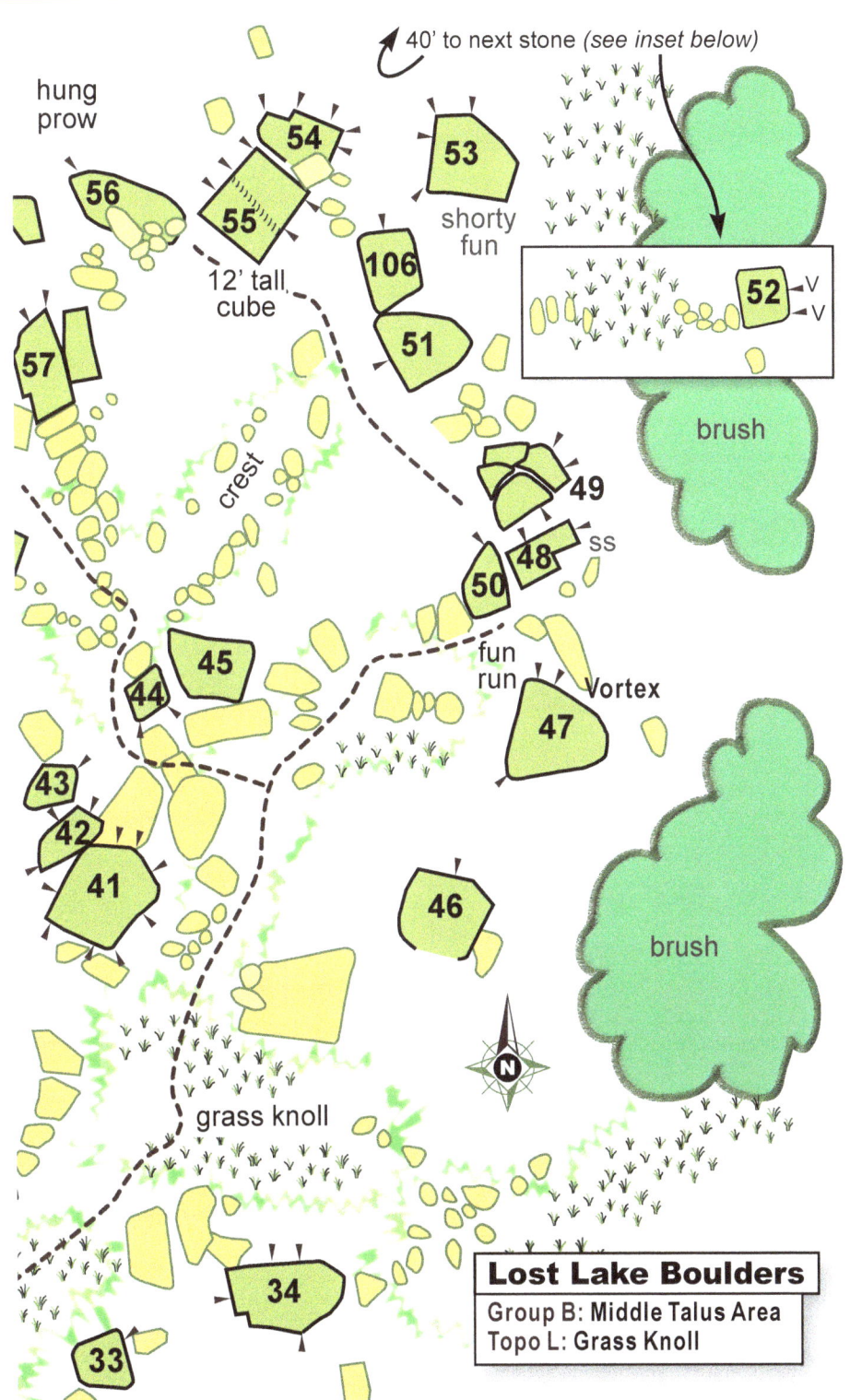

Ultra short sit starts.

V_ _____ ☐

V_ _____ ☐

Boulder #21

V_ _____ ☐

Ultra short sit start problem.

Boulder #22

V_ _____ ☐

Boulder #23

V_ _____ ☐

V_ _____ ☐

Boulder #24

V_ _____ ☐

Boulder #25

V_ _____ ☐

Boulder #26

V_ _____ ☐

Boulder #27

Matt on *Full House Boulder*

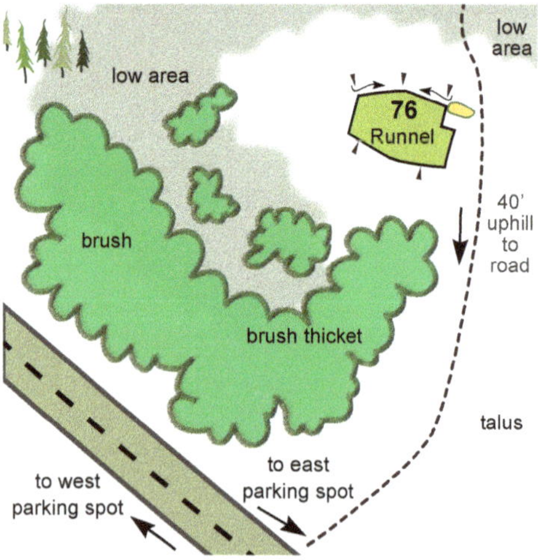

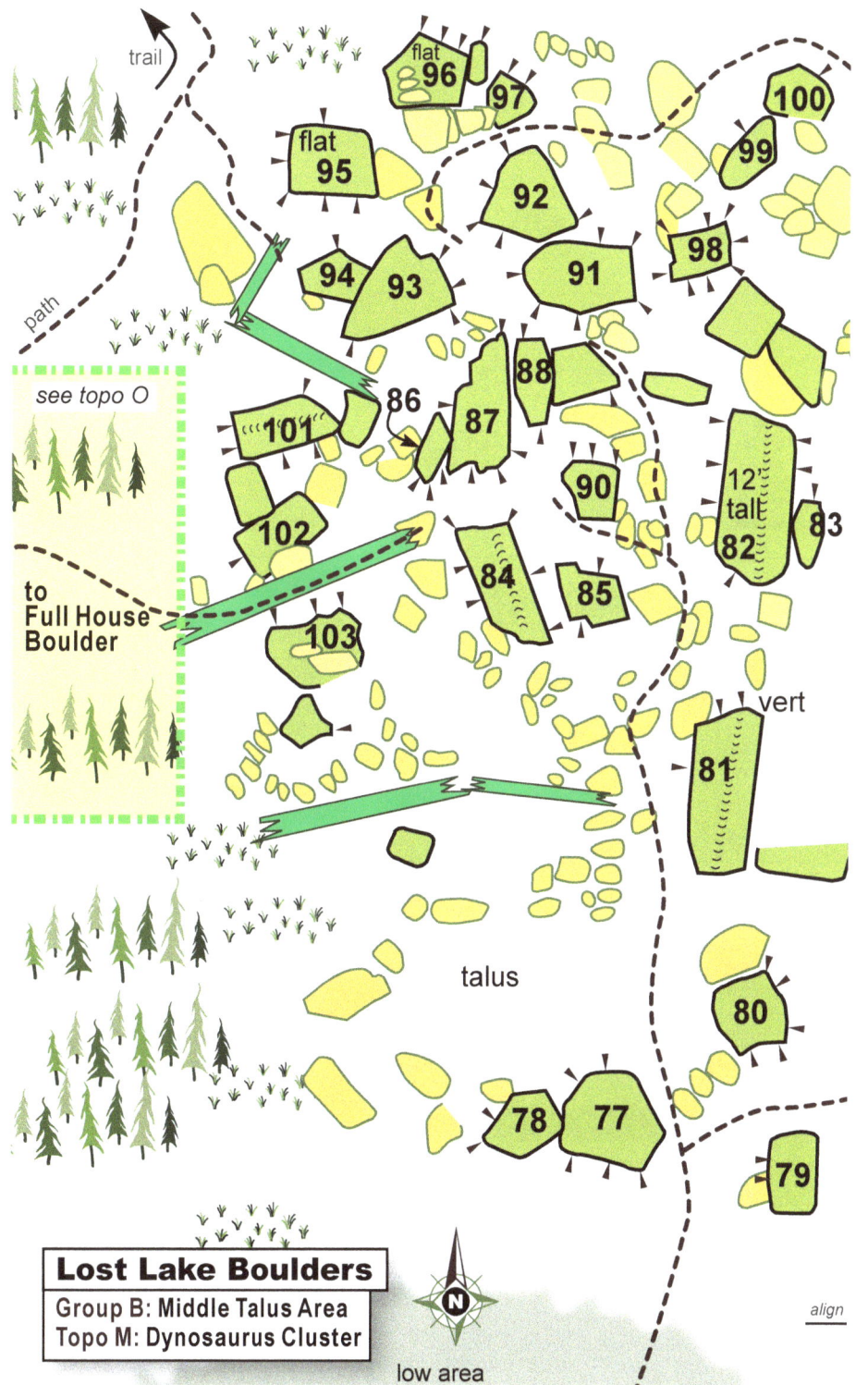

166 MT HOOD ZONE (NORTH)

V_ _____ ☐
Boulder #28
V_ _____ ☐
Boulder #29
V_ _____ ☐
Boulder #30
V_ _____ ☐
V_ _____ ☐
V_ _____ ☐
V_ _____ ☐
Boulder #31
V_ _____ ☐
Boulder #32
V_ _____ ☐
Boulder #33
V_ _____ ☐
Boulder #34
V_ _____ ☐
V_ _____ ☐
V_ _____ ☐
Boulder #35
V1 (?) _____ ☐
Short low problem.
Boulder #36
V0 (?) _____ ☐
V3 (?) _____ ★ ☐
V2 (?) _____ ☐
Boulder #37
V_ _____ ☐
Stone #38
V2 (?) _____ ★ ☐
Begin under the north side of the stone as a sit start; punch up face holds which becomes a brief prow. This prow points up high like a ships prow facing north.

LL Boulders Middle Talus Stone 38

LL Boulders Middle Talus Stone 41

Boulder #39
V_ _____ ☐
Boulder #40
V_ _____ ☐
Boulder #41
This stone offers short lines on each side, though only the west side is tapped.

V_ (?) _____ ☐
Short vertical face with a rightward angling rounded outer lip.

V3 (?) _____ ☐
Sit start, crimp a short minor rounded prow.

V_ _____ ☐
On the east side.

Lost Lake Boulders ✦ PB 167

V_ _____
On the north side.

Boulder #42

V3 (?) _____

Boulder #43

V_ _____

Boulder #44

V_ _____

Boulder #45

V_ _____

Boulder #46

V_ _____

Vortex Stone (#47)

V2 (V3ss) Vortex ★
A nice problem on the leaning east aspect. The sit start is V3.

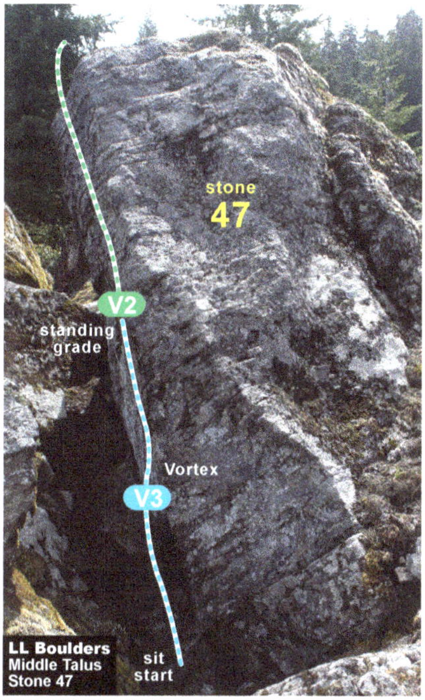

Forest Rat Boulder (#48)

A group of three minor small stones (48, 49, 50), with brief shorty problems.

V2ss Forest Rat
The triangular shaped ultra low-ball. Crawl under it to do it.

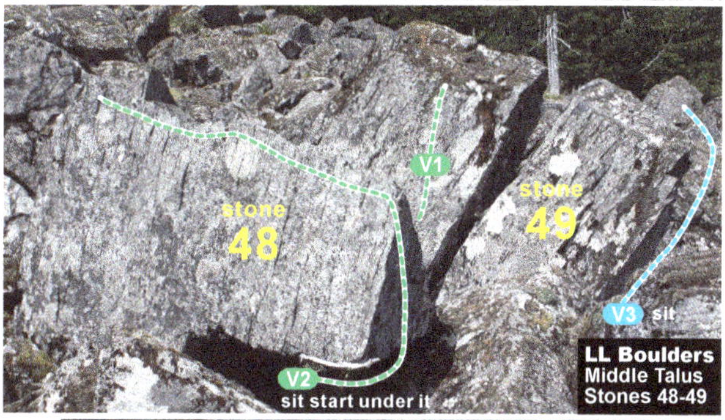

Boulder #49

V1 Toxic Waste

V3 Anti-Counter-Intelligentsia ★
Sit start shorty using left prow.

Boulder #50

V0 Enviro-nerd

Boulder #51

V_ _____

Boulder #52

V_ _____

V_ _____

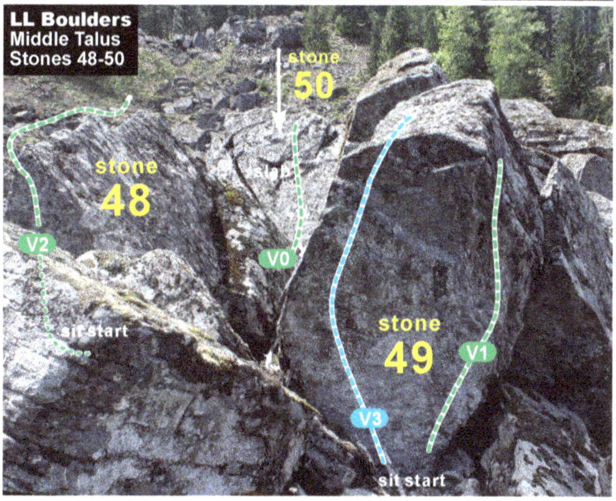

168 MT HOOD ZONE (NORTH)

Grimples (#53)

Four brief ultra low sit start lines on a squat low stone. Hmm...really?

V3ss Yes No
Go right to left along lip.

V3ss Yes But
Sit start, go center up.

V2ss Grimples
Sit start, go up prow.

VBss _____

Bluestone (#54)

All are brief short minor problems.

V0ss Lip Service
Smear the smooth face.

VBss Guerrilla Warfare
Prance over the jutting NE point.

V0ss _____
One move onto slab.

Stonehenge (#55)

A big stone with a flat vertical south face.

V6ss (?) _____
The obvious smooth vertical south face. The standing is easier than the sit start, but it's all thin crimps. Is this sent?

V2 Cool Breeze
The shorty on the right part of the same flat south face.

NORTH SIDE OF STONEHENGE:

V0 _____
V2 _____
VB _____

Boulder #56

V3 Jet Stream ★
A powerful cool looking overhung prow and a nice prize that was snagged quite early here.

Boulder #57

V_ _____
V_ _____

Boulder #58

V_ _____

Boulder #59

V_ _____

Boulder #60

V_ _____

Stone #61 (T-Rex)

Lost Lake Boulders ✦ PB 169

LL Boulders Middle Talus Stones 54, 55, 56

Tyranosaurus Rex is a very large boulder, but is not obvious because it sits in a low trough.

VB ☐
The west side easy slab walk up.

V3ss (?) ☐
Sit start at undercut and go up prow.

VB ☐
The south side easy route.

V0 ☐
The right prow on the south side.

VB ☐
Center of the east side.

V3ss (?) ☐
The hard sit start route on the east face.

V3ss (?) ☐
Sit start; ascend steep face on the north side.

Boulder #62
V_ ☐

Boulder #63
V_ ☐

Boulder #64
V3ss [?] ☐
V_ ☐

Boulder #65

V_ ☐
V_ ☐

Boulder #66

V_ ☐

Boulder #67

V_ _____ ☐
V_ _____ ☐

Pterosaur Boulder (#68)

V2ss (V3ss) Pterosaur ★ ☐
This is an ultra short stone with a very flat top, a pointy east point, and is quite easy to miss, yet it has one cool line on it. A recent revisit by other persons doing the digging yielded one extra move sequence more by getting tucked just a bit lower down into the crawl hole. All variants of this line are ultra low sit starts.

Boulder #69

V_ _____ ☐

Boulder #70

This has a few short theoretical lines.

V1 _____ ☐
V1-V2 [?] _____ ☐
V3 [?] _____ ☐

Boulder #71

V_ _____ ☐

Cube Farm (#72)

A squat flat top unit, all very short sit start lines.

V2ss Typo ★ ☐
The west point mantle.

V3ss Cube Farm ★ ☐
Transitions leftward to the west point, then mantle out.

VB _____ ☐
The south prow.

V3ss Thin Veneer ★ ☐
Short face immediately right of the south prow.

VB _____ ☐
The east prow.

VB _____ ☐
The north prow.

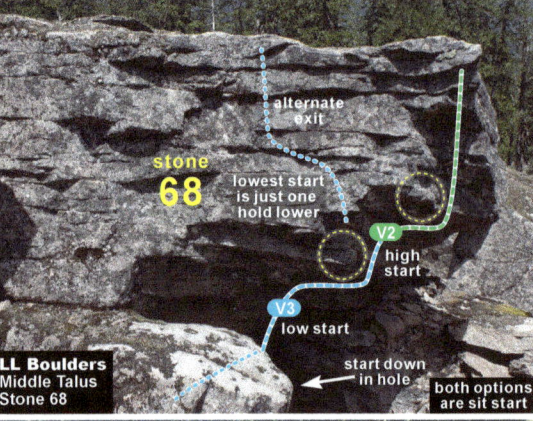

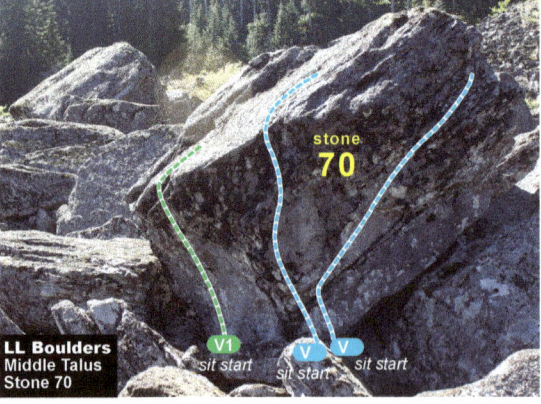

SACRED SPACE

This is a group of three main boulders facing north, and all these stones have unique worthy problems.

Stegosaur Boulder (#73)

Short west facing traverse problems.

V0 _____
Sit start, and run rail up rightward.

VB _____
Sit start, and run the crack up rightward.

Sacred Space Boulder (#74)

Unique quality lines, well worth the visit. Beta is left to right, starting on the east aspect.

V0 False Promise ★
Easy up line on the east face.

V1 Sacred Space ★
The north arête using a slight groove.

The next three problems are located on the vertical north face.

V1 Triangle Arête ★
Start on the flat face, then catch the outer high lip, and ascend that lip to the top.

V5 Triangle Face ★
Go direct up the flat vertical thin crimpy face.

V1 _____
Run the rail up leftward to the outer high point (with feet on the vertical face).

Cleaver Boulder (#75)

An 11' tall cool, slightly leaning overhung fin.

V5ss Cleaver ★
Right hand on arête, left hand on tiny face crimps.

172   MT HOOD ZONE (NORTH)

LL Boulders — Middle Talus, Stone 73, 74, 75

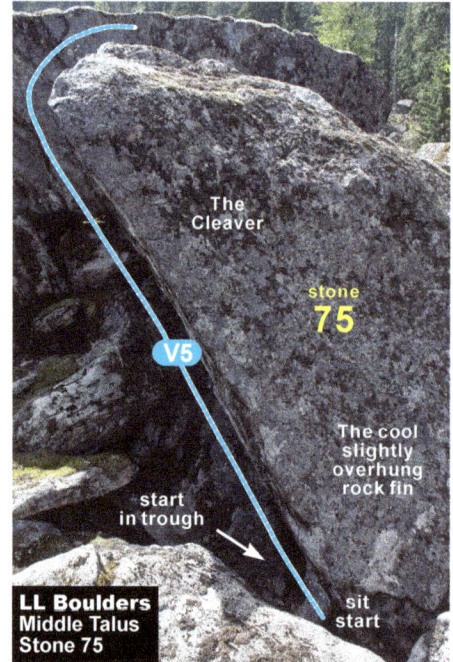

LL Boulders, Middle Talus, Stone 75

SECTION TWO

DYNOSAURUS CLUSTER

The following group of stones is quite popular, and if you're desiring to tackle some goals in the middle talus field, then this zone is a likely spot to visit first or second (for it encompasses the famous House Boulder and other large stones all near the tall fir trees at the west edge of the talus).

Descend a talus path from the paved road down past Runnel in the Jungle Stone to reach the main core pack of stones, then take a path branches left to reach the famous House Boulder. The stone beta descriptions here follow the same general flowing pattern.

Runnel Boulder (#76)

ON THE NORTH SIDE:

V0ss Runnel Arête ★   ☐
Begin low on right, traverse lip leftward to high point at center of stone.

V0 _____ ★   ☐
Jug to lip mantle. Sit start.

V4ss Runnel In The Jungle ★   ☐
Sit start; power up right along a thin seam on crimps, then traverse along top lip to top out.

Lost Lake Boulders ✦ PB 173

ON SOUTH SIDE OF THE STONE:

V1 Jungle Arête ☐

V0 Jungle Juice ☐

Boulder #77

V3ss Caught Inside ★ ☐

Sit start at incut jug, then power to the right horizontally and up a rounded rail, with feet on a vertical section of rock. This route is on the northwestern aspect of the stone.

ON THE SOUTH ASPECT:

V_ _____ ☐

V_ _____ ☐

Several minor futuristic problems.

Boulder #78

V_ _____ ☐

V_ _____ ☐

Boulder #79

V_ _____ ☐

Boulder #80

Potential VB-V3, all sit start.

V_ _____

V_ _____

V_ _____

Boulder #81

V_ _____
Minor on west face slab.

V_ _____
Possible sit start problem on north aspect.

Megasaur Boulder (#82)

On the south aspect:

V5ss The Bitter End ★
The ultra quality south face problem on a slightly overhung crimpy face. Involves using many holds, and finishing along the high left rail to the top apex of the rock.

On the west aspect:

VB _____
West side, left part of the slab.

VB _____
West side, center slab.

VB _____
West side, and the right portion of the slab.

On the east aspect of this stone:

VB _____
East side, left section.

VB _____
East side, right section.

Boulder #83

V3 (?) _____
A short small sit start problem on a jutting out blob of rock that is facing north.

Jurassic Boulder (#84)

V1 Rust Spot ★
Sit start and go straight up the well manicured flat east face.

Lost Lake Boulders ✦ PB 175

V2 _____
South end rail; keep feet on vertical face.

VB _____
North end rail and slab.

Boulder #85

V_ _____

Boulder #86

This stone is abutting up against the next stone at an angle. All are sit start lines. Beta is listed from left to right.

V4ss Nook
Tucked in a tight nook on the back side of the same block.

V3ss Bona Fide ★
Ascend outer face using both prows.

V2ss Caveat Emptor ★
Use one prow only.

V2ss Inebrians
Use the right face only.

Boulder #87

V5ss Dynosaurus ★
Powerful short vertical face with a slight offset corner. Sit start problem.

Boulder #88

V_ _____

Permian Boulder (#89)

VB-V0 Dinosaur
Ultra short problems tucked in a low pit (all three variants are sit start V0, V0, VB).

Boulder #90

V_ _____

Neolith Boulder (#91)

This tall stone actually has six problems, though none are beyond ordinary. Beta is left to right beginning on the west aspect.

VB _____
Climb the left part of the tall slab.

VB _____
Climb the right part of a tall slab.

V0 _____ ★
Tricky move with vertical start, then up slab.

176 MT HOOD ZONE (NORTH)

And three minor basic runs on east aspect.

VB _____ ☐

VB _____ ☐

VB _____ ☐

Mother Earth Boulder (#92)

A superb quality stone with a cool scallop-shaped overhanging scoop on the west face.

V2 Jack of all Trades ★ ☐
Steep line on the left part of the west facing aspect.

V0 Queen of Hearts ★ ☐
The stellar slightly hung nose, doing it all straight on.

V2 Royce Rolls ★ ☐
Super stellar problem. Sit start pulling upon a series of nice holds on a slightly overhung inner scoop of rock, then reach up left to the rounded top of the stone to finish.

Lost World Boulder (#93)

Has a cool overhung east aspect with a low trough under the stone.

V3 The Pit & Pendulum ★ ☐
Crawl into the trough under the stone, then power up the face with left hand high on the left rail.

V3 Sleeper ★ ☐
Sit start, beginning slightly right of the previous route. Climb a vertical face using a series of sloped holds.

Boulder #94

V_ _____ ☐

Mesozoic Boulder (95)

A set of short lines, best done as sit starts.

V2ss Friends ★ ☐
Sit start and ascend the left prow.

LL Boulders Middle Talus Stone 89 (Permian)

LL Boulders Middle Talus Stone 92

Lost Lake Boulders ✦ PB 177

V0ss Family Affair ★
Sit start and climb the center face.

VB _____
The rightmost face problem.

Boulder #96
Short stone with several minor north side options.

V_ _____

V_ _____

Boulder #97

V_ _____

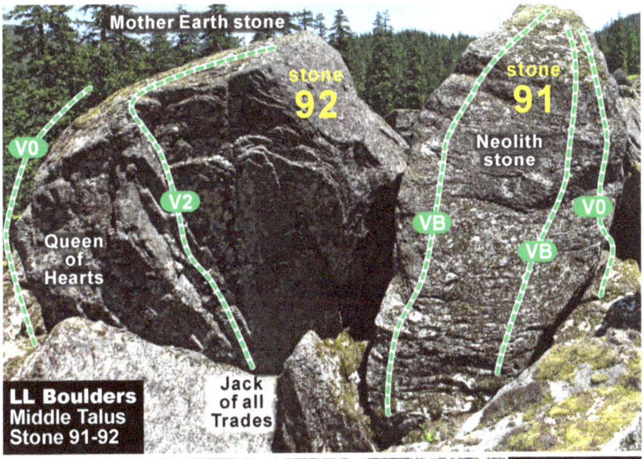

Triassic Boulder (#98)
Has eight problems all around entire stone, mostly minor warmup stuff on a short boulder, and all are sit starts.

V1 Brink of Decay ★
Interesting short hung prow on the southwest aspect.

VB Thought Control
On the north aspect.

VB Erudite Thumbsuckers
On the north side.

VB Double Standard
Situated on the NE point.

VB Smidgeonette of Idiocy
Located on the east side.

VB Idiot Proof
Located on SE point.

VB Get Down
It's on the south aspect.

VB Street Warfare
Also on the south aspect.

Boulder #99

V3ss Iter Legis
One single low brief problem.

Boulder #100

V_ _____

Paleozoic Boulder (#101)

178   MT HOOD ZONE (NORTH)

V4ss Tales from the Crypt ★
The short slightly overhung west face. Sit start.

VB _____

VB _____

Boulder #102

A short west aspect may yield something.

V_ _____

Boulder #103

V_ _____

V_ _____

FULL HOUSE

Full House Boulder (#104)

The ultimate reason to visit Lost Lake Boulders. This stone is impressive, quite large, and it's loaded with a fine host of problems all the way around it. Beta begins on the left west aspect and is described going rightward, counter-clockwise, ending on the north aspect.

V0 Stairway to Kevin's ★
First problem, located on the west face.

V0 Knockin' on Kevin's Door ★

The second problem, also located on the west face.

V1 Kevin's Gate ★
The prominent southwest arête.

LL Boulders
Middle Talus
Stone 95

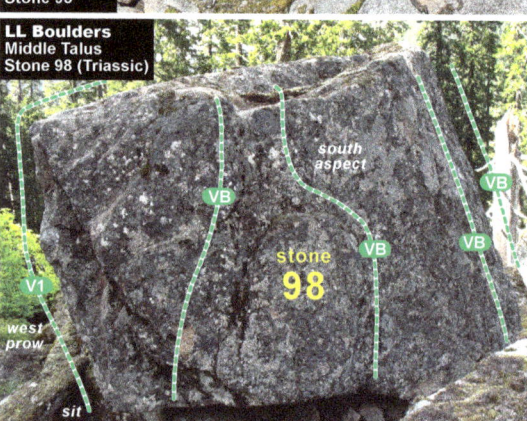

LL Boulders
Middle Talus
Stone 98 (Triassic)

V3 Raven ★
The classic south face (just left of center). Superb sequential crimpy moves on a flat vertical tall face.

V7 Borst Problem ★
This is at the very center of the flat vertical face.

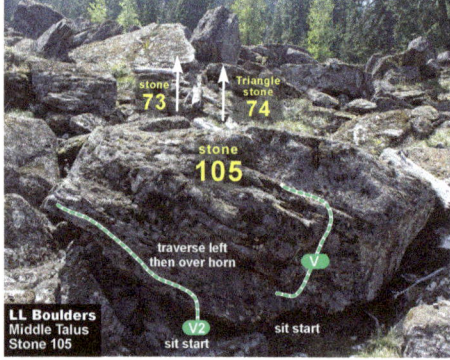

LL Boulders
Middle Talus
Stone 105

LL Boulders
Middle Talus
Stone 106

Lost Lake Boulders ✦ PB 179

Lost Lake Boulders
Topo O: Full House

stone #104

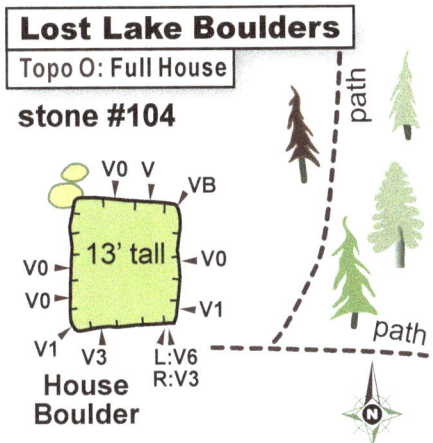

House Boulder

A few moves into the problem it abruptly cuts hard left into Raven at mid-height.

V3 Poe Arête ★

Located on the south face on the right side quite near the arête. Start on the face (just left of the arête), then transition onto arête. And it's V6 if taking the midway left split variation which stays on the face for the remainder of the ascent to the top.

LL Boulders
Middle Talus
Full House
Stone 104

V1 Yard Bird ★
The southeast arête using the east side entirely to the top.

V0 The Plate ★
East face crimps going up past a 'plate'. of rock on a slightly less than vertical face.

VB Bull Run ★
The basic northeast blunt low angled arête.

V0 (?)
North face in the very center of the angled slab.

V0 (?)
North face slab, but very close to the descent down climb steps.

EXTRANEOUS STONES:

Boulder #105
This stone is located down slope north of Stone #60 about thirty feet to the north. The stone is lowly and squat, but has several minor lines on it. Both lines are on the north aspect.

V2 [?]
Sit start, traverse left to the horn, and surmount over that horn.

VB (?)
A minor mantle up on the right part of the same north aspect.

Boulder #106
This stone is located over near #51 stone.

V1ss Tribute

V2ss Summer Breeze

V0ss Bribary

LOST LAKE BOULDERS

NORTH TALUS GROUP

Sleepy Hollow Group

The North Talus Zone (Sleepy Hollow) has been experiencing a slower route development process. Though some known grades and names are mentioned on the diagram many grades are mere raw estimates. This talus field is the furthest walk from the road, thus the refinement of the total number of routes will likely entail years of future effort. The diagram and beta listed is merely partial, focusing on some of the major boulders that are being utilized at present date. This zone has some very large boulders, several cave-like crawls under several very large stones, some hi-ball problems, and much more.

This tour describes the beta as you hike to the Dreamland stone, then northwestward past the "Pocket Cluster", and onward to the uttermost "Far North End" of the talus field.

Some colored V-scale grades in this final section are mere rough estimates of already sent lines, but will hopefully be resolved in future editions of this book.

Boulder #70 [yep!]

V0-1 (?) _____ ❏
Sit start a short problem on the east aspect of a minor low stone. Located along the XC footpath leading from the trail to the talus field.

Dreamland Boulder (#1)

The megalithic classic stone with a quality string of hi-balls (some as sit start problems). Beta begins on the north point, then east aspect, going clockwise (right to left) around the stone.

V4 (?) _____ ★ ❏
Sit start in a low trough, and power over a substantially overhung bulge. Lands upon a sloped long slab up which you will ascend to the top. North side.

V0 _____ ❏
Thin angled crack/seam on a long slab. Located on the northeastern part of this large stone.

V0 _____ ❏
Juggy angled large crack on the eastern part of this large stone.

V0 _____ ❏
Angled corner crack with obvious sloped steps for the right foot.

V4 Cody's Sister ★ ❏
Begin as a sit start and angle up left along a thin seam.

V4 Royce's Mom ★ ❏
Begin as a sit start, power up right to merge with previous line.

V3 Dreamland ★ ❏
The east face seam slanting up left. Crimp up to catch the incut crack rail, mantle, then waltz up

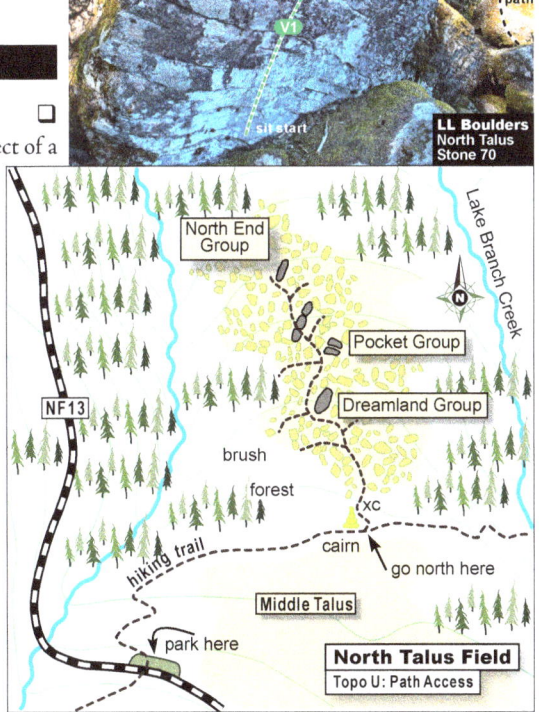

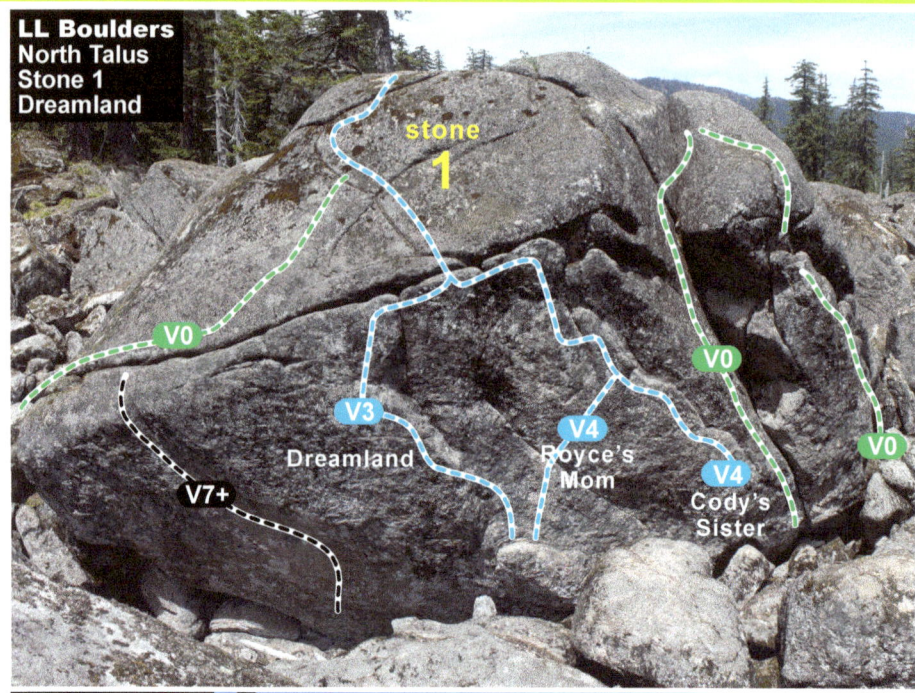

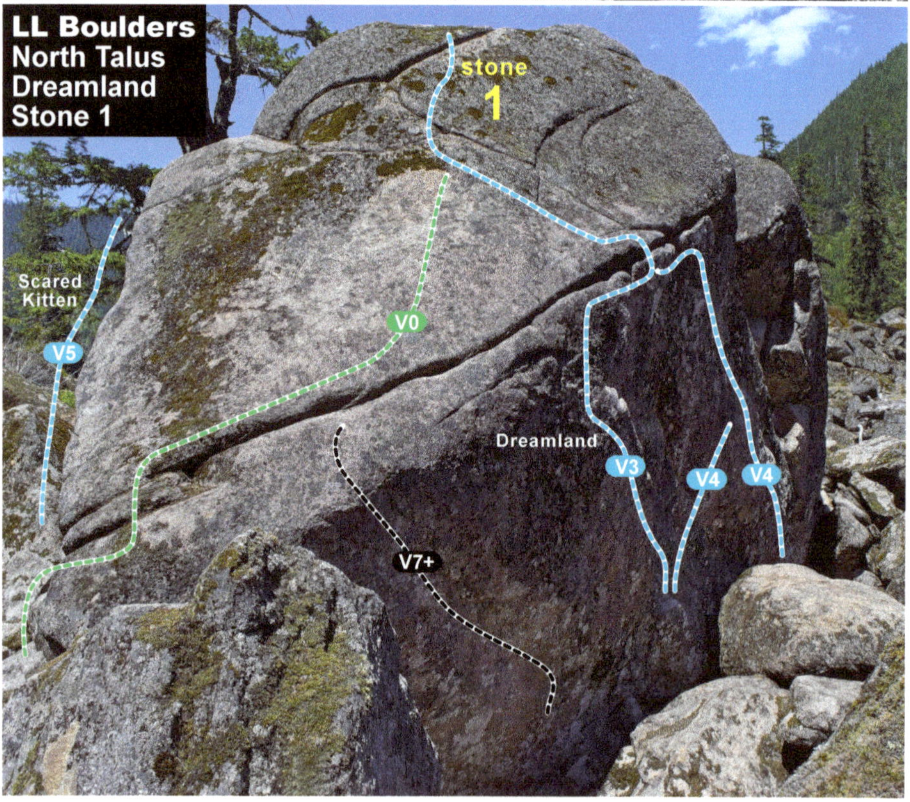

slab to top.

V0 ☐
Step over slight bulge at south tip, then cruise with feet along a crack (hands on face) up a long low angle slab (merging with Dreamland route on your way to the top of the boulder).

V5ss Scared Kittens ★ ☐
A stout line on the slightly hung SW face (sit start); use palms on a leftward rising trending rounded rail.

V2 (?) ☐
Begin just left of previous line (where the slab angles down westward) and smear onto the slab.

VB ☐
The standard down climb method getting of this giant stone using a crack on the west side.

BOULDERS 2, 3, 4, 5, 6

Boulder #2

VB ☐
South facing minor short problem.

V0 ★ ☐
Ascend the short prow.

LL Boulders
North Talus
Stone 1
Dreamland

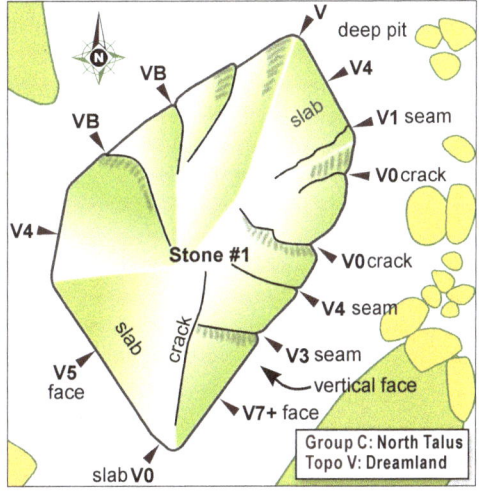

Group C: North Talus
Topo V: Dreamland

LL Boulders
North Talus
Stone 2 & 3

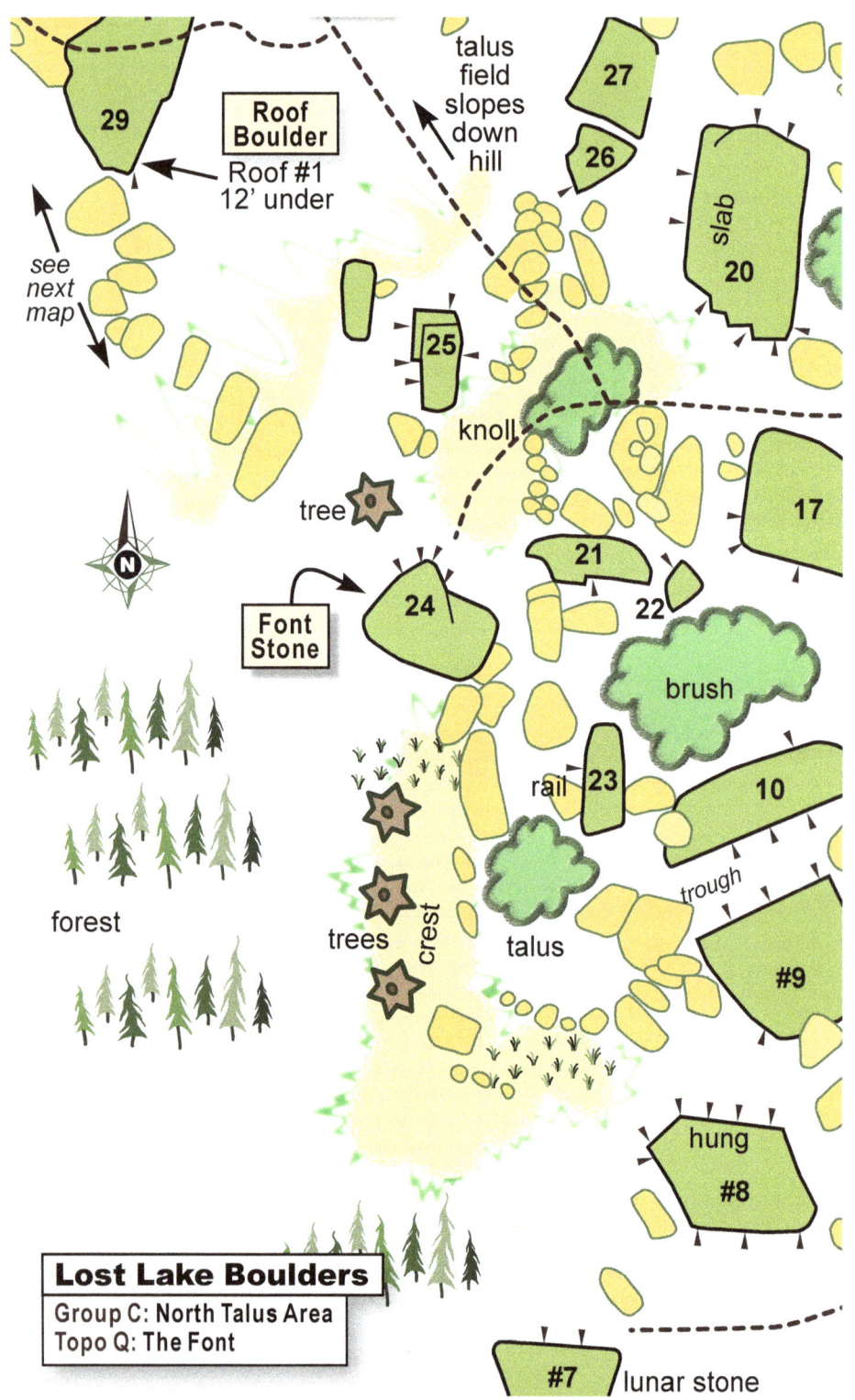

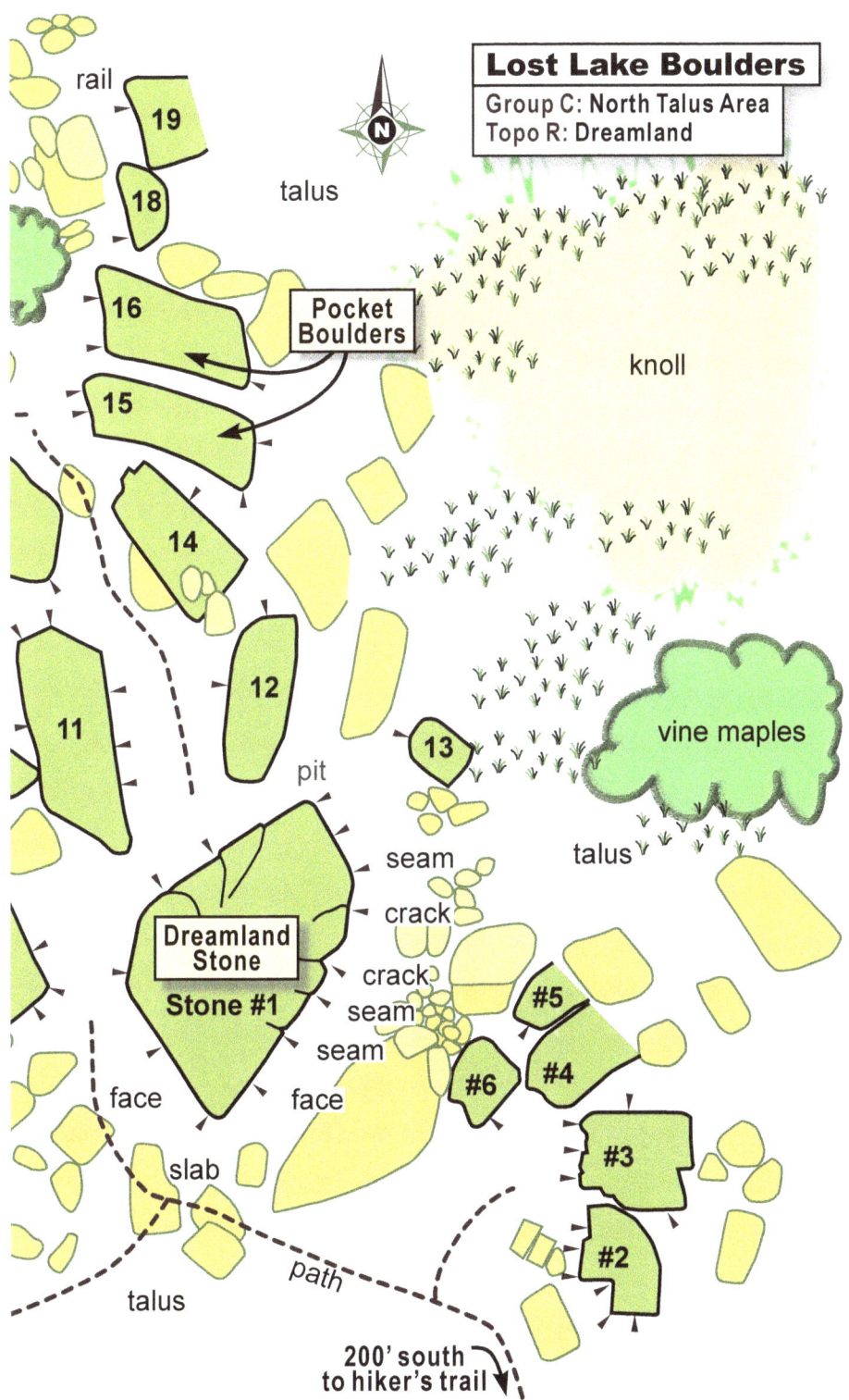

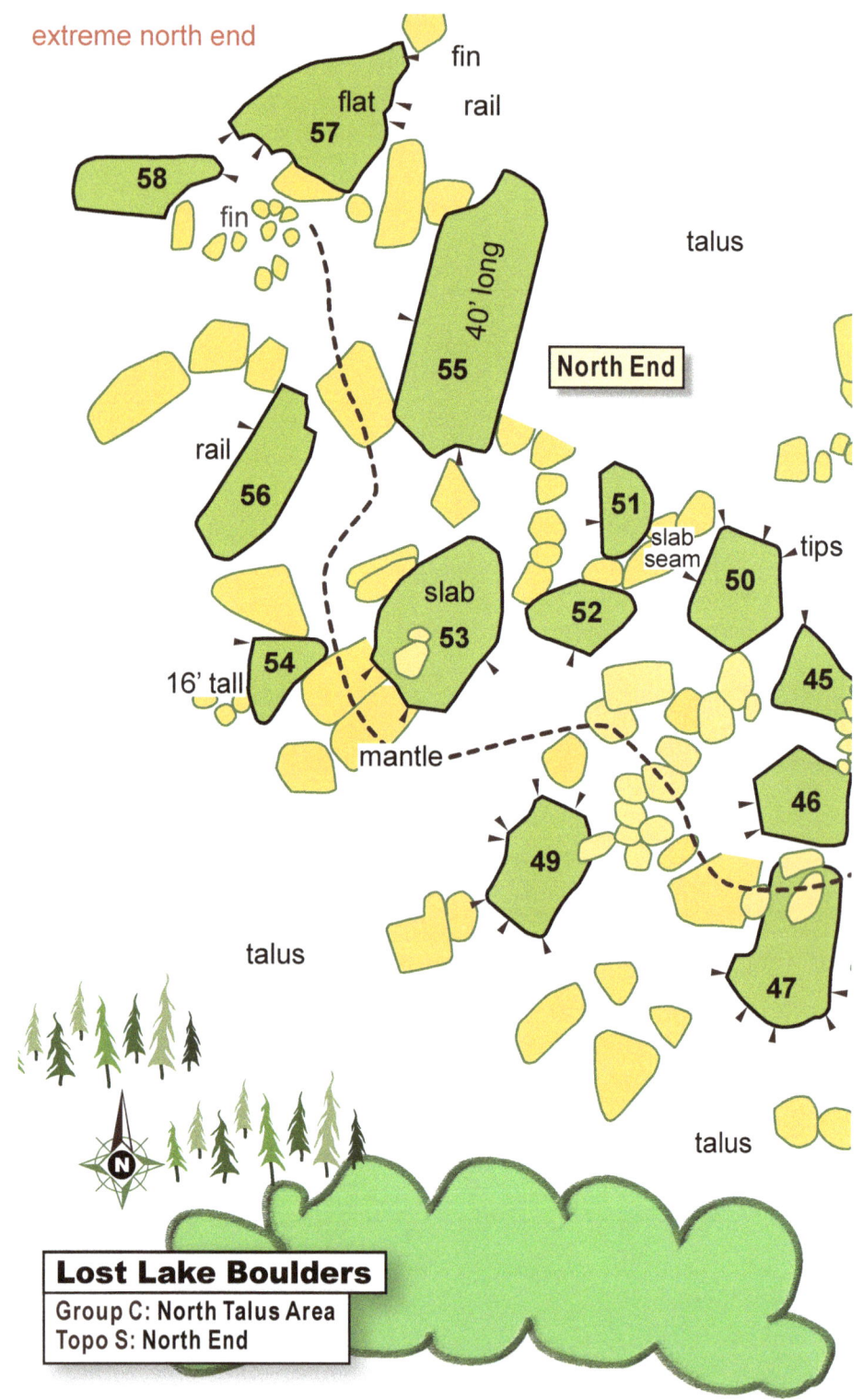

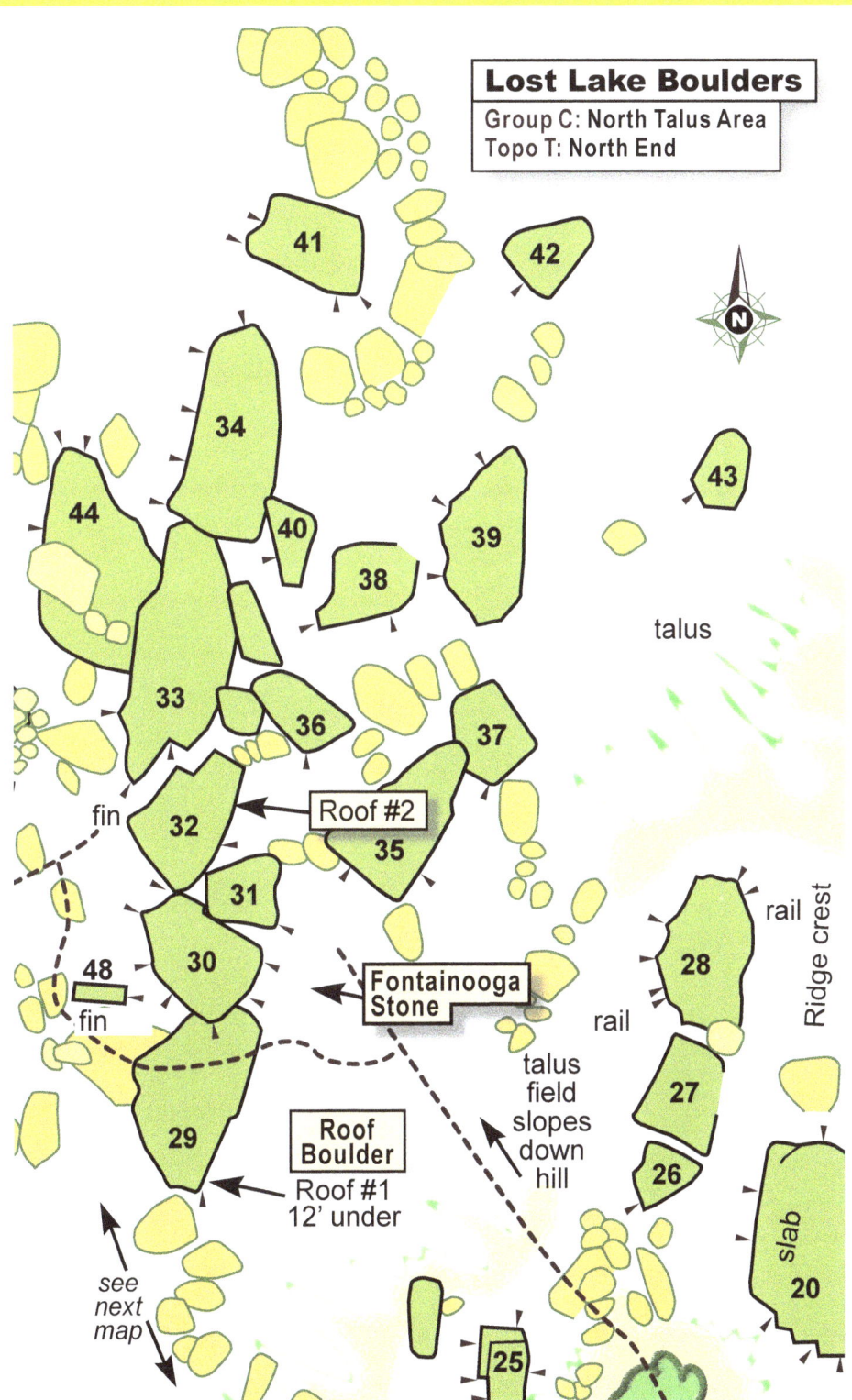

V0 ★
Climb sloped holds on the inside corner.

V0 ★
Climb a short prow.

V2 ★
Climb a slightly hung face using sloped holds.

VB ★
The leftmost last problem on Stone #2. Climb a slight hung face with left hand on a prow.

Boulder #3

V2 (?) ★
Sit start in low pit, right hand on right rail, then use various holds along the top lip, going leftward to the high point. This sole problem faces south.

V0
Minor face problem. West facing.

V0 ★
Juggy holds at a minor bulge. West facing.

V1 ★
Sit start, doing thin crimpy holds on face.

V_
May be one more viable line here.

Boulder #4

V1
Sit under the lowly pig, and muscle over it. Very short and low.

Boulder #5

VB
Minor low angle slab on south aspect.

Boulder #6

V0 ★
Smooth steep short slab that gets repeat ascents just because it looks nice.

Lunar Slab #7

Located to the southwest of Dreamland stone about seventy feet walking distance.

V2 Evening Star ★ ❏
Begin on the lower left part of the slab, smear onto the slab, then cruise up the left part of the slab.

V1 Lunar ★ ❏
Step onto the right portion of the slab and smear to the top.

Boulder #8

This is a cool looking stone uniquely overhung on several sides. The stone offers other variants beside the ones listed here.

V4 (?) _____ ★ ❏
Sit start, and power left along a sloped rail, till you reach the outer south overhung point, then power over that jutting point. South facing.

LL Boulders
North Talus
Stone 7
Lunar Slab

V5 (?) _____ ★ ❏
Begin as sit start on far left, then traverse right till you reach the central high spot, and power over the top. North facing aspect.

LL Boulders
North Talus
Stone 8

V4 (?) _____ ★ ❏
Begin as sit start under the overhung right prow, then bump a few holds up to the lip, then traverse the lip leftward till you reach the central high spot, and power over the lip to the top.

V_ _____ ❏
The west face of this stone.

Boulder #9

This stone will yield some interesting lines. The north vertical aspect of this stone is quite tall, merely because those problems begin way down in a deep trough. Beta is described clockwise beginning on the north aspect.

North Aspect:

V_ _____ ❏
North aspect – the rightmost problem.

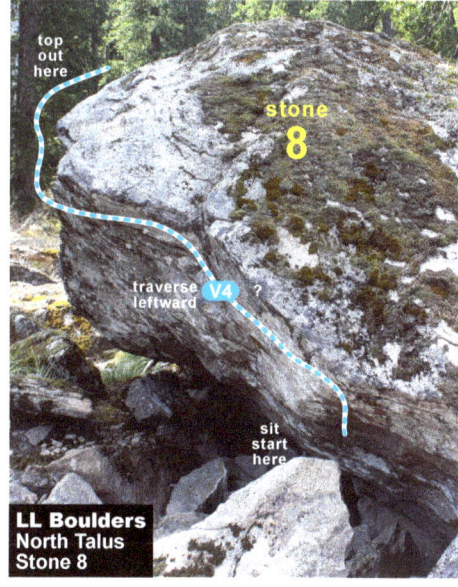

LL Boulders
North Talus
Stone 8

MT HOOD ZONE (NORTH)

V_ _____
North aspect – the middle problem.

V_ _____
North aspect – the leftmost problem.

South Aspect:

V0 (?) _____
A problem on the east face.

V3 (?) _____
Located on the east point.

V3 (?) _____
Located on the SE face.

V3 (?) _____
Located on the SW face.

Boulder #10

The stone can yield a brief selection of lines (plus maybe something on its north side).

V_ _____
On the south face.

V_ _____
On the south face.

V_ _____
On the south face.

Boulder #11

Offers a brief selection of lines.

V_ _____
On the south face.

V_ _____
On the east aspect.

V_ _____
On the east aspect.

Boulder #12

Offers a brief selection of lines.

V_ _____
On the north aspect.

V_ _____
On the west aspect.

Boulder #13

V_ _____
On the west aspect.

Boulder #14

V_ _____
On the NE aspect.

POCKET CLUSTER
Pocket Boulders

BOULDER #15 AND #16

This cluster is a great classic spot to visit. It is composed of two large side-by-side stones with unique west face aspects that provide envious entertainment. The backside of the stone will also yield a few problems.

V4 Pocket Pool ★ ❑
Sit start using both arêtes, slap up, then go right and up over point.

V3 Hole in my Pocket ★ ❑
Same sit start, but stay with the left arête, going up over the hung point.

...And the next block to the left:

V1 Apex Predator ★ ❑
The basic rounded arête.

V_ _____ ❑
The sloped left trending low rail going leftward, then up the left edge to the top.

Boulder #17

V_ _____ ❑
On the west aspect.

V_ _____ ❑
On the SW point.

V_ _____ ❑
On the south face.

V_ _____ ❑
On the SE point.

Boulder #18

V_ _____ ❑
On the west aspect.

Boulder #19

V_ _____ ❑
Interesting looking rail problem on the west aspect of this stone.

Boulder #20

Large stone with a viable selection of problems. Beta begins on the north aspect, described left to right (counterclockwise around stone).

V_ _____ ❑
On the north side.

V_ _____ ❑
On the north side.

V_ _____ ❑
On the west side slab.

V_ _____ ❑
On the west side slab.

V_ _____ ❑
Rail traverse from left to right, then top out.

V_ _____ ❑
Slightly overhung SW face using crimps.

V3 (?) _____ ❑
South point on a slight overhung bulge.

LL Boulders
North Talus
Stone 20

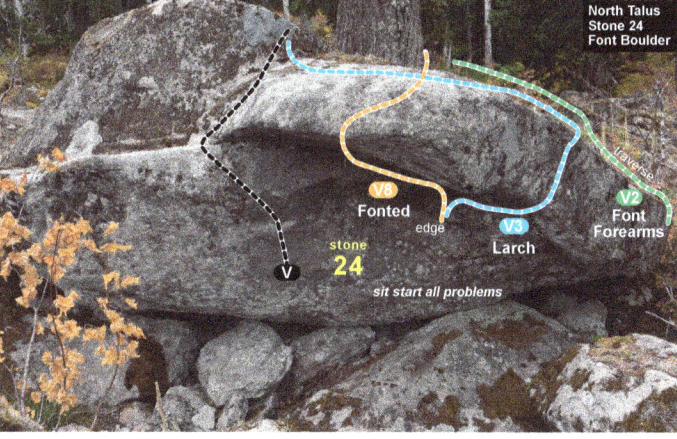

LL Boulders
North Talus
Stone 24
Font Boulder

192 MT HOOD ZONE (NORTH)

V_ _____
On the east side.

Boulder #21

V_ _____
On the south aspect.

Boulder #22

V_ _____
On the NW aspect.

Boulder #23

V_ _____
On the west aspect.

FONT FOREARM

Boulder #24

This stone is the other classic hangout spot offering fine quality low appealing lines.

V2ss Font Forearms ★

Far right, traverse sloped lip all the way around the point.

V3ss Larch Mtn Thing ★

Start on obvious edge under roof, punch out right and over.

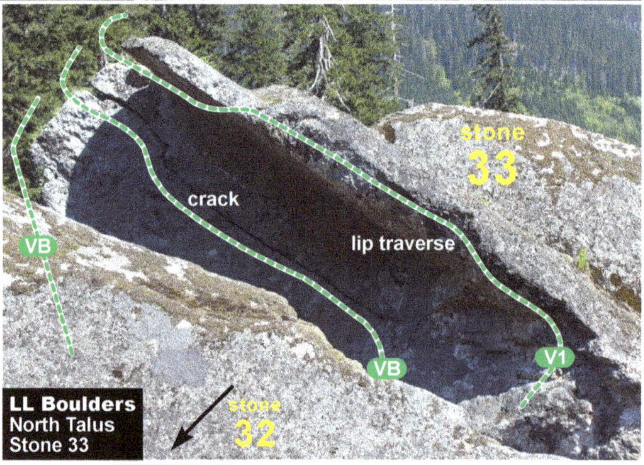

V8ss Fonted ★

Same start as above, but go left on crimps and out over roof.

V_ _____
An unfinished left trending project.

Boulder #25

Has some minor options (all tapped). Beta is left to right, beginning on the east aspect of the stone.

VB _____
On the east side.

VB _____
On the east side.

V2 _____
On the west side.

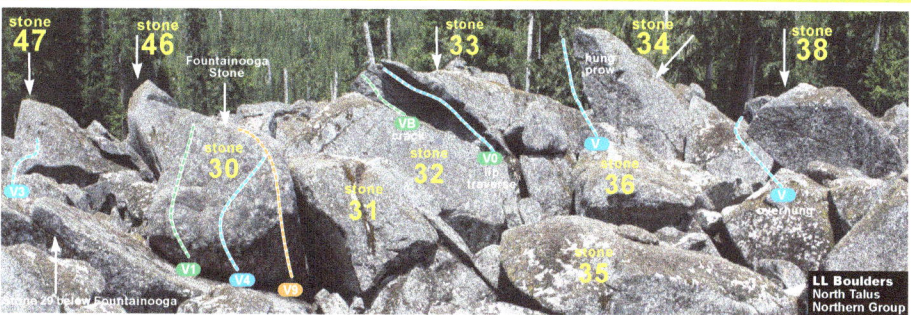

V3
On the west side.

Boulder #26

V_
On the SW aspect.

Boulder #27

V_
A minor viable problem.

Boulder #28

A large stone with a host of viable lines. Beta is described from left to right.

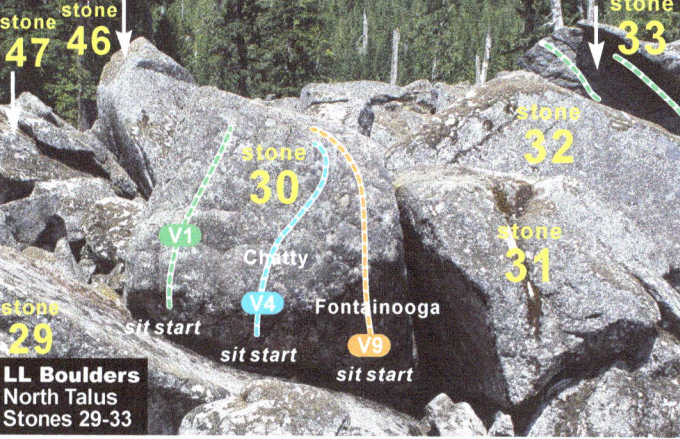

V_
Ascend the NE rail.

V_
On the north point.

V_
On the west side.

V_
On the west side.

V_
On the west side.

V_
Climb a SW rail.

FAR NORTH END ZONE

ROOF BOULDER SECTION:

Beyond a certain string of stones (Stone #24 through Stone #28) the talus field descends down a brief angled slope, then levels out onto the next final northernmost broad expansive talus zone. This section encompasses that final lower far northern zone.

Portions of this north talus field are still untapped (as of year 2024) because it entails a bit longer approach time to access, yet some boulders have seen exploratory development.

Boulder #29 (Roof)

V_
This stones underside offers a well overhung roof problem in a large cave-like crawl hole.

Fontainooga Boulder (#30)

A minor rounded block in the far north talus.

V9ss Fontainooga ★
Right low on edges, going up left on slopers on round arête.

V4ss Chatty ★
Center face starting low on slopers.

V1ss Sandstone
Left near round nose on slopers.

Boulder #31

V_ _____
Climb the SE point.

Boulder #32

THE OTHER COOL ROOF STONE:

This is the other unique well overhung roof problem in a large cave-like crawl hole.

V_ _____

Boulder #33

A large long stone with several quality entertaining lines.

VB Sharp Arête ★
Sit start and climb the sharp arête just left of the crack.

VB The Crack ★
Climb leftward out the jam crack to climb, then over onto the top.

V1 [?] Lip Traverse ★
The rounded lip traverse (going from right to left) ending at the jutting fin and crack.

Boulder #34

This is the next large long stone in a string (that series being #29 through #34). This large stone several unique problems. Beta is described left to right.

V_ _____ ★
The long west face sloped traverse going rightward to the hung prow then up that prow.

V_ _____ ★
The cool overhung prow.

V_ _____
The south face rising traverse.

Boulder #35

V_ _____
(SW aspect)

V_ _____
(SE aspect)

Boulder #36

V_ _____
Climb the south point.

Boulder #37

V_ _____ ★
Overhung south point.

Boulder #38

V_ _____ ★
The cool overhung west point.

V_ _____
Shorty on the south face.

Boulder #39

V_ _____
Something on the NW face.

V_ _____
Shorty on the west face.

Boulder #40

Lost Lake Boulders ✦ PB 195

V_ _____
Something short on west aspect.

Boulder #41

V_ _____
(west aspect)

V_ _____
(west aspect)

V_ _____
(south aspect)

V_ _____
(SE point)

Boulder #42

V_ _____
(west aspect)

Boulder #43

V_ _____
(west aspect)

Boulder #44

V_ _____
(north point)

V_ _____
(west face)

Boulder #45

V_ _____
(north point)

Boulder #46

V_ _____
(west aspect)

V_ _____
(west aspect)

Boulder #47

All problems are on the southern half of the stone. Beta is left to right.

V5-6 (?) _____ ★
Begin low on the right, and use sloped hands going left along the outer rounded lip, till you reach the upper left jugging bulge, then muscle over onto the top. Ends at the SW point.

V2 (?) _____ ★
South face crimps on a steep slab.

V_ _____
South face center of steep slab.

V3 (?) _____ ★ ☐

The SE point. Sit start on the overhung east aspect of this prow, power up onto a vertical face using crimps, landing on a low angle slab to finish.

V_ _____ ☐

Maybe something on the east face.

Boulder #48

An interesting thin rock fin tucked down in a deep trough.

V_ _____ ☐

Boulder #49

A large boulder with plenty of potential problems. Beta is described left to right beginning on the north aspect.

V_ _____ ☐
(north aspect)

V_ _____ ☐
(north point)

V_ _____ ☐
(west face)

V_ _____ ☐
(west face)

V_ _____ ☐
(SE point)

V_ _____ ☐
(south face)

V_ _____ ☐
(SE point)

Boulder #50

V_ _____ ☐
(tips on east aspect)

V_ _____ ☐
(north aspect)

V_ _____ ☐
(north aspect)

V_ _____ ☐
(west aspect)

Boulder #51

V_ _____ ☐
(west aspect)

Boulder #52

V_ _____ ☐
(south aspect)

Boulder #53

V_ _____ ☐
(SW side)

V_ _____ ☐
(mantle)

V_ _____ ☐
(east side)

Boulder #54

V_ _____ ☐
The west aspect is notably tall.

Boulder #55

A large and very long stone about thirty feet in length.

V_ _____ ☐
(west side slab)

V_ _____ ☐
(south aspect)

Boulder #56

V_ _____ ☐
A cool looking long low rail problem on the west aspect.

Boulder #57

V_ _____ ☐
(west point)

V_ _____ ☐
(west face)

V_ _____ ☐
Climb the rail.

V_ _____ ☐
Climb the short east point.

Boulder #58

V_ _____ ☐
A low rock fin juts out on the east part of this stone.

Select Additional Bouldering Sites

This chapter describes a brief number of select bouldering sites that exist in or near the Columbia River Gorge, yet were not included into PB Volume 1 book. During that next journey out of town when you're aiming for that next bouldering destination, add one of these sites to your list.

SASQUATCH HIDEAWAY

Considered to be one of the unique gems of this region, the super cool quality overhung cave-like 'hideaway' is the remnant of an old lava tube where the roof of the short low cave has remained intact (though not very deep). The inner depth of the cave opening reaches back about 25' and may yield more futuristic very low roof bouldering. The popular problems all begin near the outer lip and power a few moves out the cave lip then up the vertical outer face to the top. The little haven, in-total, yields a stellar series of ultra fun, juggy, thuggy, rambling road show entertainment that everyone is sure to enjoy. If only the site were a little closer to Portland....yet, if you can endure the drive time getting there, then definitely put this little haven on your must-do tick list.

Directions:

From the WA State Route 14 at its junction near Carson WA, drive north on Wind River Highway for 1 mile to the 4-way intersection in the center of the small town of Carson WA. From the 4-way intersection drive the Wind River Highway north for 4.8 miles. Drive east on the Old State Road for 500-feet east (about 1/10 mile), then turn left, and drive north on Panther Creek road for 2.7 miles. Where Warren Gap road meets Panther Creek road the road numbering system changes to Forest Service road NF65. Drive north on NF65 for 8.1 miles (it's a curvy road that gains elevation) till you reach a 4-way intersection (of Carson Guller Road), then continue north on NF65 another 1.9 miles. At a 'Y' go left and drive on NF67 for a total of 1.7 miles to the parking spot (the road initially goes north but trends abruptly west (at NF6701). Both NF6701 and NF121 are on the right, and NF122 and NF123 are on the left. The parking spot is just west beyond NF123.

The parking spot is located on NF67 road (this is about 300' west of the NF123 cutoff). The parking spot is a 1/3 mile west of the NF122 turnoff used to access Three Ravens Boulders. Walk NE for 450' to the south facing cave-like structure.

GPS parking spot locale alongside the gravel road is UTM 10t 586325 5087080.

GPS for Sasquatch Hideaway locale is UTM 10t 586373 5087222.

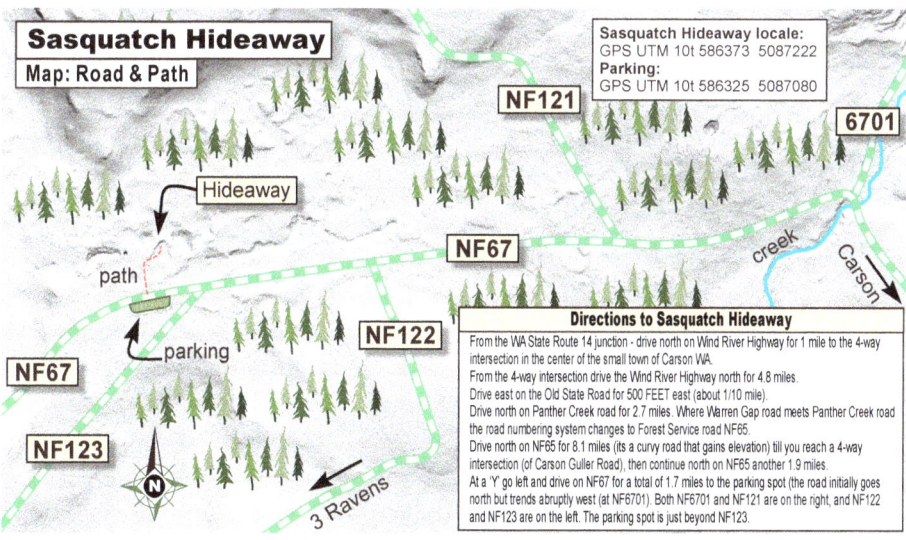

COLUMBIA GORGE

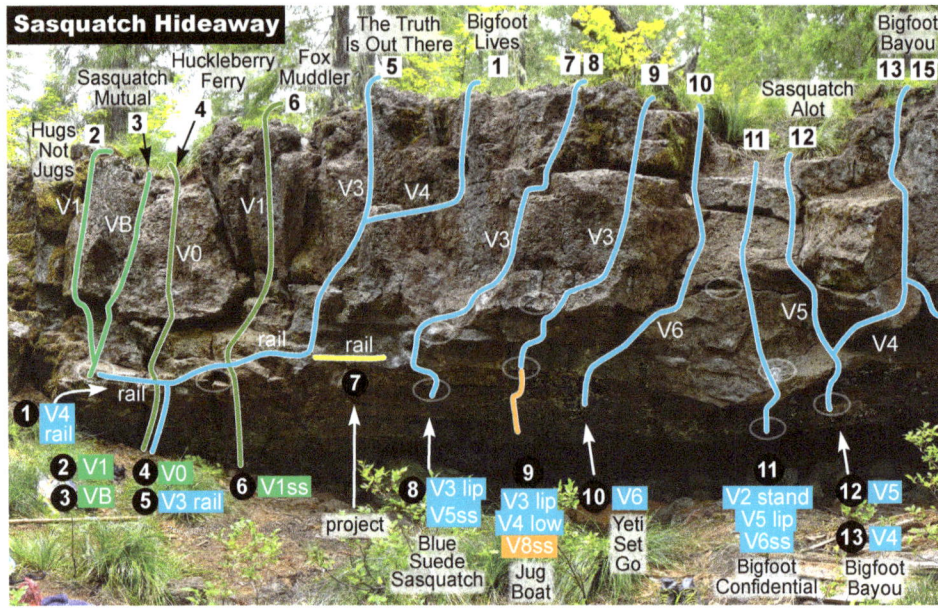

SASQUATCH HIDEAWAY BETA:

1. V4 Bigfoot Lives
Ultra long traverse rail that gains height going from left to right. Traverse rail right then follow right ward jugs to top.

2. V1 Hugs Not Jugs
Climb the arête.

3. VB Sasquatch Mutual
Climb the corner.

4. V0 Huckleberry Ferry
Climb the face.

5. V3 The Truth Is Out There
Traverse right along the rail then go straight up the face to the top.

6. V1ss Fox Muddler
Climb the overhung arête.

7. V_ project
Traverse right on rail stay low under mini roof then across face up and right to top out.

8. V3 (lip) Blue Suede Sasquatch
This problem has two starting options (V3 lip start or V5 sit start). Start low under roof on jug and do a big move to lip then up and right on the natural feature to top. Start at lip or begin as sit start.

9. V3 (lip start) Jug Boat
This problem has three distinct starting spots (V3 lip, V4 low start, or V8 sit start). Start super low on two two fingure pockets 4 hard moves tow two jugs then one big move to lip then up face.

10. V6 Yeti Set Go
Start low on to pockets throw to bottom crack then follow crack corner to top.

11. V2 (stand) Bigfoot Confidential
This problem has three distinct starting spots (V2 standing start, V5 lip start, or V6 sit start.). Start very low and throw to low lip slopper then lock off and throw up face to jug climb face.

12. V5 Sasquatch Alot
Start on low jug, and climb the left side of the feature.

13. V4 Bigfoot Bayou
Start on low jug and climb the right side of the feature.

14. V4 (V5ss) In Jugs We Trust
This problem has two distinct starting spots (V4 low edge, or V5 sit start). Start at low edge of deep roof on crimp and right corner big move to jug lip the straight out roof to lip and up middle of face.

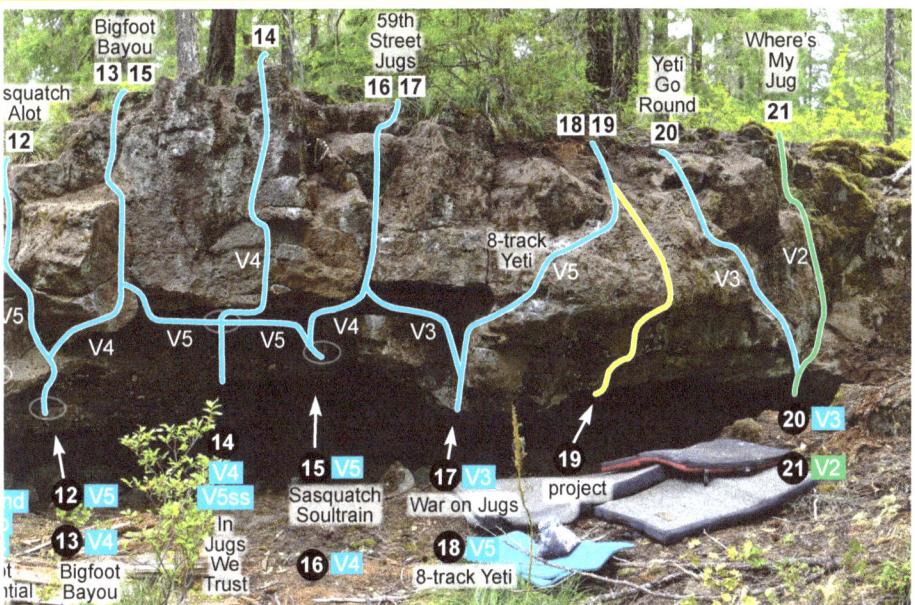

15. V5 Sasquatch Soultrain ☐
Start on corner feature in back of roof on the right side climb left to corner the up corner feature to top.

16. V4 59th Street Jugs ☐
Start in back up roof on right side climb right side out to corner then up to top.

17. V3 War on Jugs ☐
Start on low hanging jug and throw left to jug the up corner to top.

18. V5 8-Track Yeti ☐
Start on low jug and right low rail then up and right to slopper and big move to slopper the up and right on ramp.

19. V_ Project micro crimps ☐
An unfinished project.

20. V3 Yeti Go Round ☐
Climb left leaning holds up ramp to top.

21. V2 Where's My Jugs ☐
Climb up the slopers on the face.

X BOULDERS

A unique, complex packed core of quality large blocks on a south-facing sunny talus slope below the infamous Jimmy Cliff. The site offers numerous smooth basaltic stones (with no noticable phenocrysts in a deep gray matrix) that originated from the lower portion of the lava flow. Many stones (with a grittier andesitic plagioclase matrix) originated from the upper portion of the lava flow, tumbled down to intermingle into the complex. Rock nuances: crimps, smooth faces, sharp ribs, long overhung power lines, and VB slabs. Estimated to be 100+ potential problems in one primary condensed area in the initial 300' of talus slope. Only agile footed persons with diligent scrambling abilities should venture here initially, because the site has considerable jagged smaller talus debris. Seasonally, the snow may linger at this elevation until early-May, but a lengthy season of bouldering can be attained until November. Expect it to be hot in mid-summer, and on windless days. Two to three crashpads are wise, but in time the landings will likely be adjusted. As of 2016 the boulders were virtually untapped. Conveniently close to Portland (1 hour drive), no poison oak, yet site does have scenic views.

Directions

From State Route 14 at Beacon Rock, drive north on Kueffler Road (set your odometer and drive exactly 5.1 miles). This road (at 2 miles) turns to gravel on CG1400 road. Stay on this main gravel road. At 5.1 miles the road veers left abruptly, but you will turn right into a small pullout onto an old logging skid road. Park here or drive a short distance along the skid road and park at its end. The trail initially drops down to the east but becomes very apparent on a nice path that walks mostly horizontally east to the bluff in ¼ mile.

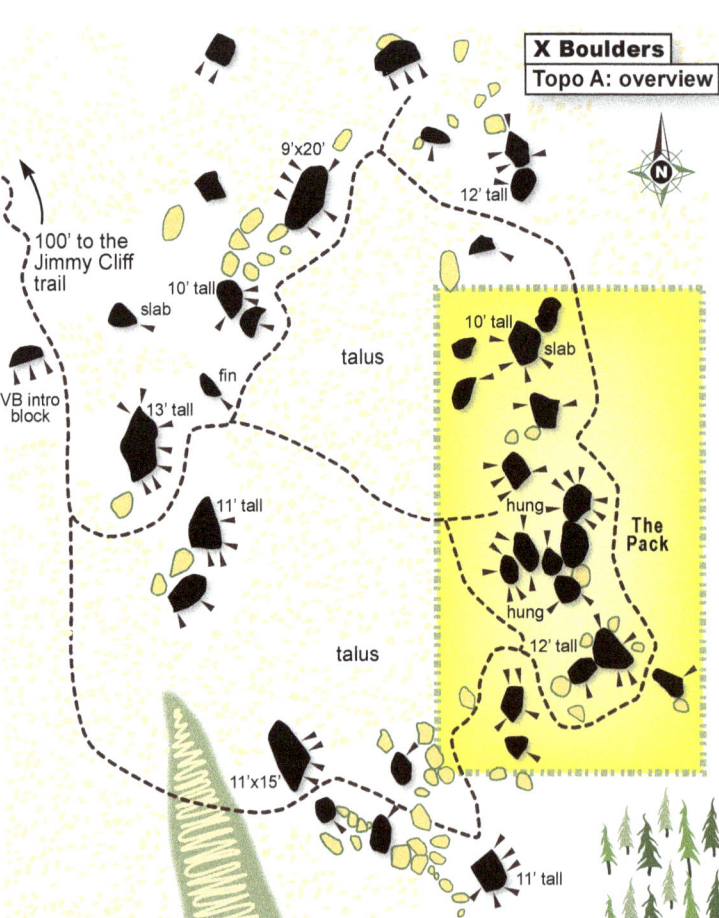

ROWENA BOULDERS

When you least expect to find roadside bouldering in this region, well here it is. Western Oregon winter weather tends to be inclement - especially in the Columbia Gorge - and on those occassions just drive to the eastside of the Cascade mountains to escape the incessant rain, to the Rowena bouldering site. This site will greet you like a long lost friend - a tiny haven packed with a variety of low-ball and hi-ball lines, and power crimp pinch-fests to fit your mid-winter bouldering routine.

Though the boulders are composed of basalt rock (which in this region tend to be smooth and slick) the slabby and vertical problems often yield a selection of ideal cruiser problems. But it's the overhung sections of stone that quickly yield stoutly powerful problems. Access couldn't be simpler - merely park the car, walk a few feet, and go bouldering.

During the Spring season anticipate some ticks, and during the Spring through Summer seasons expect vigorous low growing twigs of poison oak (mainly at the lower zone below the road) - the primary point being to use the Rowena bouldering site during the late Fall and Winter seasons.

Directions:

Drive east from Portland on I-84 freeway past Hood River. Exit at #76, then drive back west uphill on the Historical Columbia River Highway (U.S. Hwy 30) for 1.75 miles. Park along the shoulder of the road in a large gravel pullout. A massive roadside boulder will be obvious on the west side of the road at a gravel pullout. The site is located amidst a long series of 'S' road curves, in a talus slope created from an east facing rock cliff scarp. The cliff scarp tends to create a little wind-protected shadow, ideal for off-season bouldering opportunities.

To access the lower boulder zone below the road, you will need to walk (north) up the road for about 350' then step over the guardrail and descend down a talus slope to a cluster of oak trees.

The Tom McCall - Rowena overlook scenic area is atop the bluff to the immediate west. The boulders are located within the

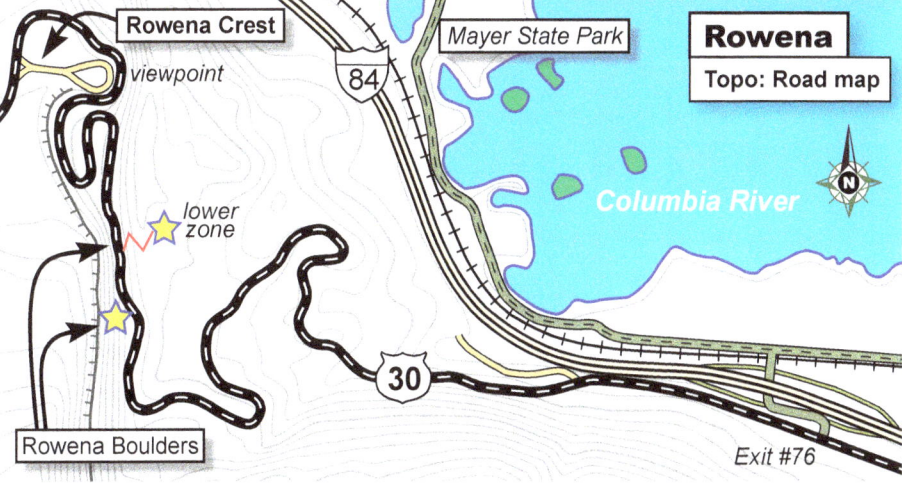

204 COLUMBIA GORGE

southwest zone of Mayer State Park.

Upper main area: GPS utm 10t 632510 5059638

The lower stone: GPS utm 10t 632530 5059824

MAIN TALUS ZONE

The first and most obvious goal is the Oak Tree Boulder, a massive square-shaped giant with a plethora of 360-degrees worth of hi-ball problems (and a few shorty's) packed all the way around it. The beta is described counter-clockwise beginning with the problem on the north side nearest to the oak tree. Some of the hi-ball problems range up to a very spicey 19' tall, so use extra crashpads if venturing high.

Oak Tree Boulder (A)

This is the noble giant boulder, a behemoth that sits right next to the paved road, and is so obviously well placed that it beckons all boulderers to a bit of fun on a brisk cold winter day.

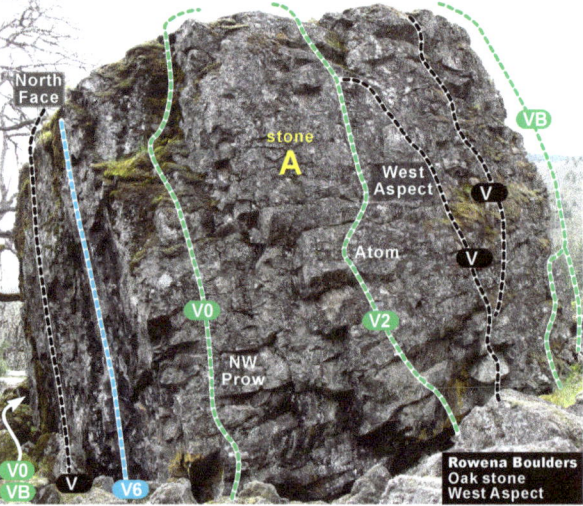

Rowena Boulders

Topo A: Upper zone

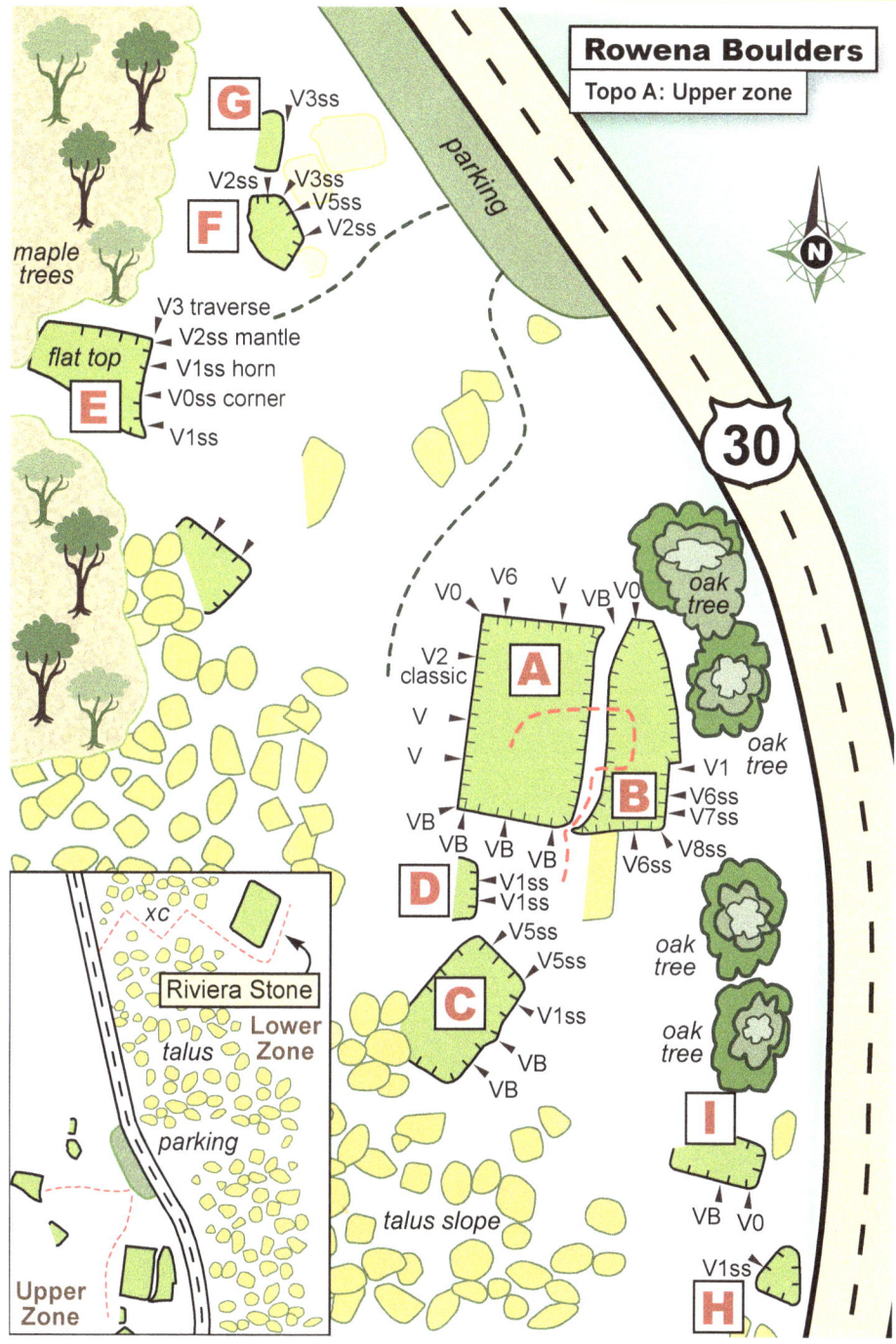

NORTH SIDE:

V0 Digital Huckster
Jug party route right next to the tree on a hung prow that ends by stepping into the slot. This line is actually on Rowena Boulder at its far northern tip.

VB Get Down
North side fat slot down climb.

206 COLUMBIA GORGE

Rowena Boulders
Oak Stone
West Aspect

stone A

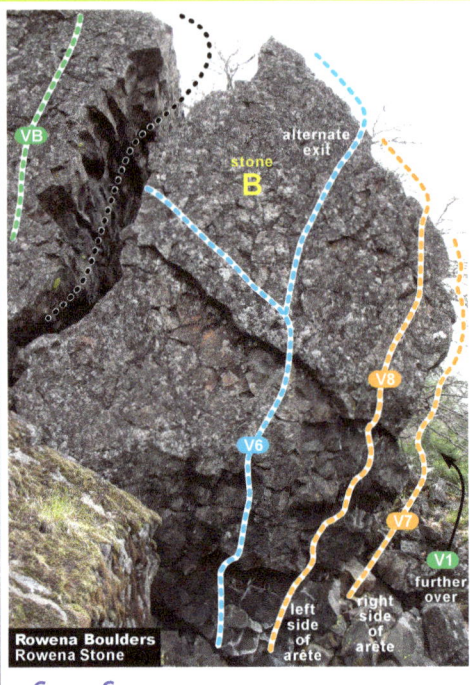

stone B
alternate exit

Rowena Boulders
Rowena Stone

V_
North hung face with crimps. Short and hard.

V6
Slightly hung face with powerful crimps on the north side of this big stone.

West Side:

V0 NW Prow
This is a cool hi-ball prow, but still a reasonable send on mostly large holds.

V2 Atom
The classic west face (on the left part) using unique crimps and foot slopers, but gives a spook when you hit the mid-height crux which is a long reach to a crimp.

V_
The center part of the west face yields this powerful send. Merges at mid-height leftward into the previous line.

V_
A potential hi-ball on the right part of the tall west face.

South Side:

VB Spiked
The SW arête. Blocky, hollow, but basic and hi-ball (two variant starts).

VB Bokeh Monster
The south face with large fun run jugs.

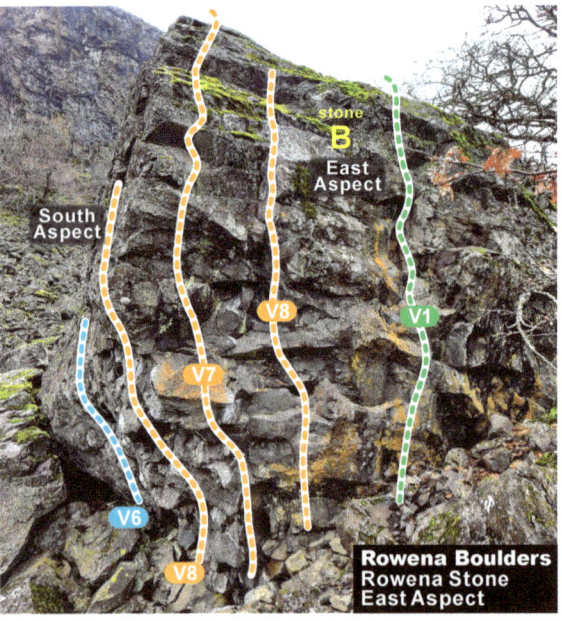

stone B
South Aspect
East Aspect

Rowena Boulders
Rowena Stone
East Aspect

VB Imperium
The other south face jugs fun run, but stay immediately left of the fat slot. Viable as an optional down climb, too.

VB Barbarian
Enter the fat slot, then get up onto the east block (Rowena block), then step over the gap onto the summit slab of the global giant. This is the common get down method.

Rowena Boulder (B)

SOUTHEAST / EAST SIDE:
This set of problems is located on the separate chunk of boulder (that creates a fat slot seperating it from the Oak Boulder giant). These are the money problems, like pure gold, quality, powerful, utterly cool stuff. Beta is described left to right.

V6ss
Powerful crimps just left of the hung arête create the ultra majestic power line. Eases when you reach the mid-height crimps. Can exit left at midway or finish direct to top.

V8ss Dynomite
Ascend the powerful overhung arête straight on beginning as a sit start.

V7ss Gravitational Pull
Immediately on the right aspect of the same hung arête, use a hung powerful sequence reaching up to catch the high crimps and arête (with left hand), then continue to top.

V1 Tick Bite
The east side of this stone. First move

is crux reaching to get established on a high hold.

Lizard Boulder (C)

Quality boulder located a mere 30' southwest of the global giant (Oak Boulder). The stone offers an excellent set of problems; most are sit start short, but with quality movement. The first two problems are on the slightly hung aspect; the easy problems are on the slabby left aspect of this stone. The beta is described *Right to Left* beginning with the hardest two problems.

V5ss E=MC² ☐
Sit start, then climb slightly hung powerful crimps using the slight hung rib.

V4/5ss E=HF ☐
Sit start, and punch up a slight overhang on powerful crimps (use left hand on the left prow) getting to the lip, then get over the lip.

V1ss Lizard ☐
Start low and crimp along near the north overhang (which is on your immediate right). Your right hand and right foot will be touching near part of the right outer prow.

VBss Tribute ☐
Basic jugs and steps.

VBss Bribary ☐
Basic steps and a reach.

Boulder (D)

V1ss Little Backward ☐

V1ss Bare Essentials ☐
Both very short. Plus two more brief variants built on the initial two problems.

The next string of stones are located directly uphill from the roadside parking spot.

Galaxy Boulder (E)

A seemingly small hung scooped boulder, but yes its got quality. This is the furthest stone uphill above the parking lot, yet when you waltz up to it and do the lines you realize just how fun these little gems are. Beta is listed Left to Right.

V1ss Time Warp ☐
On far left, minor move pulling left around lip.

V0ss Tsunami ☐
Start very low in center of stone, and bump up center corner to lip, and pull over lip using crimps. Fun line.

V1ss Extra Flavor ☐
Start on the obvious small jutting horn, then moving left to the crack (the next route), then up 'n over. Excellent problem.

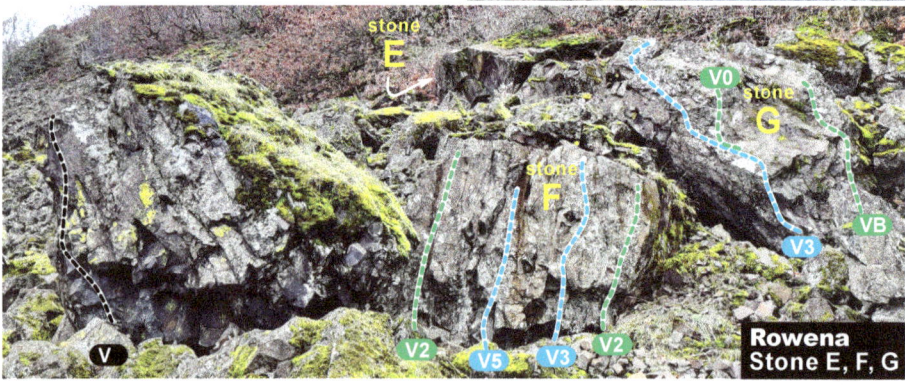

Rowena Stone E, F, G

V2ss Pororoca
On the right aspect of this stone, crimp an obvious incut, mantle over lip onto slab.

THE TRAVERSE:

V3ss Black Hole
This is the entire traverse. Start on the far right, and cruise leftward along the lip, and exit either at the center crack (V2ss) or go all the way exiting left for the full deal (V3ss).

Andromeda Boulder (F)

A short flat faced aspect directly facing the road with a flat top. About 20' from the parking area. Beta is listed Left to Right.

V2ss Noble Flaws
On the far left climb a near vertical face using the leftmost outer prow.

V5ss Rebel with a Cause
Sit start. Climb a seam weakness using various odd basalt cobble pinches.

V2ss Lost in Translation
Pinch and crimp the various odd basalt cobble blocks in the center of face.

V3ss Arcane World
It's hung just under the foot, but use crimps and pinches on face.

VB (V2ss) Methinks
On the far right north facing aspect is a 'lil minor.

Boulder (G)

NEXT DOOR MINOR

A minor stone right next door to the previous boulder. Beta is listed Left to Right.

V3ss Unlimited Reason
Traverse left along the entire lip.

V0ss Escape from Reason
Same traverse, but exit early.

VBss Say What

The next two lil' minor stones are located at the southernmost part of the Rowena cluster.

Road Dust Boulder (H)

A minor hung pipsqueek right under the car tires (next to eastbound lane).

V1ss Absentmindability
Start low on crimps, bump to incuts along top and get up over it.

Broken Boulder (I)

VB and V0 Broken
Minor left face, and broken blocky right face.

LOWER TALUS ZONE

From the gravel pullout, walk north up the paved road for about 300 feet, then go down

Rowena Boulders Riviera stone classic north prow

V6
V7
3
V6
4
V9
5
V7
6
V3
traverse
7
1
sit
V8
sit
V10
2
sit
sit
Rowena Boulders
Riviera Stone

11
12
13
sit
V8
V7
stand
V0
V3
VB
Jug
traverse
VB
traverse
V2
10
7
V3
13
V7 stand
V8 sit
8
9
Rowena Boulders
Riviera Stone

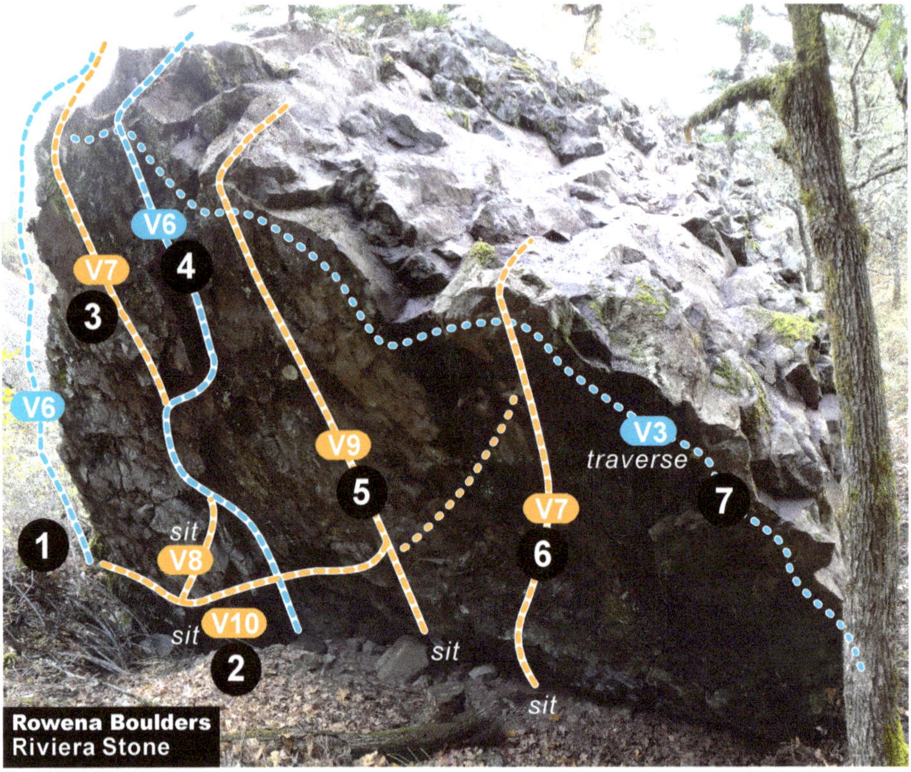

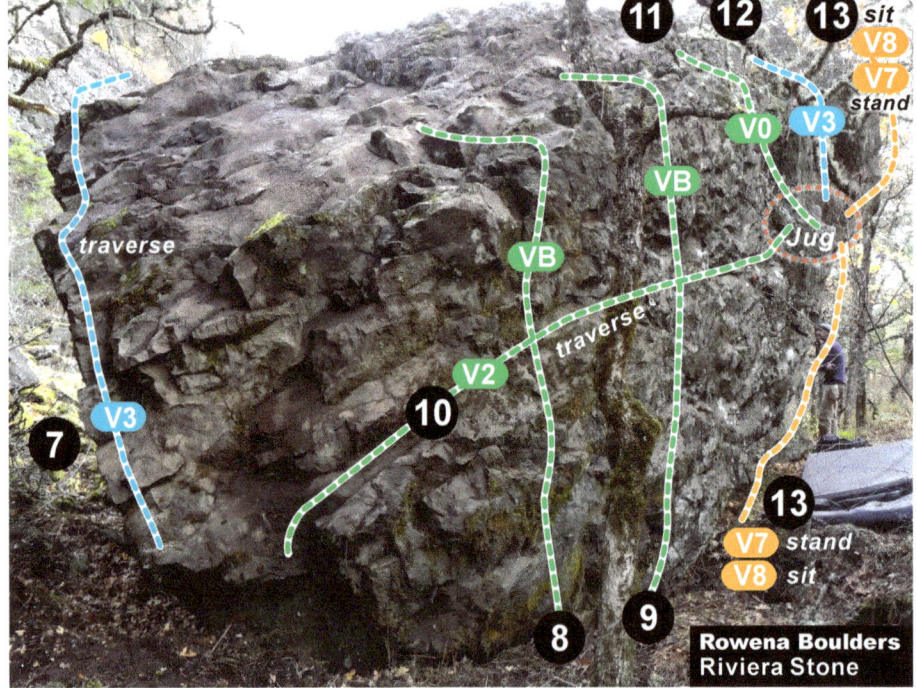

hill on a zigzag deer path descending down a rough talus slope. The Riviera Boulder is located at the base of the talus slope on flat ground.

Riviera Boulder

This global giant is a 360° circuit boulder providing stellar bouldering on all aspects, yielding some notably powerful number crunching wild beastly game. The beta begins on the seriously overhung west aspect (listed left to right) and continues counter-clockwise.

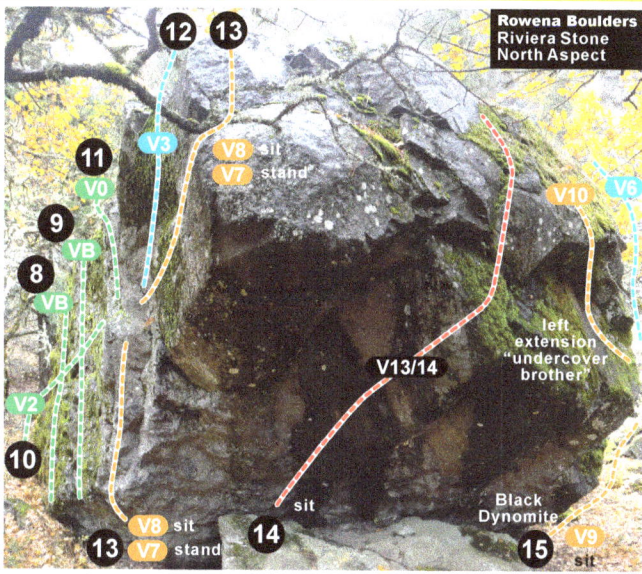

WEST ASPECT:

1. V6+ Alpha
Sit start, and climb directly up the left hung lip with your left hand using the lip.

2. V10
Begin as a sit start on your rear in the dead center of the boulder, then traverse hard left to the prow, and climb the left prow.

3. V7 (V8) Tzedekah
Low standing start is just below a big hung tooth and crimp up leftward to the top and over the lip. Sit start begins even lower on several low right-facing holds and goes up the same way to top.

4. V6 T'shuvah
If you start just below the same hung tooth, punch up slightly right-ish to tag this problem.

5. V9/V10 Tzedek
Sit start in center of the overhung stone, power straight up thin slick crimps to the top.

6. V7
Located on the right portion of this well overhung aspect. Very low sit start, and overhung crimps to attain lip, then over top.

THE TRAVERSE:

7. V3
Traverse the entire lip rail from right to left.

SOUTH ASPECT:

8. VB
Go up face just left of a small oak tree.

9. VB
Go up face just right of a small oak tree.

10. V2 _____
Traverse from the far left going right into the far V0, then upward to the top.

11. V0 _____
Just start on the fat jug and go up a rail leftward to the top of the boulder.

12. V3 Sigma
Start on the fat jug and go straight up.

13. V7/V8 Omega
Sit start underneath the overhang at the point and go up to the large jug, then rightward out the next overhang and up to the top.

North Aspect:

14. V13/14 _____ [project]
An upside down substantially overhung corner involving footwork wizardry punching outward to an outer vertical face, continuing up on several more reasonable holds to top out.

15. V6/V7 (V9) Black Dynomite
Sit start under the very belly of a very overhung prow; go out the hung prow and leftward to the reach the standing hold, and continue upward to top of the boulder. The V6 common standing start begins on the obvious midway hold.

15b. V10 Undercover Brother
A powerful hard left trending extension travels leftward even further, then goes up to the top on a series of final holds.

16. V9 Dolomite
Sit start (same as for Black Dynomite) and punch out the well overhung prow, but this time travel up rightward along the outer right lip on a series of small edges and holds.

17. V6 When I was done dying
Sit start (on the northwest aspect), climb up leftward on a vertical face using a series of small edges to reach the lip, then maneuver over the lip onto the angled top side of the large boulder.

Working against the laws of gravity on a cool cloudy day, Sam powers up a stellar problem at the *Empire*.

www.ingramcontent.com/pod-product-compliance
Lightning Source LLC
Chambersburg PA
CBHW051545010526
44118CB00022B/2584